PHILOSOPHY AND THEORY IN EDUCATIONAL RESEARCH

Philosophy and Theory in Educational Research: Writing in the margin explores the practices of reading and writing in educational philosophy and theory. Showing that there is no 'right way' to approach research in educational philosophy, but illustrating its possibilities, this text invites an engagement with philosophy as a possibility – and opening possibilities – for educational research. Drawing on their own research and theoretical and philosophical sources, the authors investigate the important issue of what it means to read and write when there is no prescribed structure. Innovative in its contribution to the literature, this edited volume enlightens readers in three ways.

- The volume focuses on the practices of reading and writing that are central to research in educational philosophy, suggesting that these practices *constitute* the research, rather than simply reporting it.
- It is not a prescriptive guide and should not be read procedurally. Rather, it is intended to illustrate the possibilities for this kind of research, and to suggest starting points for those pursuing research projects.
- Finally, attention is given to the ways in which conducting educational philosophy can be educative in itself, both to the researcher in writing it, and to its audience in reading it.

With contributions from international scholars in the field of educational philosophy, this book is a valuable guide for practitioner-researchers, taught postgraduate and doctoral students, and early career researchers in university education departments. Academic staff teaching research methods and seeking to introduce their students to philosophy-as-research without wishing to offer a prescriptive 'how to' guide will also find this book of particular interest.

Amanda Fulford is Head of Postgraduate Programmes in the Institute of Childhood and Education and Associate Principal Lecturer in Education Research at Leeds Trinity University, UK.

Naomi Hodgson is Visiting Research Fellow in the Laboratory for Education and Society, KU Leuven, Belgium, and Visiting Lecturer at Liverpool Hope University, UK.

PHILOSOPHY AND THEORY IN EDUCATIONAL RESEARCH

Writing in the margin

Edited by Amanda Fulford and Naomi Hodgson

Routledge
Taylor & Francis Group

LONDON AND NEW YORK

First published 2016
by Routledge
2 Park Square, Milton Park, Abingdon, Oxon OX14 4RN

and by Routledge
711 Third Avenue, New York, NY 10017

Routledge is an imprint of the Taylor & Francis Group, an informa business

© 2016 selection and editorial matter, A. Fulford and N. Hodgson;
individual chapters, the contributors

British Library Cataloguing in Publication Data
A catalogue record for this book is available from the British
Library

Library of Congress Cataloging in Publication Data
Names: Fulford, Amanda, editor. | Hodgson, Naomi, editor.
Title: Philosophy and theory in educational research: writing in
the margin / edited by Amanda Fulford & Naomi Hodgson.
Description: New York, NY: Routledge, 2016. | Includes
bibliographical references.
Identifiers: LCCN 2015047663 | ISBN 9781138899179
(hbk: alk. paper) | ISBN 9781138899186 (pbk: alk. paper) |
ISBN 9781315708034 (ebk)
Subjects: LCSH: Education—Research—Philosophy.
Classification: LCC LB1028 .P468 2016 | DDC 370.72—dc23
LC record available at http://lccn.loc.gov/2015047663

ISBN: 978-1-138-89917-9 (hbk)
ISBN: 978-1-138-89918-6 (pbk)
ISBN: 978-1-315-70803-4 (ebk)

Typeset in Bembo
by Book Now Ltd, London

CONTENTS

CONTRIBUTORS

Andrea R. English is the Chancellor's Fellow in Philosophy of Education at the University of Edinburgh. She received her doctorate from Humboldt University, Berlin, Germany, where she also lectured in philosophy of education and teacher education. Her work focuses on theories of learning and teaching, with particular attention to notions of reflective practice, listening, dialogue, inquiry, critical thinking, and moral and social learning. She has published on the work of Johann Herbart and John Dewey, and is currently researching the relationships between dialogic teaching, student thinking and student moral and social learning.

Amanda Fulford is Head of Programmes for postgraduate courses and continuing professional development, in the Institute for Childhood and Education at Leeds Trinity University. She obtained her PhD from the Institute of Education, University of London, undertaking a philosophical enquiry into being and becoming literate. Her research has focused on writing and reading practices in the university, and on academic literacies. Her recent research on the university and teaching and learning practices in higher education considers the dominant discourses of student satisfaction, student expectation, and student engagement, and how these drive a fundamental shift in our conception of the academy, and of the lecturer-student relationships at its heart. Her work draws on the philosophy of Stanley Cavell, his readings of the American transcendentalist writers Ralph Waldo Emerson and Henry David Thoreau, and also on the work of Gabriel Marcel, Martin Buber, and Emmanuel Levinas.

Morwenna Griffiths holds the Chair of Classroom Learning in the Moray House School of Education at Edinburgh University. Her research includes philosophical theorising and empirical investigation related to social justice, feminism, the nature of practice, pedagogy, joy in education, and creativity. Her most recent work focuses on relationships. She has written on pedagogical relations as embodied and context-dependent. Currently she is investigating social justice within all our educational relationships, understanding human relationships as just one aspect of being and living in the more-than-human world.

Naomi Hodgson is a Visiting Research Fellow in the Laboratory for Education and Society, KU Leuven, Belgium, and a Visiting Lecturer in Education at Liverpool Hope University, UK. She is the author of the recent *Citizenship for the Learning Society: Europe, Subjectivity, and Educational Research* (Wiley, 2016). Since gaining her PhD at the Institute of Education, London, in 2011 her research has focused on the figure of the researcher as a specific subject position in current modes of governance, drawing particularly on the work Michel Foucault and Stanley Cavell. In collaboration with Stefan Ramaekers (KU Leuven), she has begun to research presentations of this figure in film.

Viktor Johansson is a Senior Lecturer and Post-doctoral Fellow at Örebro University and Dalarna University in Sweden. He specialises in philosophy of education and writes on the role of children's literature in philosophy, aesthetic education, the philosophy of childhood, the philosophy of language, and the ethics of child-adult relationships. He is currently working on a book on children's philosophising in pre-schools, and on a research project on the role of picture books for learning in play and children's philosophical investigations.

Anna Kouppanou works at Cyprus Pedagogical Institute. She is an educator and a published children's author. She completed her PhD at the Institute of Education, University of London. Her thesis involved an investigation of Martin Heidegger's understanding of nearness in relation to technology, space, time, metaphor, and imagination. Her research interests include the philosophy of education and technology, phenomenology, existentialism, new media, and ethics.

Ian Munday is a Lecturer in Education at the University of Stirling. He teaches on the Initial Teacher Education and Doctoral School programmes. Ian's research activities testify to an engagement with philosophical issues in education, particularly those concerning teaching and learning. His publications have tended to focus on various approaches to performatives and performativities, and demonstrate the significance of these ideas for education. The themes explored in these terms include race, gender, the construction of authority, power relationships, and the language of schooling. Here, philosophical ideas are treated in regards to their relevance to the details of educational practice. Ian's recent research focus is on theorising 'creativity' and 'problem solving' in education.

Anne Pirrie is a Reader in Education at the University of the West of Scotland. She sees herself primarily as a researcher rather than an academic, a kind of private investigator or mischief-gatherer. This is partly because in recent times the academy has become a forum for the calculative action of individual agents driven by self-interest rather than a site of collegiality, shared knowledge, and mutual influence.

Reading is only part of Anne's job at the university. She enjoys teaching, research supervision, walking, dancing, and, above all, writing.

Stefan Ramaekers studied educational sciences and philosophy at KU Leuven, Belgium, and obtained a PhD in educational sciences in the field of philosophy of education about forms of scepticism in educational theory and practices. His research and teaching are situated in the broad field of educational philosophy and theory. For the past few years, his research has focused mainly on a critical investigation of the discourse of 'parenting' and the parent–child relationship and on the 'pedagogical' significance of educational support. With Judith Suissa (UCL Institute of Education) he published the book *The Claims of Parenting: Reasons, Responsibility, and Society* (Springer, 2012). Recently he has begun collaboration with Naomi Hodgson on research into figurations of 'parenting' in film.

Richard Smith is a Professor in the School of Education at Durham University, UK. He mainly teaches courses in the theory and philosophy of social science. His research interests are in the philosophy of social science and in philosophical issues in education, particularly higher education, postmodernity, and the epistemology of educational research. In particular, he researches the educational importance of not knowing, the moral psychology of self-belief, and also virtue epistemology. He is an Associate Editor of the *Journal of Philosophy of Education*.

Judith Suissa is a Reader in Philosophy of Education at the UCL Institute of Education, London. Her research interests are in political and moral philosophy, with a particular focus on questions to do with the control of education, social justice, libertarian and anarchist theory, the role of the state, political education, and the parent–child relationship. Her publications include *Anarchism and Education: A Philosophical Perspective* (Routledge, 2006) and (with Stefan Ramaekers) *The Claims of Parenting: Reasons, Responsibility, and Society* (Springer, 2012).

Nancy Vansieleghem works at LUCA School of Arts, Ghent Campus, in Belgium, where she teaches courses in pedagogy, psychology, and communication in (audio-) visual arts. She coordinates the research group Art, Practices & Education. Her research focus is on the potentiality of philosophy, childhood, and arts within educational (research) practices. Currently she is exploring the artistic potentiality of screen-learning by setting up collective online experiments.

Joris Vlieghe is a Lecturer in Philosophy of Education in the Department of Education Studies at Liverpool Hope University, UK. He studied philosophy and art history, and obtained his PhD in educational sciences for an investigation into the public and educational meaning of corporeality. His research focuses on how the growing presence of digital technologies alters existing school practices, and how this evolution goes together with new forms of subjectivity. He also investigates the shift from book culture to screen culture, and how this evolution affects our understanding of basic educational concepts such as literacy, creativity, and transformation.

FOREWORD

Richard Smith

In his 1983 book, *Margins of Philosophy*, Jacques Derrida offers variations on what is a constant theme in his writings. The theme is that it is a characteristic mistake of our culture, and in particular of its philosophers, to seek some transcendental guarantee of the meaning of language: God, *Logos*, Being, Reason, Mind, or perhaps an ideal language, such as that of science. Then that transcendental ideal would be situated in the centre of things, stable, pure, and uncorruptible, rather like the Sun that the escaping prisoner encounters when he leaves the Cave in Plato's (2003) *Republic*. If there are margins, then there must be something that holds the centre ground; conversely if there is some transcendental ideal at the centre, we can be sure that what is at the margins – mud and hair, and all kinds of messy and mundane ways of thinking and talking and writing – is of minor importance, if it is of any importance at all.

We can apply this analysis to educational research. If some activities, some kinds of writing, or even writing itself, are marginal to the business of educational research, then we might ask what the heart of educational research is. What is the ideal form of it? What does educational research look like when it is most nearly itself, when it is contrasted with marginal irrelevances, outmoded approaches, the luxuries of the ivory-towered university, and the dreams of mere theorists? It is not obvious that the question is entirely a sensible one, resting as it does on the assumption of a radical difference between margins and a centre ground, but now and again one seems to be offered a glimpse of an answer.

For example, recent research into the teaching of mathematics appears to have shown the value of teaching techniques used in Shanghai. Shanghai is at the top of the international schools, mathematics league table. Seventy of its teachers have recently been working with pupils in English secondary schools. Nick Gibb, the UK Minister of State for Schools, has no doubt of the value of their method, saying, 'Shanghai mathematics teaching works because it is meticulous. Every step of a lesson is deliberate, purposeful and precise.'[1] Clearly it leaves no room for chance or imprecision: these have been banished to the margins. The newspaper report (*The Guardian*, 27 Nov. 2015) that quotes him is entitled 'Chinese maths classes may add up to big gains by 2018.' Nothing, surely, could be more central in the field of educational research than the teaching of mathematics, and the reader of the report is given the strong impression that here we have something that works, a fact confirmed by academic research. Professor David Reynolds, 'who is a member of the Sheffield Hallam University committee set up to evaluate the UK-Shanghai experiment', describes himself as 'an enthusiast' for the experiment and comments that it is '"not beyond the realms of possibility" that UK pupils could get better scores in the next round of PISA[2] international tests on 15-year-olds in 2018 thanks to the Shanghai-style teaching'.

The careful reader (for there is no doubt that this newspaper report is a piece of writing, and has to be read) may, however, detect that the Minister's claim that Shanghai mathematics teaching 'works' is not wholly sound. Even Reynolds goes no further than to comment that improvement in Pisa international tests is 'not beyond the realms of possibility', a cautious note also sounded by the newspaper headline and its slightly different online version ('Shanghai teaching method "could improve UK results within four years"'). Other notes of reservation occur in both versions. One Shanghai teacher says that her UK students 'understand and answer the questions quickly. Next day I ask them and maybe they forget. In China they do a lot of work at home.' The author of the article comments that 'many children in Shanghai will have private tutoring and weekend school', which we infer is not the case for their UK counterparts. A London University researcher warns against jumping to conclusions at this stage: 'Teaching methods may differ but there's a whole lot of other explanations [for Shanghai's success], ranging from culture, to private tutoring and parental investment. To tease out the role of those different factors is incredibly difficult.'[3]

Quite a lot of inconvenient stuff, in short, seems to have been swept into the margins, not least the possibility that it is not the teaching methods that are responsible for high testing scores in Shanghai at all. Yet one important issue has been marginalised to the point of invisibility. There is no indication of just what is the purpose of this particular teaching of mathematics. For instance, it might be intended to improve children's 'mathematicity': that is, their deep understanding of the subject, something that would underpin their future development as mathematicians. On the other hand, it might be intended principally to ensure better scores in tests and examinations. The newspaper article's references to PISA suggest this. Of course, this is to set up too stark a contrast: improved mathematicity might well pay off, incidentally as it were, in better test scores; and these are in any case not negligible achievements. But we know enough by now about the dangers of 'teaching to the test' to be concerned that better PISA results, even if they are achieved, may be just that and nothing more. Reynolds is at least consistent in his refusal to consider educational aims and purposes: in a previous enthusiasm, this time for 'school effectiveness', he prided himself on eschewing 'the values debate about goals' (Reynolds, 1997). Their marginalisation appears to be part of his mission.

What else do we find in the centre ground of educational research? There is a curious lack of self-confidence, manifested by the imitation of other kinds of research, as if there was nothing distinctive about the field of education. There is a particular vogue at present for the randomised controlled trials (RCTs), which are often considered the 'gold standard' in medical research. They will tell us 'what works' in education, just as they tell us whether a particular intervention is effective in the treatment of an illness or disease. The problem of course is that the significant variables that can be screened out in medical trials (age, weight, the taking of other prescription drugs, and so on) cannot so easily be screened out in education. Different teaching approaches to reading are always liable to be confounded by the major variable of whether parents read books and value them themselves, and whether they read to their children. The contexts of education are simply too various. Whether or not the wearing of school uniforms appears to 'work' in rural Malawi tells us little about what will happen if children wear school uniforms in Leeds or Glasgow.

More broadly, the centre ground of educational research is coloured by scientism: by instinctive and unthinking worship of science, its procedures, and its vocabulary. Thus we find the widespread assumption that educational research is essentially, or even exclusively, empirical. The true researcher is the one who goes out as an heroic explorer into the 'real world' of schools and classrooms. He or she gathers data, then analyses it by measuring and quantifying it in some way. The more sophisticated the mathematics used in all this, the more 'scientific' it will all appear. It is not uncommon to hear this sort of researcher speak disparagingly of those whose research is confined to the library and who never 'get their hands dirty'.

If educational research is in some way 'scientific', naturally there must be a method for doing it: hence the plethora of books on educational research methods. There are scores of these in print, most of them bearing strong resemblances to each other. Then, too, no undergraduate or Master's programme in Education is complete without a Research Methods module, and large numbers of education academics list research methods, or methodology, among their specialisms. But the idea of method here is odder than most people notice. It has a historical basis in attempts in the seventeenth century to establish the right way to discover the scientific knowledge by which that century was rightly impressed. The classic example of this was Francis Bacon's (1620/1902) *Novum Organum*, which means, roughly, 'New Handbook of Method'. *Organum* can also be translated as 'tool kit': Bacon seems to have been alert to the importance of a title that emphasises practicality and being up-to-date. Many of today's authors have learned this from him at least.

The search for *the* method continued in the seventeenth century with Descartes's (1637/1960) *Discourse*: its full title is *Discourse on the Method of Rightly Conducting the Reason and Seeking for Truth in the Sciences*. It continued with (among other examples) David Hume's eight rules 'by which to judge of cause and effects' (*A Treatise of Human Nature*, 1739/1975, Book I, Part 3, Section 15) and John Stuart Mill's four 'experimental methods' (*A System of Logic*, 1843/2002, Book 3,

Chapter 8). There are two important things to understand about this search for method. The first is that it was widely conceived as a search for a Dummies' Guide. Bacon, for instance, explicitly states, among other remarks to the same effect, that he is attempting to produce a guide that will require little intelligence ('wits' or 'individual excellence', *Novum Organum*, Aphorism CXXII) on the part of the practitioner, but enable him or her to proceed mechanically: 'as if by machinery'. The second important point is that the search is regarded by many historians of science and social science to have been fruitless: there is no one 'scientific method'.

Empirical, pseudo-scientific research into education is, however, good business for universities. Grants can be applied for, typically for the purpose of buying the applicant out of teaching, largely for the purpose of collecting and analysing data, or to appoint a research assistant to do this. The funding that comes in can be top-sliced in order to maintain the university's library and its laboratories and other central facilities. It also goes a long way towards paying the salaries of the university's managers and administrators, including the managers and administrators of research, who generally do not do research themselves (neither, of course, do they teach). The importance of such funding – from Research Councils, industry, charities, and other sources – is so great that academics are more and more pressurised into applying for it. It is now a prerequisite for career advancement, or for any degree of job security, at many universities in the UK, that an academic whose job involves research to any significant extent should secure such funding, or at least make plausible applications for it. It goes without saying that funding is seldom awarded for non-empirical research, for instance, to give someone space and time in which to think and write, philosophically or otherwise.

At the same time, empirically-oriented research is attractive for another reason. Overseas students, particularly at postgraduate level, pay high fees to UK universities. Often their language skills, while impressive, are nevertheless not good enough to engage in essentially theoretical research. Collecting data, for instance, through interviews, and analysing it perhaps with the help of a statistical software package, is far more manageable. Thus the lucrative supply of overseas students is maintained. Marina Warner, a distinguished researcher in the field of history and literature, who resigned her professorship at a UK university in protest at the marginalisation of her specialisms, has written of how 'The incessant emphasis was on cash…accept anyone for study who could pay, unethical as that was especially at postgraduate level, where foreign applicants with very poor English were being invited to spend large sums on degrees' (Warner, 2015). None of this is to say that there is not good and valuable educational research of the conventional sort being done. But the centre ground, as I have called it, does seem cluttered: with fantasies about science, empiricism, and methodology, and what Marina Warner calls 'the incessant emphasis on cash'.

Now, it is the theme of this book that valuable educational research can equally be done by those who read, and think, and write, and who do philosophy. Yet it is not my purpose to argue that philosophy should move from the margins to the centre ground. Fortunately, philosophy secured itself against that false glory from its inception in the time of Plato and Socrates as the body of ideas and approaches that we still think of as philosophical today. It did this in two ways. First, Plato has Socrates declare, in the *Phaedrus*, that writing is no great invention. It is inferior to speech: in a dialogue with others you can question them, ask them what they meant, offer counter-arguments, and so on. Written texts, however, are like statues or portraits: they have nothing to say in response to our questions. Writing is a recipe for silence and forgetting, not for the discovery of truth through argument and for the gathering of ideas that Plato calls a kind of recollection. This relegation of writing has been powerfully influential: for instance, it is traditional for Oxford undergraduates to read their essays to their tutors rather than to submit written copies for them to read. But of course, while *Phaedrus* is a dialogue, it is one that Plato has written, and written with some care: thus there is a paradox in its dismissal of the written word, all the more so given the extensive body of Plato's writings that has come down to us. Just as we think we have seen writing being marginalised in favour of speech, then, we are reminded that we have encountered this through reading a written text. Plato's irony here is such that we are left uncertain quite which part, if either, of the binary speech/writing is being prioritised and which is being accorded lesser status.

Second, it is well known that Plato banished the poets from his ideal state, in *The Republic*: poetry is inferior to philosophy and marginal by comparison with it. But the arguments – the philosophical arguments – against poetry, put in Socrates's mouth in the dialogue, vary from the unsound to the absurd. Furthermore, many of Plato's dialogues themselves have strongly poetical passages, not least *The Republic* itself in the simile of the Cave and the Sun, and the myth of Er and his account of what he saw in his brief visit to the afterlife. The distinction between literature and philosophy is thus problematised as soon as it appears to be asserted, and the divide between different kinds of writing comes to seem as unreal as the division between margins and centre ground. As the editors of this book and its contributors know, this is profoundly encouraging for those who write about education.[4]

Notes

1 Available at: www.theguardian.com/education/2015/nov/26/shanghai-teaching-method-could-improve-uk-results-within-four-years; accessed 11th April 2016.
2 Programme for International Student Assessment.
3 Available at: http://www.theguardian.com/education/2015/nov/26/shanghai-teaching-method- www.theguardian.com/education/2015/nov/26/shanghai-teaching-method-could-improve-uk-results-within-four-years; accessed 11th April 2016.
4 I have drawn in places on elements of Smeyers and Smith (2014).

References

Bacon, F. (1620/1902) *Novum Organum*, Ed. J. Devey, New York: P.F. Collier.
Derrida, J. (1983) *Margins of Philosophy*, Chicago: University of Chicago Press.
Descartes, R. (1637/1960) *Discourse on the Method of Rightly Conducting the Reason and Seeking for Truth in the Sciences*, New York: Liberal Arts Press.
Hume, D. (1739/1975) *A Treatise of Human Nature*, Ed. L. A. Selby-Bigge, second edition, revised by P. H. Nidditch, Oxford: Clarendon Press.

Mill, J.S. (1843/2002) *A System of Logic, Ratiocinative and Inductive*, Honolulu: University Press of the Pacific.

Plato (2003) *The Republic*, Trans. D. Lee, London: Penguin.

Reynolds, D. (1997) 'School Effectiveness: Retrospect and Prospect', *Scottish Educational Review*, available at: www.scotedreview.org.uk/media/scottish-educational-review/articles/51.pdf) (accessed 30 Nov. 2015).

Smeyers, P. and Smith, R. (2014) *Understanding Education and Educational Research*, Cambridge: Cambridge University Press.

Warner, M. (2015) 'Learning My Lesson', *London Review of Books*, 19 March.

SCHOLIA

Amanda Fulford and Naomi Hodgson

The following stories give an account of how the idea for this book started, and of why we thought it *necessary* to write it. Amanda Fulford's account is based on her experiences of working in a university and delivering a research methods course, while studying for a doctorate on a part-time basis. Naomi Hodgson recounts her experience of studying on a full-time research methods Master's course prior to starting her PhD.

Amanda Fulford

It was with a sense of excitement that, in 2008, I started a new job as Programme Director for a Master's programme in education at a university in the north of England. The programme, an MA in Education, aimed to recruit professionals working in the education sector, many of whom would be serving school teachers, lecturers from further education, or trainers from the, what is termed, Learning and Skills Sector. The programme was to comprise a rigorous course of continuing professional development for those who enrolled, allowing them to pursue their subject and pedagogical interests, while critiquing the latest research and scholarship in their respective fields. Part of the course would be a year-long module on research methods. Entitled 'Developing Practitioner Enquiry', the module would prepare students with the knowledge to plan a piece of research related to their professional interests and practice. They would then conduct and report on this research in the final Dissertation module. Such modules are common; there are iterations found in nearly all taught postgraduate courses in the social sciences, albeit with different names and delivery patterns. They prepare students to conduct ethical, valid research, and present students with a broad range of approaches and practices that induct them into the field of practitioner research. Such modules are sound preparation and grounding for further study at doctoral level.

It is not uncommon for such modules to follow a fairly standard pattern. In preparing to deliver this module, I conducted some lengthy searches online to find out how different universities approached this subject. It seemed not to matter whether the courses I researched were offered in established universities, in new Higher Education Institutions, or whether they were contextualised to education, anthropology, sociology, or other disciplines in the social sciences. The general pattern seemed very similar. Of course, there were differences: courses aimed at those who were social workers, or who were employed in related fields, had an emphasis on particular practices for researching with children, or with vulnerable adults, for example. Modules on research methods aimed at those working in the discipline of psychology tended to have a greater balance of content related to experimental research designs, and on the tools to analyse statistical data in research. However, I was surprised by the degree of commonality. Most courses tended to have some sessions that provided an overview of research traditions, and while some were called 'Research Paradigms', 'Basic Orientations to Research', or 'Theoretical Frameworks', it was clear that what was intended to be covered in such sessions were issues relating to epistemology: theories of knowledge. In many cases, these introductory sessions were followed by ones entitled 'Methodology' or 'Design Frames', usually covering a range of approaches such as case study, action research, ethnography, and narrative. There were, of course, the inevitable sessions on how to collect data in research, with the most popular being the survey and the interview (these tended to be allocated a session all to themselves). Most courses included coverage of approaches to data analysis (content and thematic analysis mostly), with attention given to the use of electronic tools for data analysis (from Excel to SPSS[1]). In varying degrees, these modules might also include input on preparing a literature review, gaining ethical clearance for a research project, writing up, and presenting findings. What was clear in my investigations was that the learning outcomes from these kinds of module tended to focus on equipping students studying on them with the skills to collect, manage, and interpret data. Such data tended to be understood and categorised as either quantitative (numerical, statistical) or qualitative (verbal, observational, or artefactual).

At the time when I was undertaking these investigations, and planning the lecture series for my own module, I was also studying for a part-time PhD. But for this doctoral research I had no data – quantitative or qualitative. It was not that I had not yet begun my data collection, but rather that the kind of study I was pursuing was one in educational philosophy (there will be much more about this later in the book). There was never going to be *any* data collection or analysis. My research rather comprised reading – and a lot of it. What seemed strange to me, on reflection, was that the research methods courses I had undertaken in my own Master's programme in education, and as part of my doctoral training, were in no way directly relevant to the specific kind of research I was undertaking. But more than this, my recollections of this preparatory training had not suggested that this kind of research was even possible. Empirical investigation (understood as the knowledge gained through direct or indirect observation or experience where questions are answerable through the collection and analysis of qualitative or quantitative data) was clearly the dominant form of research. I was therefore left with a dilemma: my students should have a proper induction into the practices of research that would allow them to conduct their own investigations, and prepare them for possible doctoral work, or even for careers in academia. But would adopting the 'standard' empirical approach to teaching research methods fit with my own research commitments in educational philosophy, and the associated desire to share these with my students?

These questions were ones that were talked through in various departmental meetings, and which prompted a further range of queries from my colleagues and Head of Department. Notable among these were, first, a possible issue that if other modes of research were introduced to students (namely educational philosophy), then would students be doing more on my module than they would have to do on modules in other institutions? This was simply an issue of workload, but related to this was the question of what I would take *out* of the course in order to fit educational philosophy *in*. Second, there was the issue of the value of research in educational philosophy. I was the sole researcher in the department undertaking this kind of research, and to many colleagues, this approach was entirely new. A lack of knowledge in this area led to questions of educational philosophy's 'usefulness', 'impact', and therefore, of desirability. After all, research in education was seen to be concerned, in the main, with delivering better outcomes for pupils, with finding out what works. And if educational philosophy could not deliver that directly, why would teachers want to 'do' it, and why would their sponsoring schools want to pay for them to do it? I had a question of my own: if I was going to introduce educational philosophy to my students on the research methods module, what reading could I give them to support their emerging research ideas in this field? It simply didn't exist. The research methods textbooks on the indicative reading list that I had prepared for the module either ignored the field completely, or raised a note of caution in alerting readers to 'check with their supervisor' if they wanted to adopt a non-empirical approach.

While pondering these issues, I had dinner with my colleague, Naomi Hodgson. I began talking with her about the difficulties I was facing. I had tentatively introduced the idea of philosophical or theoretical research with my students. Their response was one both of surprise: 'I didn't know I could do research like this'. Or of delight: 'This is just what I want to do, I just didn't know this was what it was called.' Their ideas were intriguing and suggested a sophistication in thinking. One student was interested in writing about religious education in schools, and in asking instead what an education for spirituality would consist of. Another, feeling overwhelmed by the raft of initiatives brought in to manage behaviour in her primary school, wanted to examine the building of ethical teacher-pupil relationships as offering an alternative way of thinking about the classroom.

All this was fascinating, but raised the question of where, and how, to start to support these students in going forward to produce a coherent piece of philosophical research. What was needed was some kind of guidance text. We discussed the few that we already knew existed in the field of educational philosophy. Some addressed the kinds of topics in which philosophy of education tends to be interested (such as ethics, the curriculum, the aims of education); others focused on philosophical foundations of different kinds of research. But none of these seemed to address the questions at the forefront of the students' minds: what is it to do educational philosophy? How is it different from, say, empirical research – is it different at all? Where do I start if I have no data? Naomi and I discussed it further. We knew that we didn't want to write a textbook. A simple, step-by-step guide to educational philosophy was unappealing, to say the least, even were it possible to write such a book. We wanted to write a text that did not shy away from the very practical questions the students were asking (Where to start? Is educational philosophy different?), but in a way that did not replicate the approaches in many of the standard research methods textbooks that seemed to prescribe certain approaches, almost as if the researcher was choosing from a menu of options. We wanted to write a text that challenged readers to think about the issues raised in researching education philosophically, that illustrated the possibilities without being prescriptive, and that addressed the key issue of the practices of reading and writing that characterise research in the field. And so the idea for the book was born. Fellow educational philosophers teaching and supervising on the same kind of courses in very different institutions tell us that this book is needed, and that their students need this book. We hope that it goes some way to meeting that need.

Naomi Hodgson

I must confess that when Amanda first put the idea for this book to me, I was slightly sceptical. Another research methods book? Really? But as we discussed it, it became clear that this was not to be a research methods book, and could address concerns that I had had since starting out in educational research, and that I continued to contend with as a postdoctoral researcher needing to hone the skill of research funding proposal writing.

Until starting my MA in Educational Research, I had not studied education before. I was not a teacher, as many of those on the course were. My interest in education came out of my undergraduate degree in anthropology, and in particular the emerging literature on the anthropology of policy. I did my undergraduate dissertation on the redesign of the city of Liverpool as part of their bid to become Capital of Culture, and was interested in this as part of the context of engendering a sense of European citizenship through various European policies and initiatives. At around the same time, the UK government had introduced a new compulsory citizenship education curriculum. Having previously thought little about education, and the role it played in the formation of identity, of subjectivity, and our relation to the world, this seemed to raise questions. What was education currently doing, if not producing citizens? It implied that education was currently not providing the right kind of citizen. So what kind of citizen did the government want?

I proposed a study of European and UK policy on the matter, and was awarded an ESRC scholarship to study an MA in Educational Research and a subsequent PhD on this topic.

My background in anthropology by no means suggested that this would be a philosophical study. But what was to happen next reframed the questions in unanticipated and unsettling ways. While I was predominantly interested in the theoretical aspects of anthropology, the literature on methods and the empirical dimension of the field was fascinating. The ethical issues relating to the practice of ethnography and the subsequent representation of research subjects in writing, for example, suggested the study of research methods to be a rich, complex, and rewarding area of study, particularly in the interdisciplinary field of education.

In hindsight, this was a naïve view. I had not anticipated the very procedural way in which the research methods literature would describe the research process, would neatly define research methods as a list of options, and would be based on the assumption that research would be empirical, as traditionally understood. Also, there seemed to be an anxiety in the field of education, about being taken seriously, in terms of answering to the policy problems of government, to the practical concerns of teachers, and to the critical demands of contemporary scholarship.

The overbearing concern with empirical research, and the modish ways in which its critical potential were understood were, to be honest, deeply disconcerting. I was unsettled by the questions that were not able to be asked due to the orthodoxies that existed. It was in the few sessions relating to philosophical approaches that the possibility to pursue educational research otherwise was opened. The engagement with literature in the field of philosophy of education enabled me not only to articulate the approach to the study of European citizenship I wanted to pursue, and to encounter texts and ideas I otherwise would not have, but also to articulate the serious concerns I had about the way in which education and research are understood in educational research. This, then, became a central part of the account I developed; seeing educational research not only as a body of literature with which to analyse and understand education, but also as constitutive of a particular way of speaking about citizenship and education.

Throughout my postgraduate study I met a number of students in a similar position; pursuing philosophical or theoretical research and feeling alienated by the increasingly standardised ways in which research, as empirical, was taught and discussed. Unfortunately, what can ensue from this is a cynicism towards this discourse of research, and an inertia in the field of philosophy of education due to the need to attend to matters such as impact and engagement. But such matters are unavoidable at a time when securing external funding is sometimes the only way to gain or retain an academic research position: questions of methodology, relevance, and impact must be addressed in positive, value-added terms. I wanted to move away from a negative characterisation of this discourse, and find a way in which educational philosophy could articulate its value without undermining itself in the process. This is not easy, particularly when how you want to articulate what you do seems at odds with the ways in which it needs to be expressed to be evaluated by funding bodies. But, if we believe strongly in the ability – and necessity – of educational philosophy to respond to today's conditions (which you will see from reading this book that we do), then we ought to be able to articulate this in ways that are compelling to those outside the field. Not as an alternative to randomised control trials – they will still happen – but as an invaluable component in an ongoing conversation about matters of common concern. Writing this book goes some way towards that positive articulation, and I hope that it assists researchers in their own attempts.

Note

1 Excel is a spreadsheet programme from Microsoft that can be used for inputting, managing and manipulating data. SPSS (or Statistical Package for the Social Sciences) is a popular software package for statistical analysis.

PART I
Starting out

1

STARTING POINTS

Amanda Fulford and Naomi Hodgson

It makes sense to begin with some introductory remarks about what this book is, and, of course, what it is not. We are clear that this is a book about research, and about the practices of research and researching in education. However, it would be right to ask if yet another text in this particular field is needed. Indeed, there are multiple texts that currently address these practices, many of which focus on specific age phases – for example, researching with very young children – or on how to research in particular contexts such as higher education. These tend to be written as textbooks, or handbooks; they are structured guides to support teachers and practitioners, postgraduate students, or new and early career researchers, to plan and implement research projects in the field of education. They are the kinds of texts that tend to be found on the reading lists of postgraduate research methods modules in universities.

But while this is a book about research, and the practices of research and researching in education, it is *not* another research methods textbook in the sense that we have outlined above. It does not, for example, guide readers through the processes of research, from selecting a research question, choosing a methodology and appropriate data collection methods, writing a literature review, collecting and analysing data, and writing up the findings. The research methods textbooks and research project handbooks both do these things very well, and so serve a valuable purpose for researchers. This volume, though, takes a different approach in four ways. First, it addresses a form of research that we will call 'educational philosophy'. We want to avoid the over-simplistic dichotomy often drawn between empirical forms of research (where research typically proceeds through the collection and analysis of data from experimentation, observation, conversation, texts or artefacts), and philosophical/theoretical forms that are our concern here (where there is no 'data' as such, and the research tends to proceed through argument and use of sources). But we do want to focus on what might be considered distinctive about educational philosophy, while recognising that *all* educational research proceeds from questions about, or practical concerns arising from, education. Second, this volume focuses attention specifically on the practices of reading and writing that are central to research in educational philosophy. Moreover, it argues that these practices *constitute* the research, rather than that they simply support the research, and the reporting of the research through processes of writing up. Third, this book is not intended to provide a step-by-step guide for 'doing' educational philosophy. It is not prescriptive, and should not be read procedurally, as a definitive set of instructions for doing educational philosophy well. Rather, it is intended to illustrate the possibilities for this kind of research, and to suggest starting points for those interested in pursuing research projects in these ways. Finally, this book, while about research, is also about in research in *education*. But we do not understood this only as research *about* education – schooling, the processes of teaching and learning, and so on. We also give attention to the way in which conducting educational philosophy can be *educative* in itself (to the researcher in writing it, and to its audience in reading it). This is why we draw an important illustrative distinction between educational philosophy, and research in philosophy of education.[1]

This volume makes an entirely new contribution to the body of work that already exists to inform researchers in education. It is not intended to replicate the model of the many published guides on conducting educational research, and to provide a version covering research in educational philosophy. Nor does it aim to provide a basic introduction specifically to philosophy of education as a field, focusing on some of the substantive issues with which the field is concerned (such as moral education, children's rights, the curriculum, or the aims of education). We do not want to argue for the value of philosophy over other approaches to research. Rather, our aim has been to write a volume that is an academic reference work, that engages critically with the ideas of reading and writing in educational philosophy, rather than providing a 'how to' guide. The book, though, is not merely intended as a theoretical discussion of the issues. It has practical value in terms of identifying and illustrating a range of reading and writing practices for philosophical research in education, and outlines possibilities and starting points for educational philosophy.

We argue that philosophical matters underlie all forms of educational research, and that this exposes the false dichotomy between empirical and philosophical approaches to research. We claim that since the philosophical is inextricably woven into all forms of research, then philosophy cannot, and must not, be marginal to our practices of research. We make the case that philosophy, through its practices of reading and writing, *is* research in itself, and that such research can address the very practical issues facing contemporary education. We show that there is no 'right way' to approach research in educational philosophy, but we illustrate its possibilities, and the kind of questions and concerns that might form its starting points. Out text invites an engagement with philosophy as a possibility for educational research. It is aimed at practitioner-researchers, taught postgraduate and doctoral students, and new and early career researchers in education departments in universities. It is also written for academic staff who teach on research methods modules on postgraduate programmes, and who seek to introduce their students to philosophy-as-research without wishing to offer a prescriptive 'how to' guide.

Our book makes a number of key claims, which we set out throughout the three Parts of the text. Part I, 'Starting out' comprises three chapters. In Chapter 2, we consider the way that many existing research methods textbooks begin with a chronological overview of research paradigms. We provide a different kind of overview in order to show how certain questions about the nature of reality, knowledge, and our being human, recur in different traditions. We show how this illustrates the intersection of the philosophical with the empirical, and therefore how it is not helpful to continue to shore up a false dichotomy between the two. In illustrating how the intersection is a place of confluence, we show how the starting point for very different kinds of educational enquiry is in the same lived experience of education. In Chapter 3, we draw attention to the approach taken towards the empirical and the philosophical or theoretical in many of the research methods textbooks, and focus on how they discuss the place of philosophy in educational research. Here, we find that the approach tends towards either avoidance, or one that consists in seeing philosophy as an aspect of research that needs to be worked out at the outset, something that amounts to having one's philosophical position settled. We then show that philosophy, rather than being marginal to research, can comprise the research itself, and discuss what philosophy's 'methods' might be.

In Part II, 'Reading and writing educational philosophy', we illustrate the very broad range of approaches to research in educational philosophy by including examples from the research of 11 international scholars. Each contributor provides an introduction to a short extract of their published research, which is then followed by the extract itself. The contributors then analyse their extract, providing critical reflections on the specific practices of philosophical reading and writing that are evident, and that we might say constitute their 'methods' in the research.

Part III, 'How to proceed?', comprises two chapters that analyse in some detail the place of reading and writing in research in general, and in educational philosophy in particular. In Chapter 15, we discuss what we see as a difference in the place of reading in research. We describe the way reading is discussed in many of the research methods textbooks as 'reading-*for*-research'. We contrast this with 'reading-*as*-research', which we argue is characteristic of educational philosophy. We then make a similar distinction between 'writing-as-*report*' (the purpose of writing that tends to dominate the research methods textbooks), and 'writing-*as*-research' in educational philosophy. In both these chapters, we make extensive reference both to examples from the textbooks, as well as to our colleagues' contributions in Part II. In the final chapter of Part III, Chapter 16, we draw together the major themes of the volume as a whole. We use examples from other philosophical sources that illustrate the wider concerns with the relation between language and thought in particular philosophical traditions. We conclude by trying to lay out some of the starting points for research in educational philosophy, illustrating the kind of issues, problems, and concerns that tend to characterise its starting points.

Writing in the margin

In this introductory section, some attention needs to be given to what might be considered an unusual choice of sub-title for this book, and to indicating the reasons for the use of the phrase: 'writing in the margin'. The concept of the 'margin' is an interesting one, and we indicate here three key ways in which it relates to points that we want to make in this book about research in educational philosophy. Let us explore each of these briefly. Think of the connotations of the plural form of the word (i.e. 'margins'), and its sense of being at the edge or limits of something. We might talk, for example, of a person living on the margins of society, a piece of handwriting as being on the margins of legibility, or of a practice as being on the margins of safety. In all these examples, the sense is clearly that the margins relate to the very limits of acceptability, and so the term tends to be used pejoratively. This reading is supported by its etymology, coming from the Latin *marginem*, meaning 'brink', 'edge', or 'border'. We might also talk of being on the brink of madness or of suicide and, in such examples, the borderline space is well away from what we might consider mainstream. But we can also think of the margins in another way. We are used to thinking of the margins as the blank space surrounding a sheet of paper or page of a book, and these call to mind images of borders, boundaries, and empty space. Often these are spaces of which we tend to be less aware; they exist, but only at the margin of our consciousness when we write on a sheet of paper or type on a screen. They are only given attention at the outset of our work when we might have to amend the size of the margins to serve a particular purpose; subsequently, they go unnoticed.

But how does the idea of 'the margins' relate to our project here? It is in the way that philosophical research tends to be seen; it is consigned to the margins – pushed to the edge – where it tends to go unnoticed. Philosophical research in education is marginal both to the discipline of philosophy (that is, where it exists, it is rarely situated within philosophy departments in universities), and to the field of educational research (where sociology and psychology provide the dominant disciplinary frameworks). Within the field of educational research, the focus on 'what works', and the proliferation of studies that claim to deliver measurable outcomes for children and young people, put that kind of work centre-stage. The corollary of this is that research that is more philosophical or theoretical in nature, tends to be pushed into the margins. This view needs little further exemplification save to draw attention to the lack of funding generally available for such work, and to what is denied by the orthodoxies that come from a narrow conception of research that focuses on what works in the classroom (see e.g. Bridges *et al.*, 2009). So the margins are an important image for understanding the current locus of educational philosophy within the field of educational research more generally.

Following from this identification of research in educational philosophy as being *in the margins*, we want to argue strongly that this does not equate to such work being *of marginal importance* to educational enquiry. We will explore this point in more detail in Chapter 2. But even at this early stage, we want to emphasise that while some in the field of education might perceive philosophical/theoretical work research to be marginal to contemporary policy and practice, our aim is to demonstrate that this view is erroneous. We will show how philosophical concerns cannot be divorced from the practical and empirical in research on education. Moreover, we will argue that philosophy cuts in throughout research, and so it is always intersecting with empirical work. So while philosophy might be thought of by some as in the margins *because* they consider that its contribution can only be marginal, this volume starts from the view that it is, and must remain, central to all research in education.

Philosophy as research: re-thinking the margins

In highlighting philosophy as research in itself, and as constitutive of, not marginal to, educational thought, we debunk the idea that philosophy is merely an abstract concern, a 'tinkering at the edges' – or the margins. We will argue that it is not the case that philosophy has clearly marked-off marginal areas for research in education (such as conceptual clarification or discussion of issues of justification, value, and knowledge). Nor is it the case that philosophy is aimed solely at an academic audience, and that its research has little practical application to 'life at the coal face' in education, while mainstream empirical work deals with the 'proper' research that policy-makers and practitioners in education value. It is clear that research in educational philosophy can make a distinctive contribution to education, as Paul Standish points out in his introduction to philosophical approaches to research in education (2010). He shows how work in this field tends to be centrally concerned with issues of meaning and value in education, with conceptual matters, with the coherence of ideas or with the systematic establishing or refutation of a point of view. But these should not be thought of as exhaustive concerns; indeed, as Standish is keen to point out, pursuing philosophical enquiries open up from the very practical and diverse issues faced by those working in education. What this demonstrates is that research in this field is not desultory trifling with ideas at the margins of education, but rather a rich and critical engagement with central issues facing contemporary education policy and practice.

There is a further point that can be made about the notion of 'margins' that is relevant for our introductory remarks here. This imagines the margin in a positive, rather than in a pejorative sense. Imagine the margins around a sheet of paper, in a child's exercise book, or on a student's essay. These are the spaces where the writer, or a reader of the text, can annotate, make observations, embellish, reflect on, correct, or question the material. Known as *marginalia*, such comments have a long history, and are the subject of ongoing contemporary educational research (see, for example, Attenborough, 2011). One type of *marginalia*, known as *scholia* (from the Greek *skholion* meaning 'explanatory note or comment'), was common on classical manuscripts. In some cases, *scholia* were so extensive that they became works in their own right, such as those of Thomas Magister, the Byzantine scholar who compiled *scholia* on the works of Aeschylus, Sophocles, and Euripides (Mantanari and Pagani, 2011). So where does this leave us with regard to discussions of the place of educational philosophy as research? By drawing attention to the existence of *scholia*, we are not saying that philosophy is somehow to be seen as a marginal note on, an addition to, other (empirical) forms of research. This would fail to recognise philosophy's place in research and to demote educational philosophy again to the margins. Rather, our argument recognises one of the key characteristics of *scholia*: their iterative nature. They owe their existence to continual processes of thinking, revision, and development that show how ideas are never fully settled. But this is also the nature of educational philosophy (and of some kinds of research in this field that reject the obsession with certainty and proof that is so pervasive in much empirical research). As Paul Standish writes:

> Sometimes [educational philosophy is] based on a precise question one sets out to answer, or provide a solution to, but it is often concerned with an area in which one searches with less clear a destination…Sometimes argument is more loose…where the force of ideas (and the language used to express them) [are] allowed to evolve. Sometimes you don't know what you think until you have written it!
>
> *(2010: 11)*

The margins, then, are a space of critical comment, of intersection with other ideas, of re-thinking, re-wording and re-writing that open up still further lines of thought. And this kind of writing, this attention to language and the expression of ideas, is a central focus of the kind of philosophy-as-research that Part II of this book illustrates. Indeed, the second Part of our book includes contributions from a range of international scholars in the field. Their work, in its current form, is itself the result of a kind of dialogue through the use of *marginalia*. The extracts presented by the contributors are themselves the result of multiple iterations of thought and writing (and in this sense, they are no different from any other kind of reporting of research). The process of annotation (by ourselves as editors), and re-thinking and wording by the contributors in relation to their respective discussion of their extract, exhibits a further characteristic: they are educative for both reader and writer.

In Chapter 2 that now follows this introduction, we begin to consider how textbooks that support the practices of research in education tend to conceptualise research. We question the way that they provide an overview of schools of thought and research paradigms that tends to emphasise what, we think, is a false dichotomy between empirical and other forms of research. We provide a different approach to outlining these important schools of thought, by showing that they are defined by philosophical questions concerning with the nature of reality and with how we know what we know, questions that recur and are never fully settled. Given this, we argue that philosophy is there at the intersection of all these traditions, cutting in on our research questions and practices in ways that show that philosophy cannot, and should not, be marginalised.

Note

1 We illustrate the distinction between 'educational philosophy' and 'philosophy of education' in Part I, Chapter 2.

References

Attenborough, F. T. (2011) '"I don't f★★★ing care": Marginalia and the (Textual) Negotiation of an Academic Identity by University Students', *Discourse and Communication*, Vol. 5, No. 2, pp. 99–121.

Bridges, D., Smeyers, P., and Smith, R. (2009) *Evidence-Based Education Policy: What Evidence? What Basis? Whose Policy?*, Oxford: Wiley-Blackwell.

Mantanari, F. and Pagani, L. (Eds) (2011) *From Scholars to Scholia: Chapters in the History of Ancient Greek Scholarship*, Berlin: Walter de Gruyter.

Standish, P. (2010) 'What Is the Philosophy of Education?' in Richard Bailey (Ed.), *The Philosophy of Education: An Introduction*, London: Continuum, pp. 4–20.

2

RESEARCH AT THE INTERSECTION

Background – choosing from a menu of methods

Amanda Fulford and Naomi Hodgson

Philosophical or theoretical research in education is often referred to as non-empirical, or desk-based. There are a number of interrelated problems with this. First, it sets up an unhelpful dichotomy between empirical and non-empirical research. Second, it implies that, unlike 'empirical' research, which is concerned with gathering sense-data through, for example, observation, interviews, or measurement, philosophical or theoretical research is concerned only with abstract ideas, not concrete practices, experiences, or phenomena. Third, on the basis of the second assumption, philosophical or theoretical research is seen to be of less value in the study of education, where the predominant concern is with improving policy, curriculum, and pedagogy, to produce better outcomes. This concern is understandable. If we want concrete solutions to problems, philosophical or theoretical research might seem a frustrating indulgence. However, part of what we want to draw attention to here is the fact that empirical/non-empirical, theory/practice are not either/or choices that need to be made in educational research: all research starts from questions raised by observed phenomena, lived experience, existing practices, new policies, etc., and all research is underpinned by philosophical tenets, regardless of whether philosophical analysis forms part of that research or not.

So, we start here in a fairly standard way for a book about research; we look at 'schools of thought'. But the purpose here is not to provide a comprehensive overview of possible research methods, or the philosophy of research. Plenty of other guides exist that do that (see, for example, Keeves and Lakomski, 1999; Packer, 2012). Here, we provide an, admittedly selective, account of a number of dominant paradigms that have been influential in the development of Western academia, particularly in the humanities and social sciences. As we will see, however, they have equally shaped the natural sciences, and the debate about the differences between the two. The intention is to show, then, how approaches to empirical forms of research are underpinned by philosophical questions of how we know what we know, the basis of our knowledge claims – epistemology – and of the nature of what exists – ontology.

We do not provide a chronological account here, as we also show how such questions are rarely settled, but recur at various points as new questions are raised about the nature of reality and the language and practices through which we try to understand, and claim to know, it. The account given here is not restricted to the field of education, or to any one discipline of the social sciences, as these schools of thought have been influential across disciplines, albeit in different ways, and increasingly lead to an interdisciplinarity, a feature inherent to the field of education.

Where to start

Accounts of schools of thought or major research paradigms are often given chronologically. While this can be useful, particularly to show how new directions in thought were a critique of previous ones, or a response to a particular political or cultural period, there is a risk that the account can appear evolutionary, that is, presenting later schools of thought as superior, more rational, more truthful, than earlier ones. Taking this approach might imply, for example, that Plato has nothing to say about education or research or the world we live in today (which, of course, most philosophers would contest), or that positivism, the scientific objectivism found in the work of Francis Bacon, Auguste Comte, and later the Vienna Circle of the 1920s, can be dismissed out of hand or is no longer applied. It also glosses over the fact that philosophical questions are rarely settled once and for all. The crude distinctions often drawn between, say, positivist/interpretivist, or indeed empirical/ non-empirical, suggest that the researcher should make a choice between them and that, in doing so, matters of epistemology – of the basis on which we can say that we know something – can be settled in a pre-data gathering, theoretical phase. There is also a linearity to the way in which research methods texts present the process of research, which also denies the, perhaps inconvenient, persistence of questions. We will focus on such texts in more detail in Chapter 3.

Here, then, rather than taking things chronologically, we will consider different schools of thought as responses to sociopolitical conditions and recurring philosophical questions. This allows us to consider relationships between them, and to highlight the persistence of questions about the nature of the world, of human beings, and how we come to know what we know. We will start, then, with recent trends in educational research, and in social scientific research more generally, which themselves can be seen as responses to philosophical questions posed by the changing world we live in. Each characterisation is necessarily brief, but gives a sense of what is at stake in the modes of thought these philosophical perspectives enable.

Changing paradigms

A number of recent titles indicate the ways in which established research methods are no longer seen to be fit for purpose, for example, in anthropology, James Faubion and George E. Marcus's *Fieldwork Is Not What It Used To Be* (2009), in education, Patti Lather and Elizabeth St. Pierre's 2013 Special Issue of the *International Journal of Qualitative Studies in Education* on post-qualitative research, and in sociology, John Law's *After Method: Mess in Social Science Research* (2004). Law's book is a response to what he perceives to be the relatively small repertoire of methods drawn upon within the social sciences, the normativity within how they are taught, and the limitations this places on how we enquire into the complexity of the world we live in. A number of strands of thought have begun to be taken up in educational research that seek to respond to this and, in doing so, to question assumptions entailed in earlier research paradigms. Our starting point here, then, is with a relatively recent strand of thought that is starting to be taken up more widely in the study of education: posthumanism. Exploring this will set out the kind of questions to which this is a response, and lead us to consider its precursors, and the relationship of contemporary approaches to earlier influential schools of thought.

Humanism and posthumanism

The ubiquity of technology in our lives today is a significant area of study in the social sciences, from a variety of perspectives. In education, the role of technology in teaching and learning is often seen to be the solution to various problems, or to be a denigration of education and something to use with caution. Often, these accounts of technology draw on established theoretical approaches in which the human being is the primary agent. Posthumanism challenges the binary distinctions around which humanist thought has been organised throughout modernity, e.g. human/animal, nature/culture, binaries that place that which is not human as 'other' and inferior, or which assume that it has no agency of its own. The field's perhaps best-known author is Donna Haraway, whose 1991 book *Simians, Cyborgs, and Women: The Reinvention of Nature* problematised assumed distinctions between the ontologically human, nonhuman, and inhuman, informing many subsequent approaches that reconceptualise relations between human, animal, and machine, and diagnose 'how humanism ignores, obscures, and disavows the real relations among beings and things that make up the stuff of the world' (Snaza and Weaver, 2015: 1).

Humanism refers to the traditions of thought that questioned the religious or theistic explanation of phenomena. It came to dominance in particular during the Enlightenment in the late eighteenth and nineteenth centuries, as the basis for advocacy of decision-making based on scientific rationality and human progress. It advocates the central value of human potential, but for this reason has been subject to critique during the twentieth century for the evolutionary, Eurocentric, and gendered conception of Man this implied and, more recently, for its anthropocentrism.

As a critique of humanism, posthumanist approaches displace the reification of the human being in accounts of the world and attend to how 'the human', taken throughout modernity as the basic unit of reference and retaining the assurance of common sense (Braidotti, 2013: 1), is constituted in what we do and how we discuss and conceptualise it. That is, in posthumanist approaches the notion of the human is not taken as a given, with a fixed meaning. As the title of Haraway's book suggests, posthumanism provides a critique of the othering that is entailed in privileging a view of the human as male.

In humanist thought, which has characterised Western culture, Rosi Braidotti writes:

> Subjectivity is equated with consciousness, universal rationality, and self-regulating ethical behaviour, all of them equating masculinity and European civilisation, whereas Otherness is defined as its negative and specular counterpart: irrationality, immorality, femininity and non-westernness. In so far as difference spells inferiority, it acquires both essentialist and lethal connotations for people who get branded as the 'others'. These are the sexualised, racialised, and naturalised others, who are reduced to the less-than-human status of disposable bodies.
>
> *(2013: 2)*

The critique of humanism has not just emerged in the twenty-first century. In the mid- to late twentieth century, anti-humanists developed critical stances to the universalist conception of the human as exclusive, androcentric, and Eurocentric (*ibid.*). This also disrupted the organisation of disciplinary knowledge and saw the emergence of new 'fields' of study, for example, gender, postcolonial, and media studies. The radical rethinking of the category of the human by anti-humanists, indicated, for example, in Michel Foucault's identification of 'the death of Man' (1970: 387), came together in what is broadly referred to as poststructuralism (Braidotti, 2013: 3), which we will discuss further below.

To refer to the 'death of Man' is not to suggest the demise of the human species; rather, it refers to the very specific humanist conception of 'Man' that prevailed in the modern period. The anti-humanism of the mid- to late twentieth century took a variety of forms that destabilised the certainties of rationalist, Enlightenment thinking. We will return to these below, but move now to positivism as characteristic of this logical, rationalist approach. This will show how, while posthumanism provides a critical rethinking of many taken-for-granted concepts and categories, indeed, of ontology itself, humanist thought is central to the way in which the disciplines in the sciences, social sciences, and humanities have taken shape since the Enlightenment. It is also pertinent to our consideration of educational research, as although commonly associated with early twentieth-century philosophy of science and social science, positivism remains a guiding principle in methods such as 'randomised control trials', seen as the gold standard for social scientific research today (Packer, 2012: 19).

Positivism

The thorough objectivism of the school of thought known as positivism held that the meaning of the world was 'out there' to be discovered. According to this objectivist epistemology, 'objects in the world have meaning prior to, and independently of, any consciousness of them' (Crotty, 1998: 27). Positivism has taken many forms, but it was first popularised by Auguste Comte. Its name derives from an understanding of science as being based on that which can be 'posited' from direct experience rather than speculation. This objectivist epistemology 'proceeds by a study of the "given" (in Latin *datum* or, in the plural, *data*)' (*ibid*.). Comte sought to apply the methods of the natural sciences to the social, and so positivism, broadly speaking, was concerned with the establishment of the laws of nature or society by means of observation, experiment, and comparison. The later Vienna Circle School of logical positivism, which included figures such as Otto Neurath and A. J. Ayer, sought to apply the logical principles of mathematics to the study of philosophy (*ibid*.).

This 'logical positivism' took the 'verification principle' from the early work of Ludwig Wittgenstein as a central tenet, holding that 'no statement is meaningful unless it can be verified' (Crotty, 1998: 25). Those areas of study that were seen to rely on speculation – metaphysics, theology, ethics, i.e. areas unable to be based on observable phenomena – were considered by the logical positivists not to belong to the domain of 'warrantable human knowledge' (*ibid*.: 24). This claim to objectivity, value-neutrality, and certainty was questioned from within the philosophy of science, where a 'less arrogant positivism, that talks of probability rather than certainty' was later advocated (*ibid*.: 29). Others, such as Werner Heisenberg, who developed quantum theory and the uncertainty principle, raised epistemological questions over positivist science by pointing to the uncertainty in science. Niels Bohr raised ontological questions about the assumption that science can only be based on observable reality, by pointing to the unobservable reality of, for example, subatomic particles; we could not apply existing concepts to understand them as they constitute a different reality (Crotty, 1998: 29–30).

These epistemological and ontological questions recognised a contradiction in scientific practice between what it claims to do and what it does: 'Many of the so-called facts that serve as elements of these theories are not directly observed at all. Instead, they have been quite purposefully contrived and introduced as mere heuristic and explanatory devices' (*ibid*.: 30). So, far from observing a law of nature already called 'photosynthesis', for example, scientists observed a number of processes and activities, that were then defined by the concept 'photosynthesis'. Thus, the passive, neutral linking of truth to meaning is thus shown to actually entail active construction by scientists. This is not to claim, of course, that scientific discovery is meaning*less* or entirely subjective, but rather to show that, by means of language, the world is constructed in a particular way.

The epistemology based on objectively observable phenomena, as the etymology of the word data – 'given' – suggests, took the relationship between language and thought – that is, between a thing and what we call that thing – as a given. One strand of anti-humanist thought that emerged as a critique of this in the early to mid-twentieth century is referred to as poststructuralism. In a variety of ways, philosophers such as Friedrich Nietzsche, Martin Heidegger, John (J. L.) Austin, and

Wittgenstein in his later work, questioned the understanding of the relationship of language to thought found in logical positivism. The relationship between knowledge and power was a focus in particular in the work of Nietzsche and Foucault (Standish, 2004). Whereas positivist approaches had supposed there to be a natural language, poststructuralists argued that any form of speaking about something, or any discourse, to use a term associated with the work of Foucault, enables certain ways of thinking and, therefore, excludes others (*ibid.*: 490). The Enlightenment belief in the rationality of Man presupposes a right way of thinking, a normative sense of what the human man is or should be. Poststructuralist thought unsettled stable notions of identity and human development upheld by this mode of thought (*ibid.*).

Subjectivism, objectivism, and constructivism

Poststructuralist thought, then, exposes 'the possibility of certainty, of truth itself, as a chimera' (Standish, 2004: 489). In the mid- to late twentieth century, in response to rapid globalisation, commercialisation, and technologisation, postmodernist thought sought to further question the false certainties of the past (though, as Paul Standish notes, this is sometimes misconstrued as a rejection of it) (*ibid.*: 489). We now take it for granted that we will bring our own position – thoughts, values, experience, personality – to bear on any situation, but the epistemologies of subjectivism, and of constructivism – of knowledge and meaning as constructed rather than a fixed, given fact of nature – were articulated relatively recently, in poststructuralist and postmodernist thought (*ibid.*).

The account so far might suggest a binary of objectivism, on the one hand, and subjectivism, on the other. Early positivists can perhaps be associated with the former, and some strands of poststructuralism with the latter. Constructivism, however, acknowledged that we do not create meaning and impose it on the world, as implied by thorough subjectivism, nor is truth or meaning naturally out there to be discovered, as implied by objectivism; rather it is constructed out of something, i.e. the world and the things in it. This brings together the fact that humans exist in the world and cannot be understood separately from it, and that meaning is created in relation to things and actions, in the world: subjectivism and objectivism are therefore held together in the constructivist perspective.

The question of the relationship between language and thought, and between language and action, i.e. the idea that how we speak about a thing changes the nature of that thing and what we do, has implications for research, not only in terms of the methods we use and the knowledge claims we make about what we find, but also how we go about representing those findings and the researcher's role in the construction of knowledge. This draws attention to the central role of writing in the research process, from how we take notes, to how we represent or report our findings. This issue was taken up particularly in anthropology, where field notes and the representation of 'others' in written ethnographies came into question in light of the epistemological and ethical questions raised by anti-humanist, poststructuralist, and post-colonial theory and philosophy. This problematised the idea of 'culture' and the ways that the culture being studied was being represented solely by the voice of the author/researcher.

Critique and power

In what we have covered so far, some approaches have been concerned with knowing and understanding the world, while some have been concerned with challenging the existing cultural and political order, or knowing and understanding the world differently by questioning the power relations or exclusions entailed in existing approaches. We turn now to the critical tradition in Western thought, which is commonly associated with Karl Marx and with the Frankfurt School, and to which the term Critical Theory usually refers. Marx was critical of philosophy as merely interpretation and took a critical, active view of its role. Marx saw each period of history as defined by an internal contradiction, which he termed 'class struggle', e.g. in capitalist society, the struggle between capital and labour, between the bourgeoisie and the proletariat. For Marx, the ruling ideology constitutes a truth, a 'false consciousness', that maintains the oppression of the proletariat. Marx's thought was later taken up in the work of the Frankfurt School in the 1920s and 1930s, in a variety of ways, but in more cultural than economic terms, which came to prominence in the work of Adorno, Horkheimer, and later Habermas.

Marx, and later Marxist theory, were concerned then with critique at the level of the structure of society and the inequality of the agency of those in it, e.g. as seen in the distinction between the proletariat and the bourgeoisie, and with the ruling ideology, that is, the truths imposed on the masses. Thinkers such as Foucault, however, were dissatisfied with the politics that this entailed, feeling that it did not find its target. Foucault challenged the understanding of power as top-down, imposed by the state on the people, by developing historical accounts of the ways in which power was produced through particular, historically contingent discourses and practices. Through a particular form of historical analysis – archaeology – he analysed the ways in which the human sciences spoke about the human and thus how the human came to understand him/herself and how a discourse became dispersed throughout a population. It was not a matter of stripping back a false ideology to reveal a truth beneath:

> A discursive formation itself is neither true nor false because it defines which statements count as true and false. What is important is not what statements *say* or *mean* – their images, themes or concepts – but what they *do*. And what a statement does depends on its location among other statements.
>
> *(Packer, 2012: 346)*

Words are not merely a surface description of things, then, on this view, but sets of practices that order things (*ibid.*: 347). Similarly, the human subject is itself a product of these discourses and practices; there is no transcendental human subject by whom meaning is created or on whom meaning is imposed. As we saw with

Foucault's reference to 'the death of Man', the analysis of the constitution of the subject by historically contingent discourses and practices showed 'Man' to be one such construction, and denied the primacy and sovereignty of man as the exclusive source of knowledge and meaning. In later historical studies, referred to as gene-alogies, Foucault focused more specifically on power, and the relationship between knowledge and power, in the discourses and practices of the human sciences and in the production of subjectivity. It is this phase of his research, on power and knowledge, and on 'governmentality', his account of the way in which power was effected in the modern state – through the government of mentality – that has been used most widely in educational research.

More recently, in educational philosophy, it is his later work on subjectiv-ity and ethics that has been used to inform renewed modes of critique in the face of changing modes of government. Rather than simply apply Foucault's work as theory, the attitude of critique it entails has been taken up in part due to its educative aspect. His analyses of ethics, for example, in Ancient Greek philosophical texts, detail particular forms of work on the self. It is a mode of philosophy referred to as ascetic; it is not concerned with the logical analysis of practices and setting out normative principles of how to live the good life, but is concerned with the possibility of rethinking one's relationship to one's self and others as a permanent ongoing critique. While Foucault's work provided a critique of humanism, as entailing the primacy of the sovereign individual, it also recognised the possibility of critique that emerged during the modern period (see Foucault, 2000).

Foucault's work has been influential across the humanities and social sciences as well as in education. It is commonly associated with poststructuralism, and the use of such literature is generally concerned with power relations and the language and practices by means of which they are constituted. This focus on language has also been part of the concern in posthumanist literature; not only with the othering effected by the centrality of the 'human', but also with the primacy given to texts and discourse in such analyses, at the expense of the animal, material, and physical dimensions of phenomena.

So, this brings us back to posthumanism, where we started this account. The brief, selective overview given so far skips over a variety of thinkers and schools of thought. Their insights endure in current research practices in various and often unacknowledged ways. Current and emerging approaches critique and problema-tise these earlier ones, but are also made possible by them. We look at a variety of recent approaches now, that can be broadly classified as posthumanist and that are gaining attention in educational research.

Whereas anti-humanism, or the critique of humanism, was concerned with the exclusive and historically contingent notion of the category 'human' and the othering this effects, as outlined by Braidotti, posthumanism does not seek to assimilate all humans into that category. Rather, the very thinking on which the centrality of the category 'human' has been problematised is rethought. As Cary Wolfe puts it:

> [W]hen we talk about posthumanism, we are not just talking about a the-
> matics of the decentring of the human in relation to either evolutionary,
> ecological, or technological coordinates…rather,…we are also talking about
> how thinking confronts that thematics, what thought has to become in the
> face of those challenges.
>
> *(2010: xvi)*

It is not a question of a need to reject humanism entirely, but rather to show how
its 'aspirations are undercut by the philosophical and ethical frameworks used to
undercut them' (*ibid.*: xvi). To illustrate his argument, Wolfe uses the examples
of cruelty to animals and discrimination against the disabled. While it is generally
agreed that mistreatment and discrimination are bad, the humanist frameworks
for thinking about equality and ethics 'reproduce the very kind of normative
subjectivity – a specific concept of the human – that grounds discrimination
against non human animals in the first place' (*ibid.*: xvii).

This need to rethink the very frameworks we use to analyse our posthuman
condition leads Bruno Latour to ask whether critique has 'run out of steam' (2004:
225). By this he means that the criticism of humanism – by feminist, postcolonial,
cultural and other new fields of studies since the mid- to late twentieth century –
no longer gains purchase on the world we live in today; these arguments are largely
won. This is not to say that there is no longer racial, sexual, or religious prejudice,
or that inequality no longer exists. Far from it. But rather that they are no longer
upheld by the same essentialist, exclusive structures, laws, and beliefs that they were
during the modern period. Furthermore, the very conditions by which life is lived
have been changed dramatically by new media technologies, bioscientific developments, environmental degradation, and economic change and, thus, to understand
phenomena today, the agency and constitution of these must also be considered.

So, to say that critique has 'run out of steam' is by no means to say, either, that
the work of the academic is done, but rather that it might not be aiming at the
right target (*ibid.*: 225). Latour is concerned that the prevalence and acceptedness
of the idea that knowledge is constructed, rather than revealing injustice and eman-
cipating the Other, make argument and critique impossible, as nothing is accepted
as truth. He uses the example of the book written by the postmodernist theorist
Jean Baudrillard after the 9/11 terrorist attacks in New York, in which he argued
that 'the Twin Towers destroyed themselves under their own weight, so to speak,
undermined by the utter nihilism inherent in capitalism itself' (*ibid.*: 228). Latour
writes: 'What has become of critique when a book that claims that no plane ever
crashed into the Pentagon can be a bestseller?' (*ibid.*: 228). His point is that critique
in this vein glosses over what happened and what is at stake in such an event, in all
its complexity, and closes down further thinking. Thus it in some sense denigrates
the role of the academic in doing so. In rethinking critique, Latour points out that
the 'question was never to get away from facts but closer to them, not fighting
empiricism but, on the contrary, renewing empiricism' (*ibid.*: 231). His concerns
are not purely philosophical or theoretical, therefore, but illustrate very clearly the

epistemological and ontological questions raised when we start to look at how to best go about analysing or understanding the world we live in.

Latour is not rejecting the notion of critique but rather is trying to ensure that critique does some work, rather than being detached from the world we live in, in the proverbial 'ivory tower'. That it does not get so bound up in its own logic that it loses sight of what might be of concern today. His approach is not a rejection of critique, then, but rather a reminder of what an 'attitude' of critique entails. The term 'attitude' is derived from the work of Foucault, as we have seen. It refers not to a theory or method, but to an ethical and political commitment to a particular form of questioning what is accepted as truth. This is not necessarily, as Latour's work indicates, to reveal a true reality hidden beneath, but to cut through accepted truths to show how that truth is constituted, through what we say and what we do, as discussed earlier in relation to Foucault. His notion of critique is derived from Kant and Nietzsche, and was a reaction against the Critical Inquiry and Critical Theory developed by Marx and later Marxist scholars, referred to as the Frankfurt School.

The relationships between these different schools of thought continue to show how they cannot be understood solely chronologically, and as discrete entities, and further, how certain aspects of human life, questions of knowledge claims, and the nature of reality and existence, persist and recur. Matters are not settled once and for all. What is referred to as the Enlightenment, was not called this until the late nineteenth century. And although 'Enlightenment thinking' is the subject of the critique of poststructuralist and posthumanist thought, it was the philosophy that emerged during this time that enabled the attitude of critique that these later developments rely on. Each new school of thought is not an outright rejection of or replacement for what went before. Often, and particularly in chronological accounts of schools of thought, positivism comes first and is seen as inferior, even naïve, in its belief in an objectivist epistemology as able to give us access to truth. As Latour's critique of the potential nihilism of subjectivism and constructivism suggests, however, these alternatives can go so far that they deny the possibility that we can know anything at all or, by being relativist, that no one account of events or phenomena should prevail.

As part of a concern to address the prevalence of subjectivist accounts, and coming at a time when society is often understood as individualised, fragmented, privatised, and therefore as lacking a collective or public dimension, there has been a renewed interest recently in phenomenology. The origins of this approach will be discussed first before indicating how the renewed interest in it responds to current concerns.

Phenomenology

Phenomenology is associated with figures such as Edmund Husserl, a former student of Heidegger, writing in the 1930s and, later, Maurice Merleau-Ponty, writing in the 1960s. It takes up the critical impetus referred to earlier in relation to poststructuralism in its questioning of the fixity of inherited understandings and the way in which they stifle thought, while also adopting an objectivist stance in relation to the observation of phenomena (Crotty, 1998). By throwing off received understandings of the meaning of phenomena, or 'previous habits of thought', we can 'learn to see what stands before our eyes' (Husserl, 1931: 43). Otherwise, we begin to interpret or attribute meaning in advance of our seeing and experiencing and do not permit the potential new meanings of phenomena to appear to us (*ibid.*). The possibilities for human thought and the renewal of culture are, in this view, stifled if we assume in advance the meaning of phenomena. Furthermore, and of concern in more recent research, the prevailing subjectivism retains the centrality of the human understanding of the meaning and purpose of things, rather than the meaning of things themselves. This is not to return to the positivist position that there is a pre-existing meaning and truth out there to be discovered. Phenomenology allows for multiple possible meanings to be found, assuming that an object is always an object *for* someone, i.e. it has no meaning without consciousness of that thing and a particular use of it. Rather, it is to permit ourselves to experience those things anew, not on the basis of our pre-existing cultural or theoretical understanding of them. Recent phenomenological approaches, including in educational philosophy, address the concern that traditional phenomenological approaches posit a meaning 'out there' to be discovered. Instead, they address Latour's concern and 'look again' at what is the case and attend to the ways that our interactions with the material world change us and change (what we mean by) education.

The study of technology is an important case in point: we associate the word 'technology' today with digital and electronic devices and processes. Any instruments we use, however, can be referred to as technologies, in the sense that, at the point of their invention and their becoming ubiquitous, they intervened in and changed our practices and therefore what those practices mean. Seen in these terms, then, a phenomenological approach will look at what a particular technology does, how it changes the meaning of a practice, rather than assuming its meaning in advance. For example, in education, new information technologies are often understood as maximising learning opportunities and thereby enhancing human capacities, or as causing a loss of certain human skills and characteristics through the automation that these technologies allow, e.g. if I can search for something on Google on my phone at home the moment a question arises, I have no need to wait until it is convenient, go to the library, find the relevant book, and search for the answer. On a certain view, this distinction might be understood as a loss of certain traditions, the diminution of cultural and literary life, the unfettered advance of an instantaneous, consumer-demand-led culture. Taking these perspectives to the study of a phenomena decides in advance what that phenomena is, and what effect it has, and is a matter of adding detail to an already existing picture of the world.

Phenomenology's critical dimension lies in focusing in detail on everyday practices in order to see them anew. Existing practices, whose meaning and purpose might be taken for granted, or whose value is seen to be outmoded, can be assessed from an educational perspective in its own terms. New and emerging practices can be seen in terms of how they change us as human beings and our interaction with the world and each other, and thus entail analysis at the level of ontology. Such approaches require focused and detailed attention on the physical and material as well as the linguistic aspects of a practice or phenomenon, and thus are rethought in the light of new posthumanist literature. They also further trouble the distinction between so-called empirical and non-empirical approaches.

Empirical philosophy

Latour, whom we discussed above, works in the field of science studies and is commonly associated with Actor Network Theory. This is a constructivist approach, but its break with previous studies of the construction of scientific knowledge lies in its rejection of the 'social' as a source of explanation. Latour displaces the binaries referred to above – nature/culture and human/nonhuman – by treating them as symmetrical. That is to say, they are all placed on the same plane, and an account is given of an event or phenomenon based on what and how actors or agents connect with others in producing it. So, rather than actors and networks referring to separate entities, Latour's approach provides accounts of actor-networks; the relationships between things that constitute those phenomena. Laurier writes:

> Where many social theorists, and political philosophers, from Hobbes onwards, set up a binary opposition between social structure and individual agency, Latour pursues impure entities that have characteristics of structure *and* agency. They are, in other words, actors *and* networks or actor-networks. Latour suggests that those who employ an empty gulf between agency and structure do so by ignoring the dark matter of material objects that articulate, embody, coordinate and, even, author actions.
>
> *(2010: 437)*

The symmetry applies not only to nature and culture and the human and nonhuman, but also to roles; for example, the scientist is given no greater weight than, say, the butcher or the grocer in terms of what they do, what they produce, and the language they speak. Latour is, Laurier writes, 'anti-theory'. His approach is itself a critique of the tendency within the social sciences to bring theory and theoretical categories, e.g. race, gender, sexuality, kinship, to bear on phenomena and therefore to presuppose connections and asymmetries between things.

Latour's work, and posthumanist theory more broadly, mark a radical departure not only from the humanism that privileges human thought and agency and social explanations of phenomena, but also from the poststructuralism and postmodernism that called into question the very notion of truth. This is not a thoroughgoing rejection of previous schools of thought, however. Latour's arguments intersect with and question notions of positivism, objectivism, and constructivism, and in doing so, the very notions of epistemology and ontology themselves.

A further example from empirical research in this vein will further illustrate its philosophical implications. By questioning the political agency of things, Noortje Marres (2013) questions existing notions of ontology. She distinguishes her notion of experimental ontology from other conceptions of ontology: the theoretical, the political, and the empirical. Theoretical ontology refers to the classical understanding, a theory of what exists. It is a conception criticised in the field of science and technology studies for its assumption that what exists is given, not made, constructed, or performed (*ibid.*: 422). Political ontology, then, refers to 'the set of definitions that stipulate the features of specifically political entities (state, power, democracy, etc.)' (*ibid.*). Empirical ontology claims that the question of what exists is not solely a theoretical question but 'is partly settled in practices that must be studied empirically'; in STS (Science and Technology Studies) this marks the shift from epistemology to ontology (*ibid.*). The empirical conception of ontology claims:

> that what was traditionally considered the province of metaphysics, namely, the issue of what the world is made up of, is in actuality decided through specific, historical, cultural, technological and scientific interventions and as such, should be studied in empirical terms. As mentioned, this has specific implications for politics because ontology is shown to have political dimensions in and of itself. If ontologies vary over time, then the matter of what exists may be transformed from a given into an issue at stake.
>
> *(ibid.: 423)*

It should start to be clear from the account given in this chapter so far that to identify oneself strictly with a school of thought, as if it were a strict set of principles, is not possible. The questions that our experience of phenomena in the world poses, do not require us to pick an epistemology and a methodology, but rather to ask whether existing frameworks of understanding those phenomena, and the approaches used to study them, are fit for purpose. However, as indicated earlier, this is often what research methods handbooks ask us to do: to choose a method and identify oneself with a school of thought or theorist. As we have seen, theories, philosophies, and methods are not discrete entities, nor are they internally homogenous. But the list of options that prescribes those approaches deemed most suitable for enquiry in education, delimits our possibilities, and closes down the question.

Intersections

The account above gives a necessarily brief and selective overview of a diversity of schools of thought and approaches to research. While we have indicated that a dichotomy between 'empirical' and 'non-empirical' research is unhelpful, and it is a distinction that we want to resist, we have also drawn attention in the above to the way in which language shapes how we understand ourselves, what we do, what we know, and the knowledge we produce, which has political implications. In our attention to philosophical approaches to research in education, then, we do want to maintain that there is something distinctive about research in the field of philosophy of education, which is found particularly (though not exclusively) in its practices of reading and writing. This might suggest something of a contradiction: what is our position, exactly? How helpful are the terms 'empirical' and 'philosophical' in characterising educational research? Let us be clear: the intention here is not to further entrench a binary distinction between philosophy and social science, between non-empirical and empirical. As indicated by the overview above, broader distinctions between disciplines such as philosophy, anthropology, sociology, and psychology, are no more clear-cut now than they ever were. Today, interdisciplinarity is not only encouraged, but also necessary in order to respond anew to our changing conditions. The questions and challenges we face do not fit neatly into disciplinary boundaries, and we are not helped by a perception of philosophy's situating itself as superior in its ability to address them. However, we risk stifling educational questions if we leave untouched the philosophical implications of what we do as researchers.

In thinking further about interdisciplinarity and the messiness of disciplinary boundaries, we want to suggest an analogy that might serve as a focus for our current discussions. For this, we draw on various images and ideas from travelling. This is not new: Mackenzie and Ling (2009) liken research to a journey, with researchers as travellers encountering detours and delays, and Lewis and Ritchie (2010), in their study of the development of the development and support of a practitioner research network, show how the analogy of research-as-journey is particularly pertinent to education. So let us persist with this. Imagine an intersection, something like a simple crossroads, the type that motorists typically encounter on even a simple journey. At the crossroads, there are a number of road signs pointing in different directions. Each sign has on it a different destination, together with the respective distance to the destination. Some signs contain additional warnings for particular routes such as 'unsuitable for heavy goods vehicles' or 'single track road with passing places'. Cars are approaching the junction, pausing, and crossing over or turning left and right. We might think about embarking on research as having some parallels with these images. Research methods textbooks play an important role in this picture: they are analogous to the road signs at the junction. They are there to give succinct guidance to the researcher, to show the possibilities of travel, but to lay out very clearly the different destinations and to warn of potential perils along the route that might give rise to the choice of an alternative route. As we have shown, the textbooks themselves make these very claims by presenting researchers with options for research in terms of different kinds of research question, of a choice of schools of thought in which to situate one's research, of options for one's methodology, data collection methods, and of approaches to data analysis. They also lay out the pitfalls of certain routes, and provide salutary warnings.

There is a further useful analogy that we can draw here with the idea of a junction or intersection. In the normal course of events, cars approaching a junction pause only momentarily to make sure that they are taking the right road to reach their destination; their encounter with the junction is only fleeting. Once the necessary checks have been made to ensure the correct direction of travel, the cars navigate, and leave, the junction. All is settled, the journey is on track and the destination is in view. Let us further develop this image, which will help in the disruption of the tendency to dichotomise empirical versus non-empirical forms of research. Imagine two types of junction: the crossroads and the roundabout. Both can be thought of not only as a point of departure for different directions of travel, but as a point of confluence, where traffic enters from different directions, before navigating the junction to continue the journey. The junction is the space where different streams of traffic meet, each with a particular destination in mind. At the junction, different vehicles briefly share the same space, giving way to each other, and recognising the presence of the other so that their respective journeys can proceed. The junction, as the space of intersection, helps us to consider how ideas from different disciplines and traditions inform research on education. Think, for example, of a research project that seeks to evaluate the effectiveness of a behaviour management policy in a primary school. This research must take seriously ideas that come into it from different disciplinary traditions. There must be some kind of con-fluence between theories of the development of the child, and those that consider the reasons for disruptive behaviour. These are most likely drawn from psychology; but in addition, the research must take account of ideas of discipline, punishment, shame, responsibility, and authority that come from different sources, perhaps from sociology and anthropology.

These ideas of interdisciplinarity in research are not new, and our use of the image of the intersection is used not only to highlight this. But also it draws atten-tion to the richer point to be made that concerns the intersection as a shared space, or even starting point, that opens up the possibility of travel in many different directions. Research in education has such a shared space or point of initiation in that it often starts from the everyday experiences of teaching and learning, what we might call the lived experience of education. Take the example of investigating the parenting classes run by a college of further education and delivered in the com-munity. Research in this field might be informed by a number of different strands of work: policy imperatives on community and family engagement; existing aca-demic literature evaluating models of parenting; the possibility of collecting new data in the form of parents' stories; or a critique of forms of government interven-tion in family life. We can think of these strands as roads leading into the junction, but it is from this central space, where ideas intersect with the possibilities afforded by the different traditions, that research can then proceed in different directions. One route might be a detailed case study of best practice in teaching; another could be a philosophical critique of the practices of 'teaching' parenting, and the extent to which these are educative.

The point to be made here is that many research methods handbooks tend not to see the value of the intersection. If travel via difficult junctions cannot be avoided, then they provide a clearly signposted route that makes the direction of travel very clear, and ensures that the researcher's plans for enquiry are situated correctly within epistemological and theoretical frameworks, and are aligned with the most appropriate methodology and methods. But the value of the image of the intersection is its depicting a starting point for what Katariina Holma refers to as the 'complexity and multidimensionality' of the field of educational research (2009: 333). Philosophical research is simply one of the exits from the intersection; it does not have a different starting point. Philosophy is not, to extend the analogy further, on a different track. Indeed, Holma points out philosophy's and education's common interests, referring to them as 'investigational intersections' (*ibid.*). Understanding the intersection in this way disrupts the false nature of any strict dichotomy between empirical and non-empirical forms of research that many research texts suggest or imply, and which it has been one of our purposes in this chapter to show.

While the idea of research-as-journey (with which we opened this section) is relatively simple to understand, the idea of the intersection as an analogy for the confluence of ideas/traditions, and as the starting point for research in education, is somewhat more complicated. Perhaps it is not the analogy *per se* that is most helpful here, but rather the etymology of the word 'intersection' itself. Coming from the Latin *intersectionem* (meaning 'a cutting asunder'), the word comprises two elements: '*inter*' ('between'), and *secare* ('to cut'). Understanding the origins of the word is helpful in two ways: first, in appreciating the place and operation of method in empirical and non-empirical forms of research, and second, in showing how the philosophical underlies *all* forms of research. Let us deal with each of these briefly. As we have shown, with many of the textbooks that support the research process in education and the social sciences, it is as if issues related to methodology and method are part of the design frame of the research that must be agreed, tidied up, and, in some sense, tied down, at the outset of research. Such an approach precludes the need to revisit issues of method as the research progresses. But the etymological association of intersection with 'cutting in' suggests that *throughout* the research, the approach taken cuts in to, and cannot be divorced from, the investigation being undertaken. This is true of research in philosophy, but is surely also the case in other forms of research, where the practices of reading and writing that are integral to the research are also part of its methodological processes.

A further point related to the etymological associations of intersection with a 'cutting between' and 'cutting asunder' is the idea that running alongside[1] the questions and operation of research with an empirical dimension are broader philosophical questions that cut in, as it were, at various points throughout the research process. For example, an (empirically-oriented) research question such as 'How can teachers in primary education encourage self-esteem in pupils from disadvantaged backgrounds?' raises related questions that we might think of as more philosophical; in this case, questions relating to the aims of education and to what kinds of education we should value and for which we should strive, the ethics of differentiating pupils in particular ways at the conceptual level, or the practical implications of data collection. Similarly, questions of how to approach data collection with human participants as part of the planning of the design frame for the research open out onto broader philosophical questions of ethics and representation. So philosophy, and philosophical concerns, inflect what we might consider to be empirical ones, cutting in throughout research practices and processes. The analogy of the intersection (with its ideas of confluence, of starting points, and of cutting in) strongly suggests that philosophy is central to educational research in all its forms. It is not a marginal or elite practice, nor is it only appropriate for abstract enquiries into education that bear little relevance to the everyday, lived experience of teaching and learning.

Philosophy and education

It is not only in educational research of course that we find introductory guides and handbooks. In the field of philosophy of education there is a growing list of titles that set out the key approaches, issues, and thinkers that are seen to define the field. To some extent these guides exhibit the same anxiety as texts in other fields; to define the field of study, maintain its visibility, and prove its relevance to current educational questions. If the field is defined in limited terms, as a particular style of philosophy, this also shores up a distinction, which we contest, between philosophy and empirical educational research. (We will address 'styles' of philosophy later in this section.) The need to make this distinction is understandable. Furthermore, its focus on texts and concepts, rather than answering questions by empirical means that produce findings on how to improve practice, marginalises it in terms of its perceived relevance and applicability. For this reason, in the current regime, philosophical research in a practical field such as education finds it difficult to compete for funding with, for example, sociological or psychological research in education. And given the need to secure external funding, if one faces a choice, philosophical research does not appear to be the most strategically sensible one.

Earlier we discussed how philosophical questions and considerations are inherent in academic research, regardless of the field or type of research, and also that these questions arise from the same social and educational reality. Here we want to clarify what we mean by philosophy, and how a particular understanding of it (which is not limited to its traditional disciplinary definition but focuses more on practices of reading and writing) can further its educational relevance and potential. There is an assumption that a philosophical question or account is an abstract one, removed from practical concerns. This is in part due to a prevailing instrumentalism in the understanding of what research is for – improving practice, improving educational outcomes – and also in part due, perhaps, to the form that philosophy of education has predominantly taken in Anglophone countries.

A distinction is often made when characterising philosophy, between the Analytic and the Continental traditions. When this distinction is used, it refers to a traditions of philosophy largely stemming from and represented in the Anglo-American traditions of philosophy context, and work originating in Continental Europe, but particularly France and Germany, and represented by movements such as poststructuralism. The distinction is not especially helpful in understanding the history of philosophy, the interrelationship between the schools of thought discussed earlier, or the rich possibilities of meaning and thought that each has the potential to offer. So, to characterise styles of philosophy in these terms is in some ways unhelpful if our aim is to question the other binary we have discussed, between philosophical and empirical research.

But there are important remarks to be made at this point about what we mean when we say 'philosophy' here. Between philosophical traditions, there are differences in what might be seen as open to question, and how such a questioning might proceed. For example, in so-called analytic approaches based on logical deduction, an author might take a position, on the basis of prior analysis he or she is certain of, and proceed by a method of refuting alternative accounts of the matter at hand (e.g. the rightness or wrongness of something) to prove the correctness of their position, i.e. on the basis of the logical argument presented. The certainty derives not from the presentation of conclusive data, but from the logical refutation of alternatives based on, often, ideal case scenarios, e.g. an assumption of how one *ought* to act in making a moral judgment. For some, this is what the trained philosopher does.

Let's consider a classic example. Some would consider Plato's *Republic* to be a work of philosophy of education. That is not to see it as a text written with the criteria and audience of a defined field of study in mind, but as a text that in its form and content contends with educational questions and makes educational claims. For others, Plato's text is relevant to philosophy of education because it is a classic work of philosophy, and therefore is of historical interest, and because from it we can take the normative claims it makes about what a good education should consist of and why. The text contains a number of sections that clearly relate to education – e.g. the Allegory of the Cave – and these are the sections that are often taken to be relevant to education and philosophy of education. But recent readings of *The Republic* take it not, or not only, as a statement of what a good education or the good life should consist in, but refer to the form of education depicted in the dialogues between Socrates and his interlocutors, outside of the obvious 'educational' statements. The act of conversation, and the transformation of thinking that takes place within it, are taken to be a far richer description of what education consists in than is found in the book's more obvious statements about education (see Smith, 2009). From this we can see that different approaches to reading are possible, for different purposes, based on different assumptions about what a text is, should, or can do. The text will be read with different educational concerns in mind, and the writing that ensues from this will take the form of, and further invite, different forms of philosophical writing. Rather than characterising this distinction in terms of a particular school of thought or as Analytic *versus* Continental, we can perhaps more loosely characterise it as being a matter of what is considered open to question. As the earlier overview of schools of thought tried to show, questions concerning the nature of language, the nature of being, and the ways in which we claim to know, can be explored and defined in multiple ways. They are questions that recur, or take on a different inflection at different points as the world raises different questions for us.

But if philosophical research is not necessarily going to produce an answer to the question of what we should do in educational contexts, and on this understanding is not defined by a strict methodological approach, why would we do it? Isn't it a dead-end for educational research? Are we suggesting that it is an undisciplined field of study characterised by subjectivism and relativism? And if philosophy takes its cue from questions arising from our social and educational reality, just as empirical forms of educational research does, what claims are we making about its marginality?

To clarify, perhaps we can introduce a further distinction, intended to be illustrative rather than divisive or categorical. As the example of the reading of Plato above indicates, there are certain approaches to the text that entail a different orientation to the notion of education, that is, as transformative and relational rather than normative. The understanding of the relationship between Socrates and his interlocutor is not limited to a reading of what is considered right and wrong (the content) but is seen as educational in itself (the form). Dialogue, or conversation, is a speaking with and being confronted by the ideas of another that is in itself educational, but in a richer sense than is referred to by, for example, equating education with 'schooling', or with 'learning' as the individual accrual of knowledge and skills. So, the reading of the text is not concerned with finding an educational truth or principle in its content that can then be applied to education, but rather with the educational potential of the form of the text itself, and the particular language and literary devices it uses. Hence, we want to distinguish here between philosophy of education, which corresponds to the former, and educational philosophy, the latter.

As suggested, this entails a broader conception of both education and of research, not limited to the application of findings in the name of the improvement of educational practice understood as schooling. This distinction can be illustrated with reference to introductory guides to educational research. Within the broad category of research methods texts there are those specific to educational research. Part of our concern in drawing attention to the way in which the research process is characterised in such texts is to raise the question of what is, or could be, educational about educational research. For Richard Pring, 'distinctively *educational* research' 'can only be relevant if it relates to the "practice of education" – to the activities, engaged in on the whole by teachers, which have those characteristics which pick them out as education' (2015: 22). This definition chimes with much of what is assumed to count as educational research; however, we take a broader view. In the chapters in Part II we see education as encompassing not only schools and the practice of teachers, but also other educational contexts such as the university and the family, and other individuals such as the student, the parent, and 'grown-ups'. The educational, then, refers not only to what is formally taught or what it is deemed valuable to teach, but also to experiences and practices that are in some sense transformative. The criterion that educational research *be* educational, then, places a heavier requirement on the thinking it entails, and invites, than on its potential applicability to practice.

Note

1 'Running alongside' has been used deliberately here. To have written 'running beneath' suggests a hierarchy that is unhelpful.

References

Braidotti, R. (2013) 'Posthuman Humanities', *European Educational Research Journal*, Vol. 12, No. 1, pp. 1–19.

Crotty, M. (1998) *The Foundations of Social Research: Meaning and Perspective in the Research Process*, London: Sage.

Faubion, J. and Marcus, G. E. (Eds) (2009) *Fieldwork Is Not What It Used To Be: Learning Anthropology's Method in a Time of Transition*, Ithaca, NY: Cornell University Press.

Foucault, M. (1970) *The Order of Things: An Archaeology of Human Sciences*, New York: Pantheon Books.

Foucault, M. (2000) 'What Is Enlightenment?', in P. Rabinow (Ed.), *Essential Works of Foucault, 1954–1984, Vol. 1, Ethics*, London: Penguin.

Haraway, D. J. (1991) *Simians, Cyborgs, and Women: The Reinvention of Nature*, London: Routledge.

Holma, K. (2009) 'The Strict Analysis and the Open Discussion', *Journal of Philosophy of Education*, Vol. 43, No. 3, pp. 325–338.

Husserl, E. (1931) *Ideas: General Introduction to Pure Phenomenology*, London: George Allen and Unwin.

Keeves, J. P. and Lakomski, G. (1999) *Issues in Educational Research*, Oxford: Pergamon Press.

Lather, P. and St. Pierre, E. A. (2013) 'Post-Qualitative Research', *International Journal of Qualitative Studies in Education*, Vol. 26, No. 6, pp. 629–633.

Latour, B. (2004) 'Why Has Critique Run out of Steam? From Matters of Fact to Matters of Concern', *Critical Inquiry*, Vol. 30, pp. 225–248.

Laurier, E. (2010) 'Bruno Latour', in P. Hubbard and R. Kitchin (Eds), *Key Thinkers on Spaces and Place*, second edition, London: Sage, pp. 434–443.

Law, J. (2004) *After Method: Mess in Social Science Research*, London: Routledge.

Lewis, M. and Ritchie, L. (2010) *The Research Journey: Developing and Supporting a Practitioner Research Network*, [Online], available at: www.heacademy.ac.uk/sites/default/files/HF_The_research_journey_Developing_and_supporting_a_practitioner_research_network.pdf (accessed 28 June 2015).

Mackenzie, N.M. and Ling, L.M. (2009) 'The Research Journey: A Lonely Planet Approach', *Issues in Educational Research*, Vol. 19, No. 1, pp. 48–60.

Marres, N. (2013) 'Why Political Ontology Must Be Experimentalized: On Ecoshow Homes as Devices of Participation', *Social Studies of Science*, Vol. 43, No. 3, pp. 417–443.

Packer, M. (2012) *The Science of Qualitative Research*, Cambridge: Cambridge University Press.

Plato (2003) *The Republic*, Trans. D. Lee, London: Penguin.

Pring, R. (2015) *Philosophy of Educational Research*, third edition, London: Bloomsbury.

Smith, R. (2009) 'Half a Language: Listening in the City of Words', in P. Smeyers and M. Depaepe (Eds), *Educational Research: Proofs, Arguments, and Other Reasonings*, Dordrecht: Springer.

Snaza, N. and Weaver, J.A. (Eds) (2015) *Posthumanism and Educational Research*, London: Routledge.

Standish, P. (2004) 'Europe, Continental Philosophy and the Philosophy of Education', *Comparative Education*, Vol. 40, No. 4, pp. 485–501.

Wolfe, C. (2010) *What Is Posthumanism?*, Minneapolis: University of Minnesota Press.

3

PROBLEMATISING RESEARCH

Amanda Fulford and Naomi Hodgson

At this point, it might be expected that we show in detail how to do philosophical research in education, drawing on the schools of thought covered in Chapter 1, so that you can choose that which best fits your questions and perspective. But part of what we want to do here is to show why presenting approaches or schools of thought as a menu of options, as is found in many research methods handbooks, is problematic. As we will see, there is an assumption in many introductory handbooks that educational research will be empirical, and that this is distinguished from theoretical or philosophical research. The overview of philosophical 'schools of thought' in Chapter 2 shows that they are not distinct from the empirical, but rather are responses to it, and accounts of what it is.

Whatever form of research we undertake in education, the starting point is similar. As Crotty states, we do not start with a neatly defined epistemology or theoretical position that then determines what we will study, but with 'a real-life issue that needs to be addressed, a problem that needs to be solved, a question that needs to be answered' (1998: 13). Whether this issue, problem, or question lends itself to empirical study or not, the decisions we make about how to conduct the research entail epistemological and ontological questions, the answers to which bear upon how we proceed. To consider these questions is not a diversion from the path of research, from the practical question into the abstract, but rather 'it is a theorising embedded in the research act itself. Without it, research is not research' (*ibid.*: 17). It is the very making of the path.

Before we turn in Part II to look at some examples of philosophical research in education, and to particular practices of reading and writing, we want to set out more clearly what the standard educational research methods texts miss or deny in how they set out the path for research for us.

Process and procedures

We consider first the way in which many of the research methods textbooks in education and the social sciences are organised. This might seem unimportant, but, as we will show, the arrangement of content perhaps deliberately reinforces the purpose of these books: to guide readers systematically on a highly proceduralised route from identifying a research question, all the way through to the writing up of the eventual research. While, of course, there is some variety in how content is introduced and presented, many of these texts adopt a linear approach that seems closely to reflect a particular view of the research process itself. One common characteristic across many of these texts is the orderly laying out of options for the reader, often accompanied by a discussion of advantages and disadvantages of each one for research in education. The emphasis here is on researcher choice, as illustrated in Somekh and Lewin's articulation of the purpose of their text: 'The overarching premise of the book is to indicate how a wide range of researchers choose a methodology and methods which are appropriate to both the area of enquiry and their own way of seeing the world' (2004: 2). Indeed, they continue by saying that the very purpose of the discussion of concepts such as epistemology, ontology, and axiology is that 'these "paradigms and principles" contain information that will underpin the decisions you will be making if you are planning to carry out...research' (*ibid.*: 7). These aims, then, tend to determine the often dichotomous presentation of content: should your research have a research question or hypothesis? Is it situated broadly within a positivist or an interpretivist tradition? Is your approach to data analysis inductive or deductive? Perhaps this does injustice to some texts, and oversimplifies the way that much content is discussed critically and with a view to broader understandings of research. It is not that we are suggesting that all such material is unhelpful to the novice (or even experienced) researcher; there is surely a place for such texts to induct researchers into the practices of enquiry in their discipline. The issues we want to draw attention to here, though, are these: first, the way that choices are presented, and what this approach fails to recognise; second, the discussion of philosophy as an 'other' 'method' for research in education; third, the way that the researcher is situated in these discussions, particularly in relation to the adoption of researcher identity.

Many of the research texts address the thorny issue of methodology in relation to educational research – though others prefer to use the term 'design frame' (Thomas, 2013), 'research strategy' (Newby, 2010), or 'research design' (Punch and Oancea, 2014). Typically, these address the factors to be considered by researchers when choosing to adopt, for example, action research, case study, or ethnographic, narrative, or experimental approaches. While these might be grouped and discussed in terms of frameworks, under categories such as positivism, phenomenology, or Critical Theory, there tends to be little attention given to the philosophical underpinnings of the respective methodologies. This arguably can lead to a thinly justified choice of design, where the decision to adopt one methodology over another rests solely on its perceived advantages or disadvantages as outlined in the research methods text. This can blind the researcher to the broader rationale beyond the level of the purely practical. Take, for example, the choice to use narrative as a design for an enquiry into the experiences of female lecturers' progression and promotion opportunities in the engineering department of a university. Consideration of the use of a narrative methodology might focus on issues of access, the ethical issues related to discussing sensitive information, the practical issues of the time that narrative enquiry takes, and issues of 'truth' in relation to the notion of 'story'. Imagine this enquiry re-cast as an ethnographic study, with data collected through observations of the role of female lecturers within the department. Adoption of the ethnographic methodology might turn on practical discussions of how to observe and record phenomena, or of the problem of the researcher as 'insider' or 'outsider' with this approach (see, for example, Dwyer and Buckle, 2009). While all these are necessary and important considerations, the research methods textbooks tend to ignore the important broader philosophical issues that such methodologies raise: in terms of narrative, issues of the self, subjectivity, and voice; in terms of ethnography, issues of what it is to be human, to be in the world (with others), and the politics of representation.

What works?

Research on education, especially commissioned or funded research, is increasingly driven by the need to produce data and results to provide definitive answers to questions, and hence to recommend measurable outcomes that directly benefit those working in the field. For some, this is the very purpose of educational research: 'Gathering information in order to answer an education question is the *raison d'être* of educational research' (Curtis *et al.*, 2014: 1). Indeed, this idea is true of research more broadly: 'Research *is* gathering the information you need to answer a question and thereby help you solve a problem' (Booth *et al.*, 1995: 6, our emphasis). The pressure to produce and publish such research is strengthened significantly by the perceived requirement for research to have impact.[1] Under such pressure, there is an increasing tendency to undertake research that attempts to determine 'what works' both pedagogically and in terms of leadership, management, and governance. What is then deemed to be 'best practice' can thus be observed and assessed through different quality measures and indicators. As Bridget Somekh and Cathy Lewin note:

> There is increasing pressure from governments to fund only research perceived to be 'relevant' (directly relating to the implementation and subsequent improvement of policies). Based on a model from medical research, educational researchers have been exhorted…to adopt an 'evidence-based' approach…through increasing demands for 'hard data'.
>
> *(2004: 7)*

Gert Biesta (2007) similarly finds a tension in these kinds of research that drive so-called evidence-based practice, where assumptions about the value of scientific models of research, and the empirical data that they produce, ignore the moral and democratic aspects of research and decision-making in education.

Given this context, it is not surprising that the majority of research methods handbooks – especially in education – lay out what they consider to be the options for research in such a way that readers are guided towards the best methodologies and methods for ascertaining what works, and thus for producing research that has demonstrable impact. In exploring the potentialities of empirical research for investigating a language programme for pupils, Catriona McDonagh writes:

> As an empirical researcher, I was the arbiter of what happens and what counts as knowledge…My thinking was influenced by my desire for certainty, measurement and provability, which in turn influenced my research choices. I was looking for the correct answer or answers.
>
> *(McDonagh et al., 2012: 103)*

Given the affordances of empirical approaches to which McDonagh and others draw attention, how do such research methods textbooks address approaches to research that do not rely on empirical data, and how do they articulate the choice the researcher must make on which approach to adopt?

Research methods textbooks: philosophy in the margin

An overview of some of the current textbooks and guides to conducting research in education reveals, in some cases, a hesitancy in addressing the issue of philosophy as research. In other cases, there is avoidance, or a re-casting of philosophy of education in terms of how one works out one's personal philosophy of education. Some examples will serve to illustrate the difficulties here. In Gary Thomas' (2013) guide to doing a research project in education and the social sciences, there are only three passing references to philosophy. For example, in his brief discussion of the '-ologies' (which he claims will aid novice researchers in considering what questions they are asking, and crucially, how to go about answering them), he discusses both ontology and epistemology, while referring to philosophy as 'where we borrow [these] ideas from' (*ibid.*: 119). Thomas opens his discussion of the starting points of research with a consideration of the kinds of evidence that we might bring to bear on the research questions that we have. He writes:

> Usually (but not always), there will be an expectation that the kind of evidence you collect during a research project you undertake at university will be *empirical*. That is to say, you will be expected to go out into the wide world and collect data yourself rather than relying on information marshalled by others.
>
> *(ibid.: 22)*

The 'but not always' in Thomas' discussion is rather quickly dismissed: 'If you want to do a research project that is based solely on the literature, you should check with your tutor' (*ibid.*: 22).

The suspicion surrounding what Thomas seems to refer to as non-empirical approaches is further strengthened when he considers the nature of the evidence in response to different kinds of research question, and to how robust and reliable such evidence is. In his assessment, evidence that can be verified empirically gains five stars (here, Thomas uses the example of checking directions by looking them up on a map, or going to the internet; the chances of these being wrong, are, he suggests, very small). He then gives an example of a different kind of question: What is the meaning of life? A suggested approach to this question is 'Reflect on it yourself, or ask others. Read books.' This is interesting, as these suggestions for how to pro-ceed are given the lowest rating of only one star. Let us take this further. Thomas points us to the fact that there are different kinds of research question, and different categories of evidence for answering them. What we might consider to be more philosophical questions in education (such as 'What constitutes a good education?' 'What makes an educated person?' or 'What is the university for?'), are, in Thomas' analysis, not answerable through the highly rated methods he valorises. They are central questions for education, yet they seem consigned to the margins of debate.

Let us take another example. In their book on research and education, Will Curtis, Mark Murphy, and Sam Shields (2014) emphasise the researcher's freedom to choose, from a menu of methodologies and methods, those that are appropriate for the project. The choice is determined not only by the nature and purpose of the project, but also by the range of benefits and drawbacks of the different approaches to which they draw attention. The researcher is cast as something of a technician, selecting from the available tools, the correct one for the job. They write: 'Sections 2 and 3 [of their book] will help you to make the most appropriate choices in terms of the methods and strategies you employ' (*ibid.*: ix). But there is a tension in their subsequent exploration of the questions driving educational research and their dis-cussion of research design, which seems to hint at the philosophical, and the retreat into the safe territory of empirical paradigms for investigation.

Let us take as an example some of the questions that Curtis *et al.* identify as typical of the kind addressed in educational research: 'What are the most effective approaches to teaching in the classroom?', and 'Does social class matter in the class-room?'. Two important considerations seem to be missing from the subsequent discussion of these questions. First, the commentary fails to make explicit that, while the first question may be answered by analysing quantitative or qualita-tive empirical data collected through test scores or teacher and pupil interviews, the latter cannot so easily be addressed by recourse to a survey (or indeed any other empirical data collection method). The latter question is a philosophical, or a theoretical one; it is not framed in terms that suggest it is seeking a solution to a problem, nor is it one that that is amenable to empirical measurement, at least not as it is expressed. Rather, it is one for which there is no definitive answer, and opens up to further questioning.

Paul Standish summarises the difference between empirical approaches (and questions) and philosophical ones, like this:

> Philosophy *does not* involve doing experiments or collecting data empirically. Philosophy *does* involve exploring how we think and the assumptions behind our thinking, and becoming clear about the concepts we use; it *is* concerned with the nature of knowledge (and the grounds for knowledge claims); it *is* concerned especially with the reasons or justification for thoughts and opinions, and it *is* concerned with bringing clarity to thought.
>
> *(Standish, 2010: 7)*

Second, Curtis *et al.*'s commentary does not acknowledge the philosophical tenets at the heart of even the most empirical questions addressed by educational research. Underpinning the question 'What are the most effective approaches to teaching in the classroom?' are much broader questions about the nature of teaching itself, what it is to be taught, and to be a learner, and indeed what should be learned, debates that have been ongoing at least since Plato's *Republic*.

This central point, that the philosophical underpins research in education as well as more generally in the social sciences, *is* acknowledged in a research methods handbook by Somekh and Lewin when they write: 'Fundamentally, social science research is concerned with people and their life concerns, and with philosophical questions relating to the nature of knowledge and truth (epistemology), values (axiology) and being (ontology) which underpin human judgements and activities' (2004: 1).

This central place of philosophy is rarely acknowledged in such research methods textbooks, however. Rather, where philosophy does merit attention, it is only considered as an aid to better understanding the (empirical) paradigms of research. Hence, in Mukherji and Albon's text on research methods for early childhood, they claim that: 'carrying out research involves an understanding of the philosophy that underpins the research – or "paradigm"' (2015: 9). This is deemed important solely because it ensures that researchers are making informed decisions about the appropriate methodologies and methods for conducting early childhood research. So they acknowledge that all research is underpinned by a particular philosophy (or, as they put it, 'a way of seeing the world', *ibid.*: 34), and that all research has a philosophical basis, but this view consigns philosophy to the margins, to supporting decisions about selecting the paradigm in which any piece of research fits. In other texts, notably McDonagh *et al.*'s work, engagement with philosophy of education is even further marginalised; it becomes merely a tool for reflective practice and a vehicle for 'trying to work out my personal philosophy of education' (2012: 35).

These 'uses' of philosophy conceive of it as tool, or as Standish identifies from the seventeenth-century English philosopher, John Locke's, work, 'an "under-labourer" to other ways of thinking (i.e. as an assistant)' (2010: 8). But this is to misunderstand philosophy's central place in the questions we ask about education. Standish claims:

> Philosophy is less like a matter of technical expertise, instead it becomes something like an intensified version of the kind of enquiry that people generally engage in...It is precisely this kind of intense enquiry that characterizes the work of the great philosophers.
>
> *(ibid.: 8)*

Standish goes on to argue that if researchers start from the very practical questions in education (such as our example of what constitutes the most effective approaches to teaching), then the pursuit of these issues is likely to lead to the broader philosophical questions about what we know, and how to live the good life (*ibid.*: 8). This is important, and illustrates a central point in this book's argument: it disrupts the distinction that many of the research textbooks make between empirical and 'other' approaches to research (such as the philosophical-theoretical).

What Standish's insight reveals is that philosophy, far from being marginal to research in education and the social sciences, is central. So, it is clear then that educational research cannot be understood simplistically in terms of the empirical and non-empirical. Questions of value that might be pursued philosophically (for example, 'Does social class matter in the classroom?') start with the lived experience of the researcher and the researched in much the same way as more empirical problems do.

Philosophy as educational research

We now turn to how the research methods texts address (or otherwise) philosophy *as research in its own right*. As we have seen, rarely is there explicit consideration of approaches other than empirical ones. While there are references to the use of 'theoretical literature' as opposed to 'empirical research literature' (Punch and Oancea, 2014: 121), and to the use of 'conceptual and theoretical reviews' (*ibid.*: 137), it is not clear that what is being referred to here is either theoretical research or educational philosophy. Rather, it is part of a consideration of how to proceed when 'it is difficult to find large bodies of systematic empirical evidence on topics of interest, and the relevant research literature is quite small' (*ibid.*: 121). Philosophy, it seems, is important not as research in its own right with distinctive practices of reading and writing (which we will explore in detail in the remainder of this book), but rather as something that needs to be ticked off, as it were, on a checklist before proceeding with (empirical) research. It is as if any consideration of philosophy is merely a task to be tidied up or settled down before proceeding. Peter Newby writes:

> You need to be aware of and appreciate research philosophies [because] you have to understand where a researcher is coming from so that you can critique research conclusions within the prescriptions of research philosophy and to be able to comment on the appropriateness of the philosophy as a guiding framework for a particular piece of research.
>
> *(2010: 42)*

Here, what is at stake is not philosophy-as-research (our focus in this book), but rather philosophy-as-standpoint, or as Newby put it: 'Philosophy provides the lens through which to identify a research problem or to interpret or understand the implications of research data' (*ibid.*: 46). Herein lies a further assumption; that the place of philosophy in the research process in confined to the initial stages.

Peter Newby, along with others (notably Pring, 2015, and Crotty, 1998), argues for philosophy as foundational to social research, the background against which all research is conducted. However, in conceptualising philosophy's place in research in this way, it is as if philosophy is something that is there only at the beginning of research, something to be worked out, agreed, put in order, before research begins. Newby puts it like this:

> You have to consider how far working within the confines of a research philosophy requires you to use particular research methods. What it all comes down to is that by taking our understanding of research to a higher conceptual level, we become better at deciding how to work within and... outside the rules and conventions of research.
>
> *(2010: 43)*

This has implications for the researcher, who is then positioned as someone who has to 'work out her personal philosophy' prior to embarking on her research. Once she has identified herself within a particular philosophical research tradition (as a positivist, a poststructuralist, a critical realist, or a feminist, for example), this stance then determines the way she proceeds with her research. However, this view denies philosophy's place as integral to research *as it proceeds*, and that the philosophical questions raised by any research will not be settled, but are iterative and open up still further questions.

So the question of the place of philosophy in research on education, and of whether philosophy can be described as just another method to choose at the outset of research, is, as Standish notes 'a vexed one, and for good reason' (2009: i). A Special Issue of the *Journal of Philosophy of Education*, 'What do Philosophers of Education do? (And how do they do it?)' in 2009,[2] attempted to address some of these points. Perhaps the impetus to cover the topic was the self-conscious preoccupation – or even anxiety – over selecting and justifying one's method as a researcher. This anxiety is one that leads to a preoccupation with methods that characterises many of the research methods textbooks that we have described. The Special Issue's editor, Claudia Ruitenberg puts it like this: 'In faculties and schools of education, which may already suffer from "status anxiety" in the academy, the desire to have one's work regarded as sufficiently scientific can lead to an even greater emphasis on the articulation of methods' (2009: 316). In his contribution to the Special Issue, Richard Smith cautions us to 'be aware of the awkwardness of thinking in terms of having a method, still more any kind of "methodology"' (2009: 437). However, Ruitenberg reflects that philosophers of education may need to reappraise their tendency to avoid discussion of method, and to be more cognisant of the similarities between philosophy-as-research and other kinds of enquiry. All research proceeds by using an approach congruent with the theoretical framework underpinning it, and by keeping a focus on the particular questions that the study seeks to answer or explore. Philosophy, in this sense, is no different; philosophers can (and should) articulate what they do, and there is much that can be usefully said in this respect about the methods that they employ. Without this explanation of what philosophy is attempting to do, and how it tries to do this, it risks accusations that it is aloof from the practical concerns of education and that its conclusions are unfounded. As Standish writes:

> Insight into this variety of approaches [that philosophers use] is not only practically useful: it also opens possibilities of thought that otherwise escape the agenda of research. And in the end these release the kinds of enquiry into education that answers to the demands of practice in unparalleled ways.
>
> *(2009: i)*

But how we begin to conceptualise the approaches used in philosophical/theoretical forms of enquiry differs, in some respects, from the more systematic selection and operationalisation of methods found in other forms of research. While some research methodologies are strongly associated with particular data collection methods (for example, participant observation in ethnography, and unstructured conversations in narrative enquiry), the ways of pursuing philosophical enquiry are much less constrained. It would be nonsensical to talk of 'philosophy's method' (as a singular, or exclusive approach), and equally unhelpful to think of philosophy as simply another method that one selects from a list (that includes options such as case study, ethnography, comparative research, and so on). This does not preclude philosophers, though, from attempting to make explicit how they pursue their enquiries. To this end, the contributors to the Special Issue of the *Journal of Philosophy of Education* mentioned above have begun to address these points. Katariina Holma, for example, reflects back on her induction into Jay F. Rosenberg's rules of valid argumentation (Rosenberg, 1984). She thinks of her current approach in philosophy as follows: 'In methodological terms, the crucial feature…is an emphasis on the role of a thoroughgoing process of analysis and synthesis…[a] process of disassembling and reassembling (i.e. philosophical reconstruction)' (Holma, 2009: 326). It is also in the use – or 'implementation' – of the method, that philosophical/theoretical approaches differ from some broadly empirical ones. Whereas methodology and methods are generally settled at the outset of an empirical enquiry – and the subsequent work is to apply these to the substantive research, and to justify their use in the reporting of the research – it is unhelpful to think of method in philosophy as merely technique applied to a particular educational concern. This would be erroneous, as philosophical enquiry does not necessarily proceed from a point of methodological certainty, whereby the agreed design frame for the research subsequently drives the adoption of certain research and writing practices (an expectation that submitting to the paradigms of research in the social sciences demands). Rather, they are engaged in a process of reading, research, and writing in which method and content are not easily (or should not easily) be distinguished. It is as if 'one's method becomes caught up in the substance of one's research interest. Sometimes content and method are one' (Standish, 2009: i).

On this account, the way in which philosophers read and write about education constitutes research on education; such practices are 'methods' *in themselves*. The practice of philosophy of education *is* research on education. Methods, then, in philosophy, can be thought of as: 'the various ways and modes in which philosophers of education think, read, write, speak and listen, that make their work systematic, purposeful and responsive to past and present philosophical and educational concerns and conversations' (Ruitenberg, 2009: 316).

In Part III of this book we give more detailed attention to these practices of reading and writing as research. We turn now, though, to some examples from our colleagues' writing in the field of educational philosophy and theory. In the chapters that follow in Part II, a wide range of educational matters are considered using a variety of approaches. In each chapter, an extract from a piece of published research is introduced by its author(s) and is followed by a commentary on the specific practices of reading and writing that they used in the process of the research.

Notes

1 The Research Excellence Framework (REF), the system for assessing quality in UK Higher Education Institutions, defines impact as follows: 'For the purposes of the REF, impact is defined as an effect on, change or benefit to the economy, society, culture, public policy or services, health, the environment or quality of life, beyond academia' (HEFCE, 2012: 48).
2 Special Issue from 2009, edited by Claudia Ruitenberg: 'What do Philosophers of Education do? (And how do they do it?)', *Journal of Philosophy of Education*, Vol. 43, No. 3, pp. 437–449.

References

Biesta, G. (2007) 'Why "What Works" Won't Work: Evidence-Based Practice and the Democratic Deficit in Educational Research', *Educational Theory*, Vol. 57, No. 1, pp. 1–22.

Booth, W.C., Colomb, G.G., and Williams, J.M. (1995) *The Craft of Research*, Chicago: The University of Chicago Press.

Crotty, M. (1998) *The Foundations of Social Research: Meaning and Perspective in the Research Process*, London: Sage.

Curtis, W., Murphy, M., and Shields, S. (2014) *Research and Education*, London: Routledge.

Dwyer, S. and Buckle, J.L. (2009) 'On Being an Insider-Outsider in Qualitative Research', *International Journal of Qualitative Research*, Vol. 8, No. 1, pp. 54–63.

Higher Education Funding Council for England (HEFCE) (2012) *Assessment Framework and Guidance on Submissions*, Bristol: HEFCE.

Holma, K. (2009) 'The Strict Analysis and the Open Discussion', *Journal of Philosophy of Education*, Vol. 43, No. 3, pp. 325–338.

McDonagh, C., Roche, M., Sullivan, B., and Glen, M. (2012) *Enhancing Practice Through Classroom Research: A Teacher's Guide to Professional Development*, London: Routledge.

Mukherji, P. and Albon, D. (2015) *Research Methods in Early Childhood: An Introductory Guide*, second edition, London: Sage.

Newby, P. (2010) *Research Methods for Education*, Harlow: Longman.

Plato (2003) *The Republic*, Trans. D. Lee, London: Penguin.

Pring, R. (2015) *Philosophy of Educational Research*, third edition, London: Bloomsbury.

Punch, K.F. and Oancea, A. (2014) *Introduction to Research Methods in Education*, second edition, London: Sage.

Rosenberg, J.F. (1984) *The Practice of Philosophy: A Handbook for Beginners*, second edition, Englewood Cliffs, NJ: Prentice-Hall.

Ruitenberg, C. (2009) 'Introduction: The Question of Method in Philosophy of Education', *Journal of Philosophy of Education*, Vol. 43, No. 3, pp. 315–323.

Smith, R. (2009) 'Between the Lines: Philosophy, Text and Conversation', *Journal of Philosophy of Education*, Vol. 43, No. 3, pp. 437–449.

Somekh, B. and Lewin, C. (2004) *Research Methods in the Social Sciences*, London: Sage.

Standish, P. (2009) 'Preface', *Journal of Philosophy of Education*, Vol. 43, No. 3, pp. i–ii.

Standish, P. (2010) 'What Is the Philosophy of Education?', in R. Bailey (Ed.), *The Philosophy of Education: An Introduction*, London: Continuum, pp. 4–20.

Thomas, G. (2013) *How to Do Your Research Project: A Guide for Students in Education and Applied Social Sciences*, second edition, London: Sage.

PART II

Reading and writing educational philosophy

4

SATISFACTION, SETTLEMENT, AND EXPOSITION

Amanda Fulford

Introduction to the extract

The following extract considers the place of the tutorial – the one-to-one meeting and academic discussion between tutor and student – in the setting of the university. This research interest starts from a very practical standpoint: my experiences of conducting such undergraduate and postgraduate tutorials in university departments of education in the UK. It also starts from a sense of dissatisfaction. This derives not only from the way that tutorials tend to be conducted, but also from the kinds of conversations that occur in them, and with the expectations (from both students and institutions) about their purpose. The aim of the piece of research from which the extract below is taken was to explore how tutorial conversations are increasingly being used to 'deliver student satisfaction'. In particular, the extract discusses how the conversation, with its focus on what a student has to do to pass, to gain a specific mark or degree classification, is driven by the need to 'settle' student concerns. In raising issues about what kind of satisfaction can be measured using the National Student Survey, which is a now crucial element of UK universities' quality indicators, I suggest that we might think about the issue in a different way. In drawing the reader's attention to the work of the nineteenth-century American writer, Henry David Thoreau, I suggest that a tutorial discussion that is *unsettling* might ultimately be more satisfying.

EXTRACT: SATISFACTION, SETTLEMENT, AND EXPOSITION: CONVERSATION AND THE UNIVERSITY TUTORIAL[1]

The understanding of satisfaction that appears to underpin these somewhat crude measures is a very narrow one. It equates with a form of contentment, with the

(Continued)

(Continued)

positive and happy feelings that derive from everything being settled. I suggest that in the university tutorial, the conversation is characterised by such satisfying talk, the kind that is a form of settlement: of closing down and securing. Perhaps the etymology of the word 'conversation' is useful in illustrating the point here. The Latin roots indicate that in 'con-versation', we 'turn' (*vertere*) 'with' (*cum*) others. There is a sense of accord here that is entirely absent from conversation's common synonym, 'discussion' with its roots in the Latin *discutere* meaning 'to strike asunder' and from *dis* (apart) and *quartere* (to shake). Student satisfaction, in the tutorial context, derives from a conversation (rather than a discussion) which is based on the contentment derived from knowing exactly what is required to gain a pass mark in an assignment, or to achieve a certain degree classification. For the tutor, a tutorial conducted in this way gives assurance that the student, satisfied with the discussions, subsequently evaluates the module well, and scores 'Academic Support' highly in the next survey of satisfaction.

This satisfaction discourse is indicative of the ways in which both the tutor and the student tend to think, and of the power of certain discourses to author-ise such thinking. It is as if these discourses have a stifling effect. This is not to say that student satisfaction is, in itself, not an appropriate topic of discussion in the university. Nor is it the case that ensuring that students have the informa-tion necessary for them to perform to their best ability in all forms of assessment is not a right and proper approach. It is rather to draw attention to where the blinkered pursuit of the prestige that high levels of student satisfaction brings, gets in the way of other kinds of thinking, or talking. Furthermore, where there is an ineluctable link between satisfaction and the student's assessment, there is a tendency for the tutor to restrict her conversation with students to what is required to pass the module assessment. For her part, the student – keen to pass the assignment and gain a good degree classification – wants to take advantage of the tutorial to be assured of what she must do to pass. While the student must meet the all-important learning outcomes, a conversation domi-nated by such issues neglects other (less easily measured) matters such as what it is to learn, what it is that one still has to learn, and how our education can be pursued through conversation with another. But in a culture which obsesses with student satisfaction, these thorny issues are settled into more palatable, 'student-friendly' sound bites such as 'The course has helped me to present with confidence' and 'My communication skills have improved'.

Settling

The type of talk that I have described is satisfying because of the way in which it 'settles' thinking. This theme of settlement is one that is taken up in the transcendentalist literature of Henry David Thoreau and Ralph Waldo Emerson.

In these writers' work, especially in Thoreau, human becoming is marked by ideas of leaving, departure and sojourning, that are described in terms of a lack of settlement. In *Walden* (Thoreau, 1854/1999), Thoreau espouses a way of living, thinking (and crucially of using language) that disrupts ideas of security and settlement. He writes: 'I was more independent than any farmer in Concord, for I was not anchored to a house or a farm, but could follow the bent of my genius' (p. 51), and later: 'You want room for your thoughts to get into sailing trim and run a course or two before they make their port' (p. 127). Such ideas are also central to Emerson's perfectionism: our journeying (through education or cultivation) to a further state of becoming, of the self. This journeying is a necessary part of one's becoming; it is in the constant losing of the self (characterised by a lack of settlement and by leaving) that is its finding.

But we should not see Emerson's perfectionism in terms of some kind of developmental model. The perfectionist journey cannot be described with reference to particular delineated stages; it rather requires that 'A man should learn to detect and watch the gleam of light that flashes across his mind from within' (Emerson, 1841/2003: 267). Branka Arsić (2010) highlights the significance of the concept of leaving to Emerson's writing on the perfection of the self. For Emerson, 'To allow for change', she writes, 'to abandon the stationary, to overcome the fear of rupture, and to face interruption are all, in fact modes of leaving where and what one is' (p. 3). For Arsić, Emerson's 'ontology of becoming is fundamentally...an ontology of leaving' (p. 5).

In terms of the tutorial conversation, I do not want to generalise here and to claim that tutorial conversations are characterised *per se* by such settling talk. I do want to emphasise, though, that such conversations are indicative of a particular culture within some universities. It is as if something in this culture steeps those who pass through it in particular ways of thinking and talking that block and force out other ways. But, the expectations of particular outcomes of such conversations lead to certain topics being simply 'off-limits'.

Such a settling of conversation happens certainly because of the time constraints, but may also be indicative of a certain cultural expectation, a preoccupation with the latest drive to improve satisfaction, and to enhance the student experience at the expense of a space for speaking about the trickier issues of learning one's subject and with 'intellectual growth'. What would it be like, for example, if the tutorial conversation were to run along these lines: 'I hear what you say about the assignment, and about the learning outcomes, let me ask you another question: "What do you think research is for? Why should universities give attention to it in the way they do?"' What I am drawing attention to here is a re-thinking of the tutorial discussion that goes

(Continued)

(Continued)

beyond a conversation driven by accountability and service-level agreements. It is to ask whether an unsettling education can be a satisfying one.

Note

1 This extract is taken from a longer article, published as: Fulford, A. (2013) 'Satisfaction, Settlement, and Exposition: Conversation and the University Tutorial', *Ethics and Education*, Vol. 8, No. 2, pp. 114–122.

References

Arsić, B. (2010) *On Leaving: A Reading in Emerson*, Cambridge, MA: Harvard University Press.

Emerson, R.W. (1841/2003) *Selected Writings of Ralph Waldo Emerson*, London: Penguin Books Ltd.

Thoreau, H.D. (1854/1999) *Walden*, Oxford: Oxford University Press.

Educational philosophy: reading and writing practices in this extract

A close reading of this extract shows that there are a number of features that are perhaps particularly illustrative of work that we might broadly describe as 'non-empirical' or 'philosophical'. However, as we showed in Part I of this book, to draw a clear distinction between empirical and non-empirical work is to suggest a false, and unhelpful, dualism. This research on student satisfaction and the conduct of university tutorials is rooted in, and proceeds from, empirical observations. However, it does not go on to report and analyse the data from, say, interviews about, or observations of, tutorials. Instead, it draws attention to the issue of conversation in the tutorial, and attempts to understand what is happening in such conversations in the light of a body of literature – the writings of the American essayists and philosophers, Ralph Waldo Emerson and Henry David Thoreau, and secondary literature on these authors..

It is important to point out that Emerson and Thoreau were not writing about the practices or outcomes of formal education, even less the idea of the tutorial conversation or of 'student satisfaction'. Their work, though, illustrates a particular mode of thinking about our lives. Put very simply, they are advocating a way of living in a state of dissatisfaction that drives us to a continual striving for a better self. It is helpful to look at how the literature is used in this extract. The sources that are used to support the argument are more limited than would be usual in a traditional literature review, where it would be common to see multiple citations indicating the breadth of literature in any given field. The sources in the extract above are not just cited, but are given greater consideration to illustrate the developing argument.

In this sense, there is a different way of reading these sources, and of drawing on them in one's own writing. The structure of the argument is also important to note here. In the opening sections of the extract, the focus of the writing is on the tutorial conversation and the issue of student satisfaction. The discussion then moves away from these very practical concerns, and with the introduction of the subheading 'Settling', introduces ideas from the philosophical writings of Emerson and Thoreau. It is as if the two elements are juxtaposed to give the reader time to draw their own conclusions about the interconnectedness of these ideas. It is only towards the end of the extract that the ideas are woven together with a suggestion that the philosophical literature can have some bearing on this very practical concern. It is perhaps at this point that the reader, if she were not convinced that there was an issue with the way that tutorial conversations tend to proceed, might now begin to appreciate the concern being raised.

One feature of much writing in educational philosophy in particular, is the attention given to language. This should not be surprising given that writing in this field is often concerned with the clarification of concepts that tend to be used in everyday educational discourse, but which merit closer scrutiny (for example 'engagement', 'self-esteem', or 'achievement'). In the extract, this focus on language is crucial for the argument being developed. Here, the etymology of the words 'conversation' and 'discussion' is explored in order to pursue a particular line of thinking about tutorial talk with which the extract is concerned. In everyday talk, the words might be used interchangeably, but with an etymological analysis, an important distinction emerges. This then forms the basis of an argument for an (unsettling) tutorial conversation rather than a (settling) tutorial – and of course, is the starting point for exploring the nature of our education more generally.

In some traditions of writing in education, the emphasis is on drawing conclusions that will impact on practice, that is, on improving pedagogy, pupil outcomes, or policy in a particular area. In one sense, my aim in researching the university tutorial was to achieve something similar in relation to my own practice of conducting tutorials. But while this might be one (eventual) outcome of such research, others were more immediate. My aim in writing this piece (and this is only an excerpt of a longer paper) was perhaps twofold: first, to give attention to a current issue, but to approach this almost obliquely in order to gain a different perspective on it; second, to open up a space for thinking and further debate about an issue, rather than provide solutions.

5

WRITING PHILOSOPHICALLY ABOUT THE PARENT–CHILD RELATIONSHIP

Stefan Ramaekers and Judith Suissa

Introduction to the extract

This is an extract from our book *The Claims of Parenting: Reasons, Responsibility, and Society* (Ramaekers and Suissa, 2012). Our main concern was to show how the parent–child relationship has been claimed by certain languages and forms of reasoning, to the extent that it has become difficult to find other ways of talking about it and exploring its significance, at both an individual and a societal level. The idea to write the book emerged partly from our experience as parents, and our sense that dominant accounts of 'good parenting', in both policy discourse and popular literature for parents, were raising significant conceptual and ethical questions about which, as philosophers, we should have something to say. Yet at the same time, we felt a dissatisfaction with many discussions of families, parents, and children in philosophy of education, moral philosophy, and political philosophy, where parent–child relationships seemed to be framed as a sub-category within a broader moral or political theory, rather than seen as a subject for philosophical exploration in their own right. Our central premise is that childrearing and the parent–child relationship are ethical all the way down. Though this may seem like a fairly obvious thing to say since, surely, there is nothing new in asserting the ethical significance of raising children, articulating what exactly this means involves putting the experience of being a parent in contemporary conditions at the centre of our philosophical enquiry, while at the same time exposing the limitations of some of the languages within which contemporary 'parenting' is conceptualised and discussed. In probing the ethical and conceptual questions suggested by this experience, we hope to open up a space for thinking about childrearing and the parent–child relationship beyond and other than in terms of the languages that dominate the ways in which we generally think about it today.

EXTRACT: GOOD ENOUGH PARENTING?[1]

One of the main problems with the scientific discourse that dominates discussions of parenting is that it implies that there is a clearly-defined, objectively valid end-point of the parenting process and that the core of 'parenting' consists of forms of interaction that are causally related to achieving this. Implied in the language of this account is the idea that there is a right and a wrong way of parenting, and thus, in principle, a possibility of 'closure' or 'achievability' whereby one can be deemed to have succeeded as a parent. The alternative picture which we sketch out involves a focus, instead, on the particular quality of individual parent–child relationships, on the open-endedness of the process of being a parent, and on the sense in which the aims and goals that parents have cannot be unproblematically captured in a neutral, descriptive language, as they are infused with values and inseparable from the experience of individual parents within the shifting and dynamic context of their lives.

Doing, being and closure

It is important to note here that emphasising the aspects of the parent–child relationship that we have been addressing here, in contrast to the scientific account, is not a question of positing a kind of process-oriented rather than goal-oriented account of the parent–child relationship; rather, it is about showing the impossibility of identifying any single point, from outside the relationship, at which one can acknowledge that it has 'worked'. Although it is instructive to contrast the distinction between 'parenting' as a verb which connotes action and *doing* with the notion of '*being* a parent', which brings out the relational and non-task-specific aspects of the term, we are wary of approaches which posit a dichotomy between instrumental and existential or relational attitudes. [This dichotomy is addressed in an earlier chapter of the book where we discuss feminist work in the ethics of care and related work.]

Parents, as we have discussed, have, and cannot help but have, a somewhat instrumental attitude towards their children, to the extent that part of the experience of being a parent is to want one's child to be and do certain things. As Sara Ruddick puts it, 'Even before a baby is born, a mother is likely to daydream about the kind of person her child will become' (Ruddick, 1990: 105). For care theorists, this kind of thinking represents a form of paternalism that, while they acknowledge its role, they find somewhat distasteful and in tension with the essentially responsive and receptive ethical stance of caring (see Goodman, 2008: 237). As Goodman notes, their solution to this perceived tension is to argue that parental assessments of needs are acceptable if reflected through the prism of attentive love. But as Goodman comments on

(Continued)

(Continued)

Ruddick's above-quoted remark, 'such dreams are not irrelevant to parenting; they spur the process' (2008: 237). We want to suggest, on the basis of our analysis of the current scientisation of parenting, that Goodman's account can be taken further. Goodman identifies a problem within care theory that has to do with the tension between the demands on the parent to satisfy the child's needs and the demand to shape them, and suggests a conception of parenting which resolves this tension by:

> blending the 'receptive-intuitive' and 'objective-analytic' [Held, 2006] as it does connectedness and separateness. Her [the mother's] empathy motivates while her rationality evaluates. Parents are not engrossed by the child, they do not abandon themselves to the child's needs; sympathy is modulated by reflection. Once this fusion is recognized, the artificial choices between loyalty and impartiality, emotion and rationality, relationship over individuality, and context over rules are diminished if not eliminated.
>
> *(2008: 246)*

We agree, to an extent, that these tensions are at the heart of what it means to be a parent. Yet as we have begun to suggest, we see them not as something to be resolved, either in theoretical analysis, or through prescriptive recipes for good parenting, but rather as something that is lived with and explored by individual parents in the daily experience of being a parent. Undoubtedly, this experience will at times be difficult and frustrating, and will be so partly because of this inherent tension: the 18 month-old baby screaming in the supermarket aisle presents a problem not just because the parent wants to effectively stop the screaming, but because the parent may want all sorts of other, possibly conflicting, things: she may want the child to be a certain way, and may want to be a certain kind of parent; she may want her relationship with the child to be a certain kind of relationship; she may want her child not to be the kind of child who has tantrums whenever she is unhappy or frustrated; she may want her to be able to ask for what she wants without screaming; she may want to feel in control; she may want to be able to calm her child down without feeling she is controlling her and repressing her individuality; she may want her child to be assertive; she may want her to be considerate; she may want to be able to model sensitive, empathic behaviour; she may want to be able to model assertiveness; she may want to be thought of as a good mother; she may want reassurance that the child loves her; ... The list is, quite literally, endless, and not necessarily consciously articulated. Any of these desires and perceptions, or a combination of them, could be going through any parent's mind at any given moment with their child, who is behaving in a way that demands a response. To explore them, to identify what ideas, values, and motivations are behind them, which of them are in tension with others, which seem more important to the parent and why, requires an attention to the meaning of the terms in which we describe and think about what we do with and for our children.

This kind of thinking, though, cannot be done independently or in advance of the first person relational experiences of particular moments of parent–child interaction. And it is precisely this kind of practical reflection and response that is blocked, we argue, by the dominance of the scientific language. In posing as a neutral and independently valid account of what children need or which developmental goals are most important, without acknowledging that these goals reflect evaluative choices, the science of parenting obscures the point that all aspects of the process in question are infused with values and interpretation. What the scientific account asks parents to do, in other words, is to see their child as 'a child' and thus to bracket out the specific commitments and understandings they have about how they want to be as a person in their relationship with their individual child. To make a choice as a parent about what to do, or what not to do, in any given situation with one's child, indeed to describe the situation in a certain way as a particular kind of situation demanding a particular kind of response, is to make a human choice, an ethical choice. The scientific account of parenting frames discussion of 'good parenting' in terms of the causal relationship between certain parenting behaviours and certain 'outcomes' for children. But this is deeply problematic not only because, as Kagan (1998) has warned us, and as critics such as Furedi (2001) reinforce, citing his account, this rests largely on 'the myth of parental determinism', but also because it assumes that there is a logical point from where we can assess whether parenting has been successful or not, and a logical line we can draw around certain parts of our experience as parents that we can then describe as causally linked to such a point. The issue here is not a simplistic (and obviously false) rejection of the claim that there is any causal link between parental behaviour and child development. The point, rather, is that parents, like children, are agents acting in a social world infused with meaning, and that there is no self-evident way in which a particular part of their complex and infinitely varied interaction can be carved off from the rest and assigned moral significance from the outside. There is no simple sense, in other words, in which to capture this causality and reduce its inherent complexity.

In David Grossman's novel, *To the End of the Land* (Grossman, 2010), Ora, a middle-aged mother of two sons, is reflecting back on her life and her children's childhood, telling and retelling the story of her 21-year-old son, now serving in the army, in a kind of magical attempt to preserve him. At one point, she pauses in her telling, struck by the force and the almost terrifying

(Continued)

(Continued)

wonder that she expresses in the following words: 'Thousands of moments and hours and days, millions of deeds, countless actions and attempts and mistakes and words and thoughts, all to make one person in the world...' (Grossman, 2010: 454). Part of what the scientific account does, it seems, is to organise and make sense of this infinite, awe-inspiring reality, telling us which actions matter most, which mistakes we cannot afford to make; and what kind of person we will make if we do the right deeds and use the right words. The consequence of this process, however, is a loss of meaning. The contrast we want to draw out here, then, is not so much between 'process' and 'outcome', as between perspectives which offer us closure and pre-defined assessments of either the process or the outcome, and perspectives which acknowledge their intrinsic open-endedness and multiplicity of meaning. One obvious way in which a great deal of policy and practitioner guidelines based on scientific research on parenting offer a kind of artificial closure on the process of parenting is through the use of the term 'parenting styles'. We discuss this here with reference to the above points.

Parenting styles

The literature on parenting styles is too vast to cover comprehensively here, but the basic findings of the original research by Diana Baumrind are now so ubiquitous as to have become almost part of our everyday vocabulary. The prototypes of the parenting styles referred to were first identified by Baumrind (see 1966, 1967), and their description has changed little since her original work. Some of the relevant literature cites three styles: 'authoritarian, authoritative and permissive (or indulgent)', since the fourth category later identified by Baumrind, 'neglectful' parenting is, arguably, not a 'style' but an indication of failure on the part of parents to adequately care for their children. What we want to draw attention to here is the way in which this research has been taken up and presented in the context of policy and popular advice on 'good parenting', especially in relation to the above points about closure. What we are referring to is the effect on how we think about parent–child relationships, and how parents think about their own relationships, of a language that implies a kind of closure regarding what aspects of our life with our children constitute a 'parenting style' and how this will affect the kind of person our child will become.

[...]

The problem we want to emphasise here is that the infinite number of moments and the complexity of the experience of being a parent – the 'thousands of moments and hours and days, millions of deeds, countless actions and attempts and mistakes and words and thoughts' – do not fit neatly into any pre-existing account of parenting. Most descriptions of parenting styles, for example, focus on specific incidents to do with disruptive behaviour, bedtime, mealtimes or violence in the playground. These incidents, like multiple-choice problems, come pre-packaged and neatly delineated.

Note

1 This is an extract from Ramaekers, S. and Suissa, J. (2012) *The Claims of Parenting: Reasons, Responsibility, and Society*, Dordrecht: Springer.

References

Baumrind, D. (1966) 'Effects of Authoritative Parental Control on Child Behavior', *Child Development*, Vol. 37, No. 4, pp. 887–907.

Baumrind, D. (1967) 'Child Care Practices Anteceding Three Patterns of Preschool Behavior', *Genetic Psychology Monographs*, Vol. 75, No. 1, pp. 43–88.

Furedi, F. (2001) *Paranoid Parenting*, London: Allen Lane.

Goodman, J. (2008) 'Responding to Children's Needs: Amplifying the Caring Ethic', *Journal of Philosophy of Education*, Vol. 42, No. 2, pp. 233–248.

Grossman, D. (2010) *To the End of the Land*, London: Jonathan Cape.

Held, V. (2006) 'The Ethics of Care', in D. Copp (Ed.), *Oxford Handbook of Ethical Theory*, Oxford: Oxford University Press, pp. 537–566.

Kagan, J. (1998) *Three Seductive Ideas*, Cambridge, MA: Harvard University Press.

Ruddick, S. (1990) *Maternal Thinking: Towards a Politics of Peace*, London: The Women's Press.

Educational philosophy: reading and writing practices in this extract

This extract illustrates both the context in which our work was undertaken, and the distinctive methodological approach that we adopted – an approach that, while perhaps overlapping with work in other disciplines, has an important affinity with the philosophical endeavour described by Wittgenstein as 'supplying remarks on the natural history of human beings' (Wittgenstein, 1953: I, #415). Indeed, many sociological, historical, and cultural stories can be, and have already been, told about why it is that parents in post-industrial, western societies face an often overwhelming array of advice on how to bring up their children.[1] At the same time, there have been several philosophical treatments of the legal, moral, and political issues surrounding issues of procreation, the rights of children, and the duties of parents,[2] as well as some philosophical accounts of the shifts in our underlying conceptualisation of childhood and adult-child relationships.[3] While our discussion in the book partly builds on the insights of this literature, and while we are indebted to the thinkers and writers who have addressed questions such as what it means to educate children, the nature of human flourishing, the idea of introducing children into a common world, and the significance of intimate relationships, we see our project as significantly different in that it offers a philosophically-informed discussion of the actual practical experience of being a parent, with its deliberations, judgements, and dilemmas.

The discussion in this extract is illustrative of the approach we adopted in our initial conversations that led to the preparation of the book proposal, and later throughout the whole process of writing the book. In collecting material throughout this process, we often found ourselves sharing examples of descriptions of parenting (for example, in magazines and websites aimed at parents, in parenting guides and self-help books, or in policy documents and media reports on the role of parents), and expressing our frustration at the sweeping generalisations that seemed typical of such accounts (e.g. the tendency to make statements beginning with 'Children are...', 'Parents should...' or 'Research shows that...'). In trying to express this frustration, we found ourselves reaching towards an articulation of what it was that these kinds of accounts left out in their depiction of the experience of being a parent, and how they seemed to be failing to do justice to the complexities of the daily lived experience of being a parent. At the same time, we found ourselves drawn to first-person accounts of the experience of being a parent that we encountered in novels, magazines, or simply in the process of talking to other parents and to each other about our own experiences. Our actual writing process, then, often began with simply describing such experiences and sending our descriptions to each other so that we could comment on what we thought was significant or valuable in them, and then seeing how they fitted in with the general critical view we were in the process of developing. So, for example, in the above extract, imagining the scene of a mother with a screaming toddler in the supermarket, which we describe in everyday language, allowed us to make the conceptual points about the irreducibly ethical significance of parents' daily interactions with their children, and the impossibility of imposing any definitive model of choice or closure on the ways in which parents respond to such situations, in a concrete and accessible manner.

In the above extract, this tension is shown through our juxtaposition of the third-person, scientific account of 'parenting styles', with the nuanced and particular first-person description of the protagonist in the novel. What creating this tension does is to show that the first-person experiential account is irreducible to the neat empirical categories of the third-person scientific account. This also allows us to bring out the ways in which significant philosophical, particularly ethical, questions about being a parent arise from the first-person account itself. Once these philosophical questions and issues are developed and articulated, partly through drawing on the work of philosophers such as Hannah Arendt, Stanley Cavell, Bernard Williams, Martha Nussbaum, and others, as we do throughout the book, it then becomes clear how little can be conveyed through the language of the dominant, third-person accounts.

As this discussion shows, the 'data' for our work consisted of a wide range of literature, including policy documents, reports of empirical psychological research, and first-person accounts, both from the popular press and from novels. We therefore do not consider our work to be non-empirical; nor do we find it helpful to draw a sharp distinction between 'philosophical' and 'empirical'. Indeed, the work we do is about the empirical world and is based, in part, on empirical sources. Our 'methodology', then, to use a word which most philosophers are uncomfortable with, consisted in discussing this wide variety of different sources and the philosophical problems and insights that they threw up, with the aim of developing some helpful ways of thinking about the significance of the parent–child relationship. The literary and autobiographical sources (such as Grossman's novel) that we drew on were, we found, particularly fruitful in helping us to develop a central distinction that runs through the discussion in the book: the distinction between the 'first-person' and the 'third-person' account. This, we believe, is a way to remind readers that neither typical 'third-person' accounts - that purport to be based on a neutral, objective account of 'what children need' or what 'parenting style' leads to the 'best outcomes' – nor a philosophical approach which defends the ontological and ethical priority of experience or relationships as opposed to a form of instrumental rationality, can get at the full significance for parents of what it means to be a parent. Nor can they ultimately offer any valid prescriptions for what they should do in particular situations with their children. Our work thus offers an important challenge both to policies that prescribe a one-size-fits-all approach to good parenting, and to criticisms of such policies that imply that whatever parents choose to do is, by definition, morally acceptable. Treading the middle ground between these two extremes is a difficult project, but one which, we hope, our book has gone some way towards developing and defending.

Notes

1 See, for example, Dekker (2010); Edwards and Gillies (2004); Furedi (2001); Lareau (1989); Phoenix *et al.* (1991); Schaubroeck (2009), to name but a few.
2 See Archard (1993); Blustein (1982); Brighouse and Swift (2006); O'Neil and Ruddick (1979).
3 See Kennedy (2006); Stables (2008).

References

Archard, D. (1993) *Children: Rights and Childhood*, London: Routledge.
Blustein, J. (1982) *Parents and Children: The Ethics of the Family*, New York: Oxford University Press.
Brighouse, H. and Swift, A. (2006) 'Parents' Rights and the Value of the Family', *Ethics*, Vol. 117, pp. 80–108.
Dekker, J.J.H. (2010) *Educational Ambitions in History: Childhood and Education in an Expanding Educational Space from the Seventeenth to the Twentieth Century*, Frankfurt am Main: Peter Lang.
Edwards, R. and Gillies, V. (2004) 'Support in Parenting: Values and Consensus Concerning Who To Turn To', *Journal of Social Policy*, Vol. 33, No. 4, pp. 627–647.
Furedi, F. (2001) *Paranoid Parenting*, London: Allen Lane.

Kennedy, D. (2006) *The Well of Being: Childhood, Subjectivity, and Education*, Albany, NY: State University of New York Press.

Lareau, A. (1989) *Home Advantage, Social Class and Parental Intervention in Elementary Education*, Philadelphia, PA: The Falmer Press.

O'Neil, O. and Ruddick, W. (Eds) (1979) *Having Children: Philosophical and Legal Reflections on Parenthood*, New York: Oxford University Press.

Phoenix, A., Woollett, A., and Lloyd, E. (Eds) (1991) *Motherhood: Meanings, Practices, and Ideologies*, London: Sage.

Ramaekers, S. and Suissa, J. (2012) *The Claims of Parenting: Reasons, Responsibility, and Society*, Dordrecht: Springer.

Schaubroeck, K. (2009) *Een Verpletterend Gevoel van Verantwoordelijkheid. Waarom Ouders Zich Altijd Schuldig Voelen*, Breda: De Geus.

Stables, A. (2008) *Childhood and the Philosophy of Education: An Anti-Aristotelian Perspective*, London: Continuum.

Wittgenstein, L. (1953) *Philosophische Untersuchungen/Philosophical Investigations*, Trans. G.E.M. Anscombe, Oxford: Basil Blackwell.

6

THE EDUCATIONAL MEANING OF 'PRACTISING'

Joris Vlieghe

Introduction to the extract

In the following piece of work I write about 'school' practices, and more precisely about a form of training and exercise that is usually seen as archaic and utterly ineffective. This is not because I particularly cherish a long bygone past, or because I take delight in going against what is commonly believed to be true. On the contrary, I explore this practice as part of a research project that looks at things that happen in school contexts from the standpoint of human embodiment (a perspective that is often forgotten or dealt with in a stereotypical way). The thoughts presented here speak to my fascination for the peculiar phenomenon of gathering bodies within the four walls of a classroom and demanding that they do exactly the same things at the same time, over and over again. Arguing that this is part of what makes (or made) a school 'school', I want to come to an understanding of what precisely happens there, what is being experienced, and what is made (im)possible by this practice. Moreover, this work is also an attempt to introduce 'new' schools of thought to the field of educational philosophy. Of course, one of these schools is anything but 'new', *viz.* the phenomenological tradition, but it has been mostly 'forgotten' today. The same applies to the work of the contemporary Italian philosopher, Giorgio Agamben, whose ideas – until a few years ago at least – have received little or no attention from educationalists. The following extract tries to address this oversight.

EXTRACT: THE EDUCATIONAL MEANING OF 'PRACTISING': A PHENOMENOLOGICAL AND AGAMBENIAN ACCOUNT[1]

In this text I deal with the *educational* value of activities that typically take place in school contexts. More precisely, I focus on practices such as getting to know the

(Continued)

(Continued)

text of a poem by heart while reciting it, mastering the tables of multiplication by repeating the appropriate mathematical formulae ('four times nine is thirty-six'), as well as reiterating sets of the most elementary bodily movements during gym class. These concern the repeated and collective training and exercising of (basic) skills, under the supervision of a teacher who imposes a fixed rhythm. In many European languages there exist expressions to refer to this activity, such as *üben* (German), *(s')exercer* (French) and *oefenen* (Dutch). In (British) English this activity can be circumscribed as the 'practice of practising' (cf. Laws, 2011).

Although there are a few notable exceptions, such as the work of Otto-Friedrich Bollnow (1978) and, more recently Malte Brinkmann (2008), this phenomenon is mainly dealt with in a condescending manner. Usually it is regarded as a practice that stems from those unenlightened days in which we used to discipline children by cracking the whip, or it is seen as a practice of secondary significance only. However, I will develop here a positive and substantially educational account, regarding it as important in its own right. Therefore, I revisit some of the insights defended by Bollnow, but at the same time I also criticise his views and offer still another account, which is based on the work of Giorgio Agamben.

I should clarify here that I am not interested in a normative concept of education, in view of which certain activities should be evaluated as useful or harmful, as worthwhile or obsolete. On the contrary, I concentrate on a practice that traditionally takes (or took) place inside classrooms and to investigate what it precisely *means* to perform it. I deal with the 'practice of practising' as being a proper 'pedagogical form' (Masschelein and Simons, 2010). This is to say that it is typically something we do at school. Of course, there exist numerous examples of practising that take place outside educational institutions (e.g. rehearsing a play for the amateur theatre at home), but my contention here is that when it is performed inside the classroom (e.g. playing the recorder together) it still concerns something different. In my view there exists a typically *educational* form of practising, which has been a major constituent of the historical reality which we have known in the West since modern times and which we call 'school' (cf. Stiegler, 2006).

So, the main question I pose here is: What *is* practising and what makes it a *typically* educational activity? To Bollnow, there exists a significant difference between *learning* and *practising*, because the object of learning is knowledge (to know something, *wissen*), whereas practising has to do with acquiring a skill (to be capable to do something, *können*) (1978: 26–27), and knowledge and skill are two different things. One either knows something or does not know it, meaning that there cannot be a situation in between. Learning is then the activity in which the student moves from one side to the other, i.e. from ignorance to insight. She cannot further perfect her knowledge by learning more intensively: in that case she might only deepen or extend the knowledge she already possesses. According to Bollnow, this is in great contrast to practising, an activity during which the student tries, through repetition, to perfect a skill she already possesses, although not as yet completely. Every *real* ability is at the same time a dis-ability (*können* is essentially *nichtkönnen*): complete mastery would turn us into mere machines. Absolute ability equals death, so Bollnow says (*ibid.*: 34–35). Practising consists thus of remaining in relation with a *constitutive inability*, rather than of beginning with a situation of complete lack of ability to end up with complete mastery. It concerns a neverending process of improving on an ability and therefore a continuous work on the self. So, even if, in order to acquire knowledge, one inescapably also has to repeat from time to time, this repetition cannot be properly called *practising*: here, rehearsal only serves keeping the student's knowledge intact or to broaden it. It is merely a matter of learning something one did not possess, or acquiring again what one had forgotten. As far as *practising* is concerned, on the other hand, repetition is essential and constitutive.

All this might sound convincing, but I believe that the opposition Bollnow introduces is only correct in a limited number of cases, e.g. when *learning* the correct translation of words into a foreign language as opposed to *practising* woodcraft or a musical instrument. The first case is indeed only a matter of knowing or not knowing that *un livre* is the same thing as a book, while the second example necessarily implies the possibility of improving one's sculptural or musical abilities. The problem is, however, that the typical cases of 'school' practising, such as mastering the alphabet by repeating the abc should, according to the definitions Bollnow gives, be categorised as learning *and not as practising*: this is because there necessarily comes a moment at which the student reaches complete mastery. Moreover, the activity of reciting the alphabet is not something that allows for further improvement. If, for instance, one desires to gain another skill, say being able to recite the alphabet in the reversed order, it will not do much good repeating the alphabet.

Therefore, Bollnow's approach to practising typically applies to highly complex cultural or sportive activities, like painting or archery. Moreover, as Brinkmann (2008: 291) claims, what seems to be really at stake in Bollnow's analysis is that practising is ultimately self-exercise: a continuous attempt to overcome oneself, which is a response to an existential obligation towards self-perfection. In that sense, the object of practising is in the end immaterial: it does not really *matter* if a student engages with painting or archery. The only criterion is that practising concerns a skill that is not as easy to get a hold on as reciting the alphabet is, and that never cancels out what he calls 'constitutive

(Continued)

(Continued)

disability'. Hence it is difficult to relate Bollnow's ideas to basic forms of practising that are characteristic of school practice, such as reciting over and over
again the geometrical definitions of the triangle. In the remaining parts of this
essay I will argue that the subject matter *does* matter and that the opposition
Bollnow wants to defend actually relates to *another* dimension of pedagogical
practices he discusses, *viz.* the difference in the experience of *können* (being
able to do something) while learning or practising.

Rather than opposing knowledge and skill, I argue that *both* can be the object
of learning and practising. More precisely, *learning* can be defined as essentially
consisting in strengthening ourselves, i.e. in adding something to ourselves that
we formerly did not know or were not able to do. This might happen with or
without repetition and this might happen with or without formal education.
Practising, on the contrary, is an activity in which we relate to something we
already know or already are able to do. Of course, there remain very important differences between reciting the tables of multiplication and rehearsing the
cello, but the common denominator in both cases is that we relate to something
we *already possess*, albeit partially. This, in my view, is the decisive point. It
explains why *re*-hearsing and *re*-peating are essential. It also explains why practising is typically a school activity or a proper 'pedagogical form'. This is because
students are asked to do things they otherwise would not. School is a particular
time and place that first allows for this *re*-lating to texts, numbers, movements,
etc. to take place. And so it seems that the *collective* and *bodily* dimensions of
school practice are not without significance: at school students are physically
gathered and are asked to do exactly the same things at the same time.

In the concluding part of this text I elaborate the idea that practising
is essentially a way of relating to something (a subject matter, a domain of
knowledge, a skill) we already 'can', so to speak, with the help of Agamben.
This move also enables me to clarify why the collective and bodily dimension,
typical for the school, is important. As Agamben (1999) himself indicates, his
whole philosophy is concerned with the question of what we precisely mean
when we say 'I can'. Contrary to a widespread opinion, he argues that we only
experience being creatures of possibility *at the precise moment* that we find
ourselves at the limits of possible self-realisation. This is to say that when we
just actualise the potential to do this or that, e.g. when we are able to see this
or we are able to see that, we never experience that we *can*, in this case: we do
not experience the potentiality for vision itself. It is only at the moment that the
relation to any concrete actualisation is suspended, that we might sense what it
is all about when we affirm 'I can see.' This would be the case for instance when
we find ourselves in a completely darkened room and experience, *not in spite
of but due to* this condition of utmost impossibility, that we *can* see (*ibid.*: 181).

Therefore, a *true* experience of possibility is not a matter of strengthening one's own position in life, but rather consists of a moment during which our existence is not any longer a private affair (something that we as self-sufficient subjects can appropriate and call our own). This means, counterintuitive as it might sound, that the 'I' in the expression 'I can', is no longer a foundational and self-sufficient subject that realises itself through the concrete things it 'can' do. Rather, it disappears. The only thing that remains is an anonymous, though affirmative experience of existence as possibility – and this is what Agamben refers to with the phraseology 'potentiality' (*ibid.*).

In view of this analysis, practising appears as an educational pursuit that requires students to relate to themselves and the world in a manner that has not so much to do with extending their field of actual possibilities, as is the case in learning. It is not a transition during which we move from a lack of possession (*nichtkönnen*) to a condition of possession (*können*). Rather, what takes place is a suspension of private positions and interests *vis-à-vis* a piece of knowledge or a skill we possess. So, it seems, the opposite takes place: practising concerns the passage from a condition of self-possession (*können*) to a situation of dispossession (*nichtkönnen*). Seen from this perspective Bollnow's 'constitutive disability' should not be defined as a condition that allows for perfecting ourselves *ad infinitum*, but rather a desubjectivating experience that grants the possibility of educationally relevant transformation.

In sum, the significance of practising resides in the possibility of experiencing what it means that one *can* count, spell, move, etc. – in the sense of potentiality, rather than of the actualisation of private possibilities. Something one already possesses is taken up, again and again, and as a rule together with others and in a very embodied way: when reciting the tables of multiplication in a group or performing, collectively, repetitive gymnastic exercises, it is as if a collective body takes a subject matter up and by repeating it separates it from all concrete surplus-value the acquisition of this subject matter might have *vis-à-vis* the students' own individual existences. A collective of bodies does the job and the self-possessed subject disappears. Of course, to deal with numbers or physical movements in this particular way is not something we are inclined to do outside the walls of educational institutions. Exercising is therefore a typical 'pedagogical form'.

Note

1 This text is part of a presentation I gave during a symposium on 'Agamben and Philosophy of Education' held at the 2011 European Conference on Educational Research in Berlin. A revised version of it appeared as Vlieghe (2013).

(Continued)

(Continued)

References

Agamben, G. (1999) *Potentialities: Collected Essays in Philosophy*, Trans. D. Heller-Roazen, Stanford: Stanford University Press.

Brinkmann, M. (2008) 'Üben – elementäres Lernen. Überlegungen zur Phänomenologie, Theorie und Didaktik der Pädagogischen Übung', in K. Mitgutsch, E. Sattler, K. Westphal, and I. Breinbauer (Hg.), *Dem Lernen auf der Spur. Die pädagogische Perspektive*, Stuttgart: Klett-Cotta, pp. 278–294.

Bollnow, O.-F. (1978) *Vom Geist des Übens. Eine Rückbesinnung auf Elementäre Didaktische Erfahrungen*, Freiburg: Herder.

Laws, C. (Ed.) (2011) *The Practice of Practising*, Leuven: Leuven University Press.

Masschelein, J. and Simons, M. (2010) *Jenseits der Excellenz. Eine kleine Morphologie der Welt-Universität*, Trans. F. Opperman, Zürich: Diaphanes.

Stiegler, B. (2006) *La Télécratie Contre la Démocratie. Lettre Ouverte aux Représentants Politiques*, Paris: Flammarion.

Vlieghe, J. (2013) 'Experiencing (Im)potentiality: Bollnow and Agamben on the Educational Meaning of School Practices', *Studies in Philosophy and Education*, Vol. 32, No. 2, pp. 189–203.

Educational philosophy: reading and writing practices in this extract

This text demonstrates a particular *philosophical* approach to educational issues, *viz.* phenomenology. Although I criticise one of its protagonists (Bollnow), the kind of argumentation I develop is phenomenological right through. This means that I want to come to an accurate and detailed understanding of the meaning of a given 'phenomenon', in this case, 'practising'. More precisely, my analysis focuses entirely on the experiences we have when practising. My central claim is that, if we stay true to what we *actually* experience, the most essential characteristic of this activity is *not* that it concerns the perpetual attempt to perfect a skill (although this might hold true in many cases of practising), *but* that it consists in taking a certain (disempowering) relation towards skill or knowledge one (partially) possesses.

An obvious criticism to raise here is why we should turn to philosophy to find all this out: a qualitative investigation mapping students' real experiences might do this job far better than the philosopher sitting behind her desk. But, it is equally obvious that semi-structured interviews do not automatically reveal the truth about things: the hard core of the researcher's work consists in discovering common themes, (dis)connections, (ir)regularities, etc. in whatever the interviewees report, and – more importantly – finding appropriate words and categories to disclose something the interview transcriptions do not disclose by themselves. In that sense, her work is not much different from that of a phenomenologist, *viz.*, to give a precise and rich account of a phenomenon, and to do this in such a way that is both convincing and makes sense. The audience should not only come to a (ideally) complete understanding of the phenomenon, but also be presented with an account that is plausible and recognisable.

The main difference is, of course, that in the philosophical work I have presented I did not engage in a conversation with students, but with other theorists, one of them even living and writing in a time that is not ours. They offer words and definitions of these words, as well as words that indicate connections, similarities, and oppositions between things. The work I have presented tries to see whether Bollnow's and Agamben's words can help to give an adequate understanding and recognisable description of the phenomenon at hand. Recall that Agamben is not an educationalist, so what I essentially try to do is *check* whether or not his ideas are meaningful in the world of everyday school life. And recall that Bollnow's thought is somewhat forgotten, so again, my work might be seen as a *check-up*: do these ideas still make sense or not?

I said that I engaged in a conversation with two other authors, but in a sense this is not accurate – not phenomenologically accurate anyway. It is perhaps more appropriate to say that this kind of work actually consists in *a conversation with oneself*: looking at words and conceptual clarifications others have developed, one tests whether they make sense for oneself. For that matter, Bollnow and Agamben too could only write what they did by continuously testing their ideas in combination with their own experiences. And, again, this is also what the reader is supposed to do: *check up on her own experience* to see whether or not the definition of practising I distil from my analysis articulates clearly and convincingly what she might experience herself.

A basic presupposition behind this is that the reader and the author have *equal* access to the phenomenon in question. Even if they have not (had) actual experience of it (which I doubt in the particular case of practising), they can at least imagine what it would mean, and thus check my analysis against possible experiences. This implies that it is utterly misguided to say that philosophy is antithetical to empirical research. Moreover, this kind of research comes up with words, conceptual clarifications, and hypotheses that might inform what is traditionally called empirical research.

Finding the right words to articulate dimensions of experience is not easy. First, it takes careful analysis, and at this point phenomenology is very close to ordinary language philosophy: we have to consider what we precisely mean when we use a certain expression in a particular context. For instance, my argument is based on the idea that it makes sense to distinguish between learning and practising, but that it is not meaningful to connect this distinction to the opposition of knowledge and skill whenever 'school' contexts are involved. In order to find the required degree of precision and nuance, it is also necessary to use language itself in a very conscious way. Language is not *just* a means of communication reporting on research results, but *itself* plays a part in the arguments philosophers make. For instance, throughout my text I abundantly italicise words and expressions. When I write 'that a *true* experience of possibility is not a matter of strengthening one's own position in life', it does make a difference that 'true' is stressed in this way. It indicates that when we only take into consideration the type or definition of possibility expressed in the second part of the sentence (self-actualisation), we might miss out on an experience of potentiality that is more subtle. This is, however, not to say that defining possibility in terms of self-actualisation is not a true idea. So, the use of italics helps to articulate something that is difficult to express directly and which in this example goes beyond the plain and superficial opposition between true and false. Something similar is to be found in my attempts to stress the 'can' part in the expression 'I can' to point out an experience of being-able that is about being able *as such* (rather than being able to do *this* or being able to do *that*).

Second, phenomenological analysis also demands the willingness to broaden one's horizon. For instance, I draw from literature from various linguistic contexts. The research I have presented is to a large degree inspired by the fact there exists in certain languages a unique word for the practice of practising, which suggests that it has some generic or even essential traits that sets it apart from other pedagogical activities. Moreover, in order to find a solution for what I see as shortcomings in Bollnow's account, I turn to a philosopher who has written virtually nothing about education. Nevertheless, an engagement with Agamben's concept of potentiality might help us to come to terms with the difference between learning and practising, or to see that opposing skill and knowledge is in the end of lesser importance than opposing *können* and *nichtkönnen*. Furthermore, to arrive at innovative views, it pays to seek out paradoxes, *viz.*, to come and see that the most profound experience of what it means to be able is preconditioned by a lack of ability.

All this might of course sound like intentionally making things more complex than they are, and like having little to do with day-to-day educational reality. I do not think that philosophers of education should attempt to prescribe precise advice to teachers and policy-makers, or to critically assess pedagogies on the basis of some so-called 'deeper' insights that people without philosophical training lack. Nonetheless, philosophical work can be a valuable background when people in the field have to make decisions, or have to give shape to their own role as a teacher. I just want to point to the analyses others have made (e.g. Biesta, 2006) regarding a way of thinking and speaking that has become dominant today, *viz.*, to consider education and learning as virtually synonymous. This means that the only thing that really matters is the acquisition of competences and the optimisation of individual learning outcomes. This precludes other possibilities for conceiving of education that might be of importance nonetheless. Showing that practising is not merely a dulling and inefficient pedagogical tool (and surely a bad practice when learning is all that matters), my analysis might open new spaces of thought in which to look at education differently.

Reference

Biesta, G. (2006) *Beyond Learning. Democratic Education for a Human Future*, Boulder, CO: Paradigm.

7

LISTENING AND THE EDUCATIONAL RELATIONSHIP

Philosophical research from a phenomenological perspective

Andrea R. English

Introduction to the extract

My research focuses on the interconnection between democratic forms of participation and critical thinking. The aim of my research is to understand exactly how educators can support critical, democratic participation. The premise of my research is that, as human beings, we experience certain limitations, that is, we not only experience what we know and can do, but also what we cannot do and do not yet know. This is particularly important when considering questions of moral learning and moral education. In this extract, I seek to illuminate an essential role of the teacher in moral education that is not commonly addressed, namely, the role of the teacher as *listener*. My interest in listening has grown partly through my work with a research network on listening and education, and an earlier version of the extract was originally published in a journal Special Issue put together by members of this network.[1] Since that article, I have further developed my research on the teacher-learner relationship and on what I call 'discontinuities' (such as doubt, uncertainty, and struggle) involved in the experience of teaching and learning (English, 2013). My aim in investigating the experience of the teacher as listener is to illustrate what kinds of interactions help or hinder moral learning. In particular, this extract highlights the notion that moral education entails listening to students, not to hear if they can simply obey external demands, but rather to hear if they are in a struggle to move beyond self-interest for the sake of recognising others.

EXTRACT: LISTENING, MORAL GUIDANCE AND THE EDUCATIONAL RELATIONSHIP[1]

Although Johann Herbart[2] did not explicitly develop a theory of listening, his theory of moral guidance radically calls into question the assumed linearity

(Continued)

(Continued)

between listening and obedience to external authority with consequences for our understanding of the role of critical listening in educational relations. Using Herbart's theory of moral guidance as a basis for my examination, I identify three necessary (but not sufficient) guiding principles of listening in forms of teaching that seek to begin and maintain the educational relation. I use the term 'critical' to describe the teacher's listening in order to refer to the fact that the teacher is listening for ways to understand how the learner is judging herself and is evaluating what is heard on the basis of the distinction between egoism and having regard for others. I define the educational relation as the relation between teacher and learner that supports the learner's striving toward moral self-determination, and thus neither imposes the will of the teacher onto the learner nor forces the learner to blindly conform to societal norms. The three guiding principles of listening can be described as follows: (1) listening to know where the learner is, (2) listening to know when to cultivate discontinuity in the learner's experience and, in turn, to support the learner's expansion of her circle of thought, and (3) listening to know when to end the task of moral guidance. I examine each of these here.

Listening to know where the learner is

Of these three principles of listening, the first one is meant to orient the teacher's listening toward finding out how the learner thinks on his or her own; that is, the teacher is listening to find out where the learner is starting from in the learning process. Herbart argued that the teacher must come to understand the learner without initial prejudices because only in this way can the teacher determine where the learner can and should grow. He asserted that the teacher must listen to all of the child's 'innocent wishes' without 'prematurely (seeking) to correct them,' for these can be connected to the child's 'opinions and views' (Herbart, 1806/1902: 243; 1806/1887:121–22).[3] The teacher's listening here, which I call listening to know where the learner is, is oriented toward the learner in order to understand how the learner thinks so as to gain an initial impression of how the learner's thoughts might influence actions.

Listening to know when to cultivate inner struggle

The second principle of listening guides the teacher to know how and when to initiate the learner's self-critical and reflective thought. Following this principle, the teacher seeks to listen to know when to cultivate discontinuity in the learner's experience and, in turn, to support the learner's expansion of thought. Listening here is not neutrally listening to the learner's views, nor listening with the aim of affirmatively leading the learner to take on the views of the teacher. Rather, listening involves finding ways to problematise the learner's self-understanding, insofar as it is informed by egoism and self-interest rather than by respect for and recognition of the other. On this account, listening in teaching is an essential component of dialogue with the learner. The aim of dialogue in this context is to understand whether the learner is acting too quickly on self-interested ideas without careful consideration of the situation at hand. In this way, the teacher uses questions that seek to mediate between the learner's thought and action in order to cultivate the learner's process of coming into conflict with herself, and the teacher listens to see if this inner conflict or inner struggle is taking place. We can say that the teacher thereby seeks to cultivate discontinuity within the learner's experiences by interrupting the learner's experience, so that the learner begins to stand outside the self, gain distance on initial intentions, become self-reflective, and form critical judgments about those intentions.

To understand this sense of listening, we can turn to Herbart's example of how a teacher as moral guide would respond differently to two different learners, each of whom is caught in a lie (1806/1902: 240; 1806/1887: 119). He explained that if a teacher hears a child telling a 'self-interested lie' for the first time, then the teacher must correct the learner harshly, so that the learner recognises the gravity and consequences of his act and wants to correct himself, so as not to risk losing the respect he had previously won. However, if the teacher begins to recognise that a child has become a 'deliberate liar,' the teacher must approach the situation differently. As Herbart notes, if the teacher were to use harsh corrective words to the child who has already made a habit of lying, the child would only become 'more deceitful and insidious' (1806/1902: 240; 1806/1887: 119). This child knows the teacher disapproves, but his habits show that he is not concerned with this disapproval. Herbart argues that the only way to deal with such a situation is not by isolated reprimands, but by supporting the learner's process of expanding his 'circle of thought' so that he can discover and value the meaning of respect, and choose other options for action.[4]

In both of these cases, the teacher is looking at, and listening to, the whole individual as a historical being. Although both students are telling a lie, the teacher is hearing the lie differently. This difference in what the teacher is hearing leads to a different understanding of how to interrupt the learner's experience. In the first case, the teacher is interrupting the learner's experience by pointing out to the learner how this first lie does not fit into the series of good choices (telling the truth) he has made thus far. The learner's self-reflection and self-questioning are promoted here so that the learner learns not to change good choices just because a self-interested opportunity has arisen. In the second case, with the child who has become a deliberate liar, the teacher is also determining

(Continued)

(Continued)

how to interrupt the child's experience. The child here, however, only sees one way: his way of doing things, that is, lying, rather than telling the truth. So, to interrupt this learner's experience, the teacher must cultivate the learner's ability to expand his horizon of thought and experience by presenting the learner with other ways of being in the world, so that he begins to question his own judgments, see himself differently and see the possibility to make different choices.

Thus, the second principle of listening delimits the idea that the teacher listens to each learner not just in one isolated moment, but as a person who is in the process of change and growth. The teacher on this model must constantly make connections between the individual learner's present and past choices, and evaluate how these relate to future possibilities for change. This type of pedagogical judgment of the whole person requires a teacher who can support the expansion of the learner's 'circle of thought' in multifaceted directions, which means presenting the learner with alternative ways of seeing the world, new ideas and different knowledge or experiences that present different options for action. Listening thus informs the teacher's understanding of what subject matter to teach the learner, thus connecting the teacher's task of moral guidance with the task of instruction.

Although the first two principles identify conceptually distinct aims of listening, in practice, these aims are closely connected. The teacher must understand both where the learner is starting from in the learning process, and where the learner still needs to grow, and this understanding may become clear in the same moment. In both cases, the learner is being 'discovered' by the teacher. As Herbart says, neither practical experience nor *a priori* principles alone can tell us how to educate another human being: the individual must 'be discovered, not deduced' (1806/1902: 83; 1806/1887: 9). Each individual learner is unique and can only be understood by the teacher in the moment, that is, through lived experiences and interpersonal interaction. In this way, the teacher is making the learner the 'point of orientation' for all decisions (1806/1902: 113–14; 1806/1887: 30, translation modified by AE). In today's diverse classrooms, it is increasingly important for teachers to understand how to discover each learner as a unique individual, without imposing prejudices or making assumptions about learners.

Further, both of these two principles of listening in teaching involve determining how to initiate learning processes that aim to help the learner understand, as Herbart states, the 'disharmony' within himself. By listening to know where the learner is starting from, the teacher can find the good within the learner; that is, the teacher can find out where the learner is already acting with inner freedom and out of respect for the other. This good within the learner – the warmth for the good that the learner has already cultivated – provides the grounds upon which the learner can create an idea of good as his own evaluative criteria for judging himself, and is therefore an indispensable starting point for the educational relation. By understanding where the learner is starting from, the teacher can understand how to support the learner's growth by helping the learner recognise self-developed notions of good and bad. To aid the learner in this process of self-understanding, the teacher must listen to find ways to initiate discontinuity in the learner's experience: the teacher 'aims to get the learner to separate from himself; for [the learner] must educate himself.'[5] In other words, the teacher is attempting to help the learner recognise his own negative experience – the interruption in his thought or action that has now thrown him off (his own) course – and inquire into this negative experience, question himself, understand his inner struggle, and find strength to move on.

On this understanding, teaching entails seeking out moments when the cultivation of discontinuity is necessary for the learner's growth, so that changes of fixed self-interested habits become possible. This sort of teaching cultivates the learner's belief in her own perfectibility in the moral realm: the learner begins to see that she can change and that, by not doing so, she has something to lose, so that she wants to change. The true basis for moral inner struggle is that the good has been recognised, felt, and cultivated as a warmth for the good; once we have had the experience of honesty and loyalty among friends, the opportunity or even desire to lie weighs more heavily on us. In other words, after one has had the experience of the good, one then has something to lose: namely, one's self-respect, the basis for the respect of others.

Listening and the end of moral guidance

Finally, the third guiding principle of listening in educational relations is reflected in Herbart's considerations of the end of the task of moral guidance. At the point when learners demonstrate an ability to make their own informed, self-determined decisions, the teacher as moral guide has the task of ending moral guidance. Herbart underscores that moral guidance is self-undermining; it must seek out its own end.[6] To do this, the teacher must listen to know when to end the task of moral guidance because the learner has become his own guide. By listening to learners, the teacher seeks to determine if they have individually learned to endure the struggle and recalcitrance of negative experiences constitutive of moral decision-making processes and to act in recognition of the other. Herbart asserted that when the learner 'can pursue his right way independently,' then the teacher must drop 'all claims of moral guidance [*Zucht*]' and 'confine himself to sympathetic, friendly, trusting observation' (1806/1902: 239; 1806/1887: 119). The teacher-learner relation

(Continued)

(Continued)

changes at this point, as does the dialogue between them: all advice from teacher to learner has 'the purpose of getting the learner to think about the matter for himself' (Herbart, 1806/1902: 239; 1806/1887: 119). As the process of moral guidance ends, the learner takes on a stronger role of initiating dialogue with the teacher by asking for advice regarding problems and dilemmas. The change in the teacher-learner relation that results from an educational relation is a change that involves the learner's self-transformation; the learner now 'possesses both praise and blame within himself, and can guide and impel himself by their means' (Herbart, 1806/1902: 248–49; 1806/1887: 125).

The third principle illuminates the role of listening in concepts of the educational relation developed by various contemporary philosophers. Nigel Tubbs, for example, examines the task of an educator to 'negate' herself [7] by cultivating the learner's doubt. Nicholas Burbules states that authority in education must be self-undermining.[8] Dietrich Benner underscores that the educational relation is based in educating to 'promote the learner's self-activity,' a task that entails forms of teaching and educating that seek out their own end.[9] The principles of listening developed here extend such notions of the educational relation by highlighting the less considered, yet indispensable, role of listening in teaching.

On this account of the nature of the educational relation, the learner's self-transformation cannot occur in spite of, but only in the context of educational relations that support discontinuity in a learner's experience brought about by inner struggle. The end of the teacher-learner relation does not mean the end of the individual learner's inner struggle (although the nature of this struggle changes as the learner changes). Rather, the end of the teacher-learner relation means that the learner's relation to her own negative experiences, to the interruptions in her experiences of the otherness of the world, has changed: the learner no longer needs a teacher to interrupt her experiences, and promote her reflective inquiry into the nature of the negativity of her experiences – into her own doubt and felt resistance of the world and others. Instead, she is able to recognise the interruption in her experiences and initiate such reflective inquiry on her own.

Notes

1 This extract is taken from English, A. (2013) *Discontinuity in Learning: Dewey, Herbart, and Education as Transformation*, New York: Cambridge University Press, pp. 43–48. It is from the section entitled 'Listening and the Educational Relationship'. I have modified the headings and added subheadings to the extract for the purposes of this article. It has been reused with permission, Copyright © Andrea R. English 2013.
2 Johann F. Herbart (1776–1841) was a German philosopher and was a philosophy student of Johann Gottlieb Fichte at the University of Jena, and later worked as professor of philosophy at Göttingen University, and at the University of

Königsberg, where he took the former post of philosopher Immanuel Kant. Herbart made it a central aim to investigate educational questions and is considered one of the foundational thinkers in modern pedagogy. His followers started an educational movement known as Herbartianism, which was popular in the late nineteenth and early twentieth centuries in the United States, Europe, and other parts of the world. For more information, see Dunkel (1969), and the *Encyclopedia* entry on Herbart (English, 2014).

3 The first citation 1806/1902 is the English translation of Herbart's original German text, cited as 1806/1887.

4 On this point, see in particular pages 1806/1902: 213ff., and, 1806/1887: 100ff., and Herbart's concept of multifaceted educative instruction.

5 Herbart, J. F. (1851) 'Aphorismen zur Pädagogik', in G. Hartenstein (Ed.), *Johann Friedrich Herbart's Sämmtliche Werke*, Vol. 11, Part 2: 'Schriften zur Pädagogik', Leipzig: Leopold Voss, pp. 419–506.

6 Compare Herbart, 1806/1902: 239, 248–49; and, 1806/1887: 125, 128–29.

7 Tubbs draws this current of thought from the Socratic tradition, continuing Tubbs, N. (2005) 'Philosophy of the Teacher', Special Issue of the *Journal of Philosophy of Education* Vol. 39, No. 2, p. 318, through the Continental tradition of philosophy such as that of Heidegger, although he does not mention Herbart.

8 Burbules, N. C. (2007) 'What Is Authority?' in William Hare and John Portelli (Eds), *Key Questions for Educators*, San Francisco: Caddo Gap Press, pp. 17–21.

9 Benner, D. (2001) *Allgemeine Pädagogik: Eine systematisch-problemgeschichtliche Einführung in die Grundstruktur pädagogischen Denkens und Handelns*, Weinheim: Juventa, pp. 78–79.

References

Benner, D. (2001) *Allgemeine Pädagogik: Eine systematisch-problemgeschichtliche Einführung in die Grundstruktur pädagogischen Denkens und Handelns*, Weinheim: Juventa, pp. 78–79.

Burbules, N. C. (2007) 'What Is Authority?' in William Hare and John Portelli (Eds), *Key Questions for Educators*, San Francisco: Caddo Gap Press, pp. 17–21.

Dunkel, H. B. (1969) *Herbart and Education*, New York: Random House.

English, A. (2013) *Discontinuity in Learning: Dewey, Herbart, and Education as Transformation*, New York: Cambridge University Press, pp. 43–48.

English, A. R. (2014) 'Herbart, Johann F.', in D. C. Phillips (Ed.), *Encyclopedia of Educational Theory and Philosophy*, Thousand Oaks: Sage Publishers, pp. 373–376.

Herbart, J. F. (1806/1887) 'Allgemeine Pädagogik aus dem Zweck der Erziehung Abgeleitet', in Karl Kehrbach (Ed.), *Joh. Friedr. Herbart's Sämtliche Werke in Chronologischer Reihenfol*, Vol. 2, Langensalza: Hermann Beyer und Söhne, pp. 1–39.

Herbart, J. F. (1806/1902) 'The Science of Education', in *The Science of Education, its General Principles Deduced from its Aim, and The Aesthetic Revelation of the World*, Trans. Henry M. Felkin and Emmie Felkin, Boston: D. C. Heath & Co.

Herbart, J. F. (1851) 'Aphorismen zur Pädagogik', in G. Hartenstein (Ed.), *Johann Friedrich Herbart's Sämmtliche Werke*, Vol. 11, Part 2: 'Schriften zur Pädagogik', Leipzig: Leopold Voss, pp. 419–506.

Tubbs, N. (2005) 'Philosophy of the Teacher', Special Issue of the *Journal of Philosophy of Education*, Vol. 39, No. 2, p. 318.

Educational philosophy: reading and writing practices in this extract

When I read a philosophical text, my perspective is largely influenced by the philosophical tradition of phenomenology. This tradition is concerned with how human beings perceive and interact with the world and others, which tells us something about what it means to be human and to be educated. In this way, having a phenomenological 'lens' on texts allows me to read the texts in order to understand phenomena we cannot readily observe in the real world. The extract is an example of writing in which such phenomena, namely, 'listening' and 'inner struggle', are foregrounded and discussed philosophically. My focus in reading and analysing Herbart's texts was on discovering how Herbart understands educative teacher-learner interaction, on which basis I aimed to draw conclusions about the nature of the teacher's listening in moral education.

As I mentioned in the extract, Herbart did not develop a theory of listening explicitly, but his theory of moral guidance entails implicit notions of what it means to be a teacher, including how a teacher should listen. Generally speaking, when I read a philosophical work, I have two aims. First, I aim to trace how the author uses particular ideas and concepts throughout his or her text in order to determine what that author means by such concepts. Second, I read a text to understand to what extent the concepts in the text can contribute to the questions I am trying to answer. For example, in using Herbart's texts as source material for an article, I tried to understand how he uses the idea of 'moral guidance' in teaching, and what he means by that term. At the same time, I sought to answer my own questions about what is required of teachers to listen to learners in a way that supports critical thinking and moral development. These questions allowed me to discover and pay attention to particular ideas in Herbart's text, that, had I not been thinking about the concept of listening, I might not have seen. This is shown in the extract, in which I focus on Herbart's description of the aims of moral guidance. From that description, I was able to create an argument about what teachers are listening *for* when supporting students' moral learning. Although I am following the argument of the author, I am also using my own questions to frame what I pay attention to in the text and, in that way, create my own argument about what I view as relevant to education today. Philosophical research is particularly important because it brings new questions to bear on philosophers' texts from previous eras, which allows us to critique past philosophical ideas or to show how we can learn from them. In this way, philosophical research helps us as a society to maintain our relationship to the past through continued conversations about significant educational ideas.

Writing in educational philosophy always has at least an implicit relation to educational practice, because it aims to clarify a matter relevant to education, and education happens between human beings who are in the world. My aim in writing theoretically about teaching is not to provide teachers with specific, concrete strategies to use to accomplish specific educational goals. However, I do have the aim of making ideas explicit (for example, ideas about listening in teaching, as found in the extract), so that educators can begin to think about connections between theory and practice on their own. In the extract, which represents only part of my theory of listening, I explicate principles of listening that are aligned with certain ways of acting in teaching. These principles can serve to guide the practice of teachers, even though they do not tell teachers exactly what to do. I use examples carefully in philosophical writing, because although examples help to give us a picture of how an abstract idea connects to practice, they also can serve to limit our imagination about what is possible in educational practice. I used Herbart's examples (as seen in the extract) to show how a teacher listens in moral guidance, because I found these helpful in illuminating distinctions between different ways of listening. In my philosophical writing, I also draw conclusions about educational policy, although this is not seen in the extract. I view philosophical research as important for broadening our vision of what is possible in education; it can make important contributions to discussions and debates of educational policy.

Note

1 The research network is entitled 'Listening Study Group' and was originally formed and led by Sophie Haroutunian-Gordon. Since 2014, I have served as lead on this network. I began to develop the three ideas of listening discussed in the extract in my article, English, A.R. (2011), 'Critical Listening and the Dialogic Aspect of Moral Education: J. F. Herbart's Concept of the Teacher as Moral Guide', in Sophie Haroutunian-Gordon and Megan Laverty (Eds), *Philosophies of Listening*, Special Issue of *Educational Theory*, Vol. 61, No. 2, pp. 171–189.

References

English, A. R. (2011) 'Critical Listening and the Dialogic Aspect of Moral Education: J. F. Herbart's Concept of the Teacher as Moral Guide', in S. Haroutunian-Gordon and M. Laverty (Eds), *Philosophies of Listening*, Special Issue of *Educational Theory*, Vol. 61, No. 2, pp. 171–89.

English, A. (2013) *Discontinuity in Learning: Dewey, Herbart, and Education as Transformation*, New York: Cambridge University Press, pp. 43–48.

8

DIFFICULTIES OF THE WILL

Philosophy of education through children's literature

Viktor Johansson

Introduction to the extract

The philosopher Ludwig Wittgenstein famously stated that in philosophy, 'What has to be overcome is a difficulty having to do with the will, rather than with the intellect' (1980: 17). There are recurrent scenes of interactions between teacher and student, and children and their elders, in his texts. Although they serve the purpose of setting up comparisons with actual language use, these comparisons do not necessarily provide the best examples of the emotional complexities in scenes of adult-child interactions. The extract shows an attempt to use children's literature to complement Wittgenstein's investigations by showing how the frustrations, dejections, and even the depressive sense of hopelessness that both student and teacher may experience is an inherent part of having a clear view of the dissonances that may occur in student-teacher and children-adult interactions. To explore the emotional aspects of such interactions, I turn to children's literature, just as the American philosopher Stanley Cavell, who has engaged extensively in discussions about the relation between philosophy and literature, turns to romantic literature: 'not for illustrations, but for allegories, experiments, conceptual investigations, a working out of this complex of issues, and I claim that that is what they are, that's what produces these texts' (Cavell, 1986: 229–230).[1] Or as Cavell puts it later in the same text: 'I want story-telling to be thinking...' (1986: 238). The following extract is an example of how philosophical readings of children's literature can be a form of philosophising that works with difficulties of the will.

EXTRACT: 'THE WORLD IS A DEAF MACHINE': SHAUN TAN AND THE EMOTIONS OF DISTANCE[1]

I have begun to develop a Cavellian and Wittgensteinian account of the child's exclusion from communities of reason and language that emphasises the child's struggle to take a position in those communities and how both adults and children, teachers and students, and readers and writers, might get lost in those struggles. Australian artist and author Shaun Tan, famous for his graphic novels and picture books, creates words and pictures that give a sense of the depression involved in children's dissonances and loss. In his picture book *The Red Tree* (2011) (published as a collection with notes from the author and two other stories, *The Lost Thing* and *The Rabbits* under the fitting title *Lost and Found*) we follow a child, whose gender is undetermined, through a day.[2] The story begins with the child sitting in a bed with a glum posture, black maple leaves slowly filling the bedroom, with the words 'sometimes the day begins with nothing to look forward to'. These words set the scene for exploring the emotional and affective aspects of what I call dissonance. This child can't see anything to look forward to. There is nowhere to go, no openings to go on with herself or her community and as the next page reads, 'things go from bad to worse'.

As the story continues, the child walks the streets. We read, 'darkness overcomes you'. Though the streets are filled with people, the child is aloof. The people on the street, busy with other things, are turned so that they cannot notice the child or the gigantic dark fish floating above her stooped head, shadowing her steps. I get the sense that something heavy and overwhelming, an impenetrable emotional darkness overcomes the child.

'[N]obody understands', the next page reads, and we see the child sitting with a diving helmet in a position indicating that it's cold, with fluid up to the ankles, in a bottle. The bottle placed in barren dark landscape. We now have a sense of what this depressive state may consist in. The phrase 'nobody understands' is thematised in other words and other depictions in the book. The next phrase is 'the world is a deaf machine without sense or reason'. The theme climaxes when a number of pictures depict the phrase 'sometimes you do not know what you are supposed to do...or who you are meant to be...or where you are'. It is possible to take this theme in two ways. '[N]obody understands' may be the source of much of the depression, but it may also be the result of depression. The child is disconnected and the heavy dark fish that no one else notices despite its remarkable size both establishes the disconnection and is followed by it.

'Nobody understands' also indicates that there is a somebody that could understand the child. The child is disconnected from something or someone. The child is disconnected from the world – 'the world is a deaf machine'. This machine, depicted as a large square surrounded with monumental buildings full of people that seems equally disconnected, is also, we are told, without sense and reason. It is not only that nobody understands the child, but the child cannot find sense or reason in the machinery of the world. However, in the depiction of the phrase 'without sense or reason', the deaf machine is reinterpreted. Now the child is climbing a stair, leading nowhere, in a city of words, a city made out of cuttings from papers and signs. Languages are mixed, words put together in nonsensical phrases, and although the picture contains a few phrases that almost make

(Continued)

(Continued)

sense, the context makes them incomprehensible. This picture gives a sense that language is overwhelming, that the child is lost among words. The world is deaf to the child, but it is also incomprehensible to the child. The established ways of adulthood are deaf, and they are nonsense to those marginal to the established conventions of linguistic usage.

Cavell is sensitive to such adult deafness, but Tan's picture book adds something exceedingly important. The buildings of words and letters give a fragmented glimpse of a language that I may attain but do not reach. It is a reminder of how I as a child fought my way to be acknowledged in a linguistic community and how that fight may result in loss and depression. In Tan, not finding sense or reason in the world of adulthood is set in the context of overwhelming emotional pressure.

Being emotionally locked out from language and reason is not the only sense in which the child is disconnected. The phrase 'sometimes you just don't know what you are supposed to do' indicates that even though the world is deaf and does not understand the child, the world has expectations. There are things the child is supposed to do. But what things? We see the child on stage wearing a costume and surrounded by all kinds of weird creatures doing some kind of performance. The stage is full of signs with nonsensical words. It is easy to see how this setting may raise the question of what the child is supposed to do, but an uncanny quality of this picture is not the stage in its centre, it is the audience surrounding the stage. All that is shown of the audience are their hats turned so that I sense their gaze directed towards the child. No faces are shown. Cigarette smoke between hats reminiscent of chimneys in an industrial landscape. It is as if there is a dark, massive, machine-like, impersonal expectation on the child. It is no wonder that I can discern a tear on the child's cheek.

Expanding on what it may mean that a picture of a cube suggests a certain use to us, Wittgenstein proposes that 'we're at most under a psychological, not a logical, compulsion' (Wittgenstein, 1953: § 140). This remark is helpful to understand Wittgenstein's project. A picture or a word may be used in many different ways (Wittgenstein, 1953: § 139). However, we seem to be inclined to see a picture in a particular way, as a cube for example, or a cube as a dice. Tan gives life to the expectation as psychological. The child is not looking for a logical must, but for a belonging among its elders. The oscillation between the psychological expectation and the logical must become a powerful, but incomplete, picture of Wittgensteinian philosophical critique. We may be inclined to read Wittgenstein's saying that 'a picture, that lay in our language, held us captive' as suggesting that we are held captive by the expectations (or our experience of it) of our fellow speakers (1953: § 115). We are, so to speak, stuck in the mud of finding the right use of the picture or word, blind to other possible uses and then we are lost when we find that we don't really know what those expectations are.

I find the oscillation between psychology and logic repeated in the *Investigations*, from its beginnings with St Augustine's account of his own learning of language, the examples of shopping for apples and the builders passing slabs, to the famous rule-following and private language remarks, to the discussion of seeing aspects. Wittgenstein seems to say that logic may not be the best help in diagnosing loss here (which is not to say that it cannot be of some help). I am suggesting that a picture book is very helpful.

Wittgenstein is not suggesting that philosophers' logical investigations of concepts such as 'cube' can be replaced by a psychological and therapeutic account. The psychological compulsion is introduced by saying 'we might be inclined to express ourselves like this' (Wittgenstein, 1953: § 140). Looking for psychological explanation of use is not that much better. Neither psychological expectations nor logical solutions will solve the child's problem of not knowing what to do, or say, or what the words that surround the child can mean. When Wittgenstein adds psychological compulsion to his account he is reminding us that there are many processes that we are prepared to call 'applying a picture of a cube'. This goes for how I use Tan's book as well. The emotional dimension it adds suggests only one inclination in attempting to grasp dissonance in our interactions.

Hence, not knowing what he or she is supposed to do, the child is left logically riddling out the nonsensical words, or finding ways to please its audience's expectations. In the picture I see a child who has given up on this task, too tired to go on. In the *Investigations* it is the teacher that gives up when the student's capacity to learn seems to have come to an end (Wittgenstein, 1953: § 143–144, 217); in *The Red Tree* it is the child's spade that is turned. But Wittgenstein, read through Tan, can be read as saying that though adults may be held captive by a particular application of a word or a picture and thus lost when facing other possibilities, we can feel equally lost by the sense that there is nothing at all that can tell us what to do. The latter is the position Wittgenstein seems to want for us, but as Cavell has famously remarked: 'It is a vision as simple as it is difficult, and as difficult as it is (and because it is) terrifying' (Cavell, 2004: 52). Tan tells me how this feels. Distance and dissonance can be emotionally overwhelming.

Still, Tan complicates matters further. It is not only a matter of industrial expectation of what the child is supposed to do, the child says that 'sometimes you just don't know…who you are meant to be' and 'or where you are'. Whereas 'what you are supposed to do' is depicted with an audience expecting something, the 'supposed to be' and 'where you are' depicts the child alone. The first

(Continued)

(Continued)

with the child standing facing towards a wall full of different obscure drawings, sketching a picture of herself in the exact same position she stands in. The second phrase is conjoined with a picture of the child in a vast and strange landscape of rolling hills, one hill with what seems to be a cemetery on top of it. These pictures give some sense of hope. In the rest of the book the child's surroundings seem overpowering. The child is small in a large, deaf, dark, and pressuring world. But now the child draws the answer to what it is supposed to be. Being lost is not only bad. It also means that the child has the opportunity to reorient itself. Not knowing what to be opens for taking responsibility for one's own being.

When we return to the child's bedroom 'suddenly there it is right in front of you/bright vivid/quietly waiting/just as you imagined it to be'. An attentive reader will expect this. Several pictures show a small red leaf. Now a red tree is growing on the bedroom floor, first small with just a few red leaves, then as the child enters the room, the tree is in full bloom covering the room. The child is smiling.

The child is lost and eventually finds something, which is where we arrive with Wittgenstein and Cavell. We must lose ourselves to find ourselves. But notice how differently Tan arrives there. Of course the arrival in the case of a picture book is even more vague than in these rather obscure philosopher's texts. The pictures and few words in Tan's book open for many different emotions and interpretations. Both the philosophers and Tan begin with the problem of going on, with a teacher, with a community, with the world. They emphasise that going on may be difficult. However, whereas the philosophers emphasise the reflective sense of loss – in Wittgenstein losing our selves is a matter of being lost for words, we do not know what to say and how to go on in language – in Tan this loss in language is emphasised as an emotional loss. The child is lost because her emotions disconnect her from the world and words of the adults and this emotional disconnection may also result in disconnection with words. Emotional loss marks the extreme difficulty with which children grow into communities of language and the deep emotional struggle involved in losing and finding ourselves; a difficulty that for Wittgenstein and Cavell, despite their emphasis on philosophical problems being embedded in the very lives of men and women, children and adults, seems less emphasised in their accounts of children.[3] As suggested by children's literature scholar Kimberley Reynolds, Tan's use of nonsense and the very few words that carry the story mark the limits of language as a cure for loss; it underlines how human interaction involves more than words (Reynolds, 2007: 101).

Notes

1 The research presented in the excerpt is part of Chapter Three of the doctoral dissertation *Dissonant Voices: Philosophy, Children's Literature, and Perfectionist Education* (Johansson, 2013).

2 Others have presumed that the protagonist of Tan's story is a girl. To me, this is not at all clear. See Reynolds (2007: 99–101).
3 For an interesting exception, see Cavell's retelling of his son's reaction to the funeral of Cavell's mother (Cavell, 2010: 461–462 and 467–468).

References

Cavell, S. (2004) *Must We Mean What We Say?*, Cambridge: Cambridge University Press.
Cavell, S. (2010) *Little Did I Know: Excerpts from Memory*, Stanford, CA: Stanford University Press.
Johansson, V. (2013) *Dissonant Voices: Philosophy, Children's Literature, and Perfectionist Education*, Stockholm: Stockholm University, Department of Education.
Reynolds, K. (2007) *Radical Children's Literature: Future Visions and Aesthetic Transformations in Juvenile Fiction*, London: Palgrave Macmillan.
Tan, S. (2011) 'The Red Tree', in *Lost and Found*, Sydney: Arthur A. Levins Books.
Wittgenstein, L. (1953) *Philosophical Investigations*, fourth edition, Trans. G.E.M. Anscombe, J. Schulte, and P.M.S. Hacker, Oxford: Wiley-Blackwell.

Educational philosophy: reading and writing practices in this extract

So, why turn to children's literature to learn this about children? What does it mean to turn to children's literature 'not for illustrations, but for allegories, experiments, conceptual investigations, a working out of this complex of issues', and to 'claim that that is what they are, that's what produces these texts'? Or what does it meant to say that I, following Cavell, 'want story-telling to be thinking'? How is such philosophical procedure a matter of working on the will?

This small extract from recent philosophical writing refers not only to a work of children's literature, but also, more specifically, to a picture book – a particular form of storytelling, and a distinct form of thinking. The point of turning to such a work is to be able to philosophically work on my own, and the reader's, will, as I suggested by way of introduction in the quote by Wittgenstein. However, the picture book provides means that go beyond the mere use of words. It is storytelling that utilises a wider range of modalities, where the colour, perspectives, and motives of the picture become significant. This multi-modal form of storytelling adds a different and more aesthetic perspective on the issue of the child's dissonant interactions with the world than is possible with a philosophical account. The difficulty here is how to clarify the relevance of the aesthetic perspective or experience of reading the picture book to the philosophical issues discussed. In order to do that, it is not enough just to read the picture book; we need to make a reading of it and bring out what this reading of it does to us. Moreover, such a reading of a literary and artistic work is set in conversation with philosophical texts and ideas. It is such conversations that can become a working on the will, an opening for an emotional and aesthetic sensitivity to the issue of interaction between children and adults.

In the extract I offer a reading of Tan's picture book that accounts for my aesthetic and emotional experience of engaging with the story. For example, I describe how my imagination gives me a sense of the overwhelming emotional struggles of a child trying to find a place and meaning in the world. In this particular case this involves accounting for experiencing both the words *and* the pictures. The words 'the world is a deaf machine' are set in the context of previous phrases and pictures. That is the reading. The reading is philosophical since the experience of the text and its pictures is set in the context of a philosophical discussion, namely, a discussion of, and supplement to, Wittgenstein and Cavell's views of childhood. The literary experience thus changes the impression of the philosophical issue. It changes the conversation. So, part of what I was trying to do here is to tie the emotional aspects of my reading of the story to a philosophical conversation. That is one way in which storytelling becomes thinking.

Here it is important to recognise that my philosophical conversational partner in this extract is Wittgenstein. Wittgenstein even thought that philosophy should be a form of poetic work (Wittgenstein, 1980: 24), but surely not all kinds of philosopher would invite this conversation. Not even philosophical outlooks that themselves involve literature are necessarily receptive to conversations with literature in which literature contributes a perspective on educational reality. Although many would agree that literature is an important form of critical reflection on the human condition, this view of literature – which itself makes the conversations between literature and philosophy as a method possible – has been under attack from many influential philosophers for the last few decades (see e.g. Derrida, 1976: 158; Fish, 1980: 242–244; Eagleton, 1997: 145–146). The critique of literature as a means for understanding extra-literary realities has shown that, at best, literary language and fiction are bound to the text of their own work. The attempt to step out from the text and say something about an extra-textual reality thus becomes a step away from the literary. This could be seen as quite an innocent move. However, it may be argued that such a stepping out of the text, and carrying assumptions from the fictional context to orient oneself in reality, tends to form unwarranted ideological prejudice. The philosopher of education who engages with literature, it seems, is thus left to reveal and criticise such assumptions and prejudices in literature.

In this extract I did the opposite by letting the literary account destabilise philosophical assumptions. The criticism of that aspiration shows that we need to be careful so that our experience of the literary text does not solidify ideological presumptions, in this case, about children and their experience of dissonance with their elders and the world. One could suggest that this is the same with a philosophical argument; it too can solidify ideological presumptions. In my extract, the literary examples are used to destabilise philosophy. In that context, educational research needs to use both literature and philosophy against and with each other.[2]

To see how this turns out, think of the many examples of unruly children we find in children's literature. Sometimes when we read about those children in fictional accounts, our experience of the unruliness is not that different than it would be if we were involved with them as parents or teachers, observed them as empirical researchers, or read an account of a researcher's observation of them. However, sometimes when we read those accounts as literature, our experience can be very different. The unruliness may turn into something funny or whimsical, something scary or provocative. We may get a sense of the absurdity of certain conventions, and so on. The literary experience shows further ways of seeing a phenomenon and gives it new significance. That is what this extract attempts to do. Wittgenstein's texts are surprisingly rich with situations of dissonant interactions between children and adults, where the adult's instructions do not seem to make sense to the child, or the way the child acts on the instructions does not make sense to the adult. When Tan tells the story of the child turning to a world that does not make sense, a world that is like a 'deaf machine' that still places expectations on the child, we experience those dissonant situations differently. All of a sudden we see and feel how they can involve being alone in the presence of our elders. In this extract that is how children's literature is used as form of philosophical study of children.

Putting the picture book in conversation with philosophers is an attempt not just to say something but also show something. Many philosophers influenced by Wittgenstein have pointed out that in his philosophy we must pay as much attention to what he says as what he shows by saying so (Burbules *et al.*, 2008: 5–9).[3] Being emotionally involved in the philosophical expression of a position makes it possible to see different aspects of that phenomenon. The point of showing here is not directed to a clear something – that of course could be said – what is shown are the difficulties of our will, the temptation to take a limited view of what is involved in the conceptual understanding of a phenomenon. What is shown is not so much that emotions are essential to the dissonant reactions between children and their elders, but that the temptation to leave emotions out is nonsensical once we have experienced the emotional aspects of these interactions (Kuusela, 2008: 109–110). To show something – not merely say something in a text – conditions the act of writing, which means that we cannot show something without full attention to both what we write and the manner or the method of the writing. Manner and method depend, of course, on what we want to show. Writing becomes a work on our will, or, in a sense, our seeing.

Such work on the will, or seeing, may easily fall into dogmatic ideology that affirms presumptions. From the reading of Tan, one may get the sense that not understanding the world and not being understood *are* depressing. That's the way it is. Likewise, from Wittgenstein's examples, one may get the sense that dissonance is an intellectual and philosophical problem. However, in this extract, the method consists in using literature as, what Wittgenstein called, an object of comparison that is meant to clarify the problem of dissonant interactions – one thing to compare with among many other comparisons (Kuusela, 2008: 125). The experience of reading Tan is compared to other experiences of the phenomenon, in this case with Wittgenstein's discussions of logic and psychology, but also with the more hopeful aspects of Tan's story culminating in the child finding the red tree.

The method of using children's literature in educational philosophy outlined here can be summarised in three suggestions: (1) One needs to be careful about which philosophers one engages with, since not all philosophical outlooks are open to certain uses of literature; (2) In order to avoid solidifying one's experience of a phenomenon, one needs to think of literature (and philosophy) as objects of comparison, which are comparable with the phenomenon and not models of reality; and (3) As objects of comparison, readings of literature not only say something about a particular educational phenomenon, but also show us something about it.

In conclusion, let me say something about how philosophising with children's literature has relevance for education. *First*, if this is a form of philosophising that attends to both the saying and showing of philosophical thinking, the text itself is educational. It begins in the acknowledgement that a philosophical effort has an intrinsic pedagogy (see Johansson, 2014: 65–69). *Second*, in the particular case of educational philosophy, and especially in how I used literature to explore dissonant reactions between children and their elders, the philosophical education consists in showing further aspects of the educational phenomena at hand. This showing is meant to affect the will of the philosopher and the reader of philosophy. It is a way to explore modes of seeing a phenomenon that goes beyond the temptation to see them within the limitations of our established concepts, even beyond the limitations of the words, as well as the pictures and emotions, we use. A picture book in conversation with the philosopher's investigations can give a sense of what it means to be a child entering the world of adults.

Notes

1 This essay, 'In Quest of the Ordinary: Texts of Recovery', has also been published as Chapter Three in Cavell's *In Quest of the Ordinary*. However, the version I refer to here has a question and answer section, from which this quote is taken, and which is not contained in the chapter version in Cavell's book.
2 Throughout the last decades of the twentieth century many philosophers of literature and literary theorists, inspired by Derrida's deconstruction, Foucault's archaeology of knowledge, and Marxist historicism, developed criticism of using literature in the way I propose. However, philosophers working in the light of Cavell's work have argued that literary fiction has the power to cast doubts on our most firmly held presumptions and shed further light on our most vital (philosophical) problems. For a recent discussion, see Harrison (2015), Gibson (2007), and the editorial introduction to Eldridge (2009).
3 Wittgenstein introduces this distinction in his early work. See Wittgenstein (1922: 4.1212 and 6.522). He has many different ways of emphasising the notion of showing in his later work, for example, when he compares his remarks to sketches of a landscape and calls his reader a viewer of it, or when he describes his form of philosophising as presenting a surveyable representation of how we look at matters (Wittgenstein, 1953: Preface and § 122). For further discussion, see Diamond (2004), Conant (2004), and Kuusela (2008, Chapter 3).

References

Burbules, N., Peters, M.A., and Smeyers, P. (2008) 'Showing and Doing: An Introduction', in M. Peters, N. Burbules, and P. Smeyers, *Showing and Doing: Wittgenstein as a Pedagogical Philosopher*, Boulder, CO: Paradigm Publishers, pp. 1–15.

Cavell, S. (1986) 'In Quest of the Ordinary: Texts of Recovery', in M. Eaves and M. Fisher (Eds), *Romanticism and Contemporary Criticism*, Ithaca, NY: Cornell University Press.

Conant, J. (2004) 'Why Worry About the *Tractatus*?', in B. Stocker (Ed.), *The Post-Analytic Tractatus*, Aldershot: Ashgate, pp. 167–192.

Derrida, J. (1976). *On Grammatology*, Baltimore, MD: Johns Hopkins University Press.

Diamond, C. (2004) 'Saying and Showing: An Example from Anscombe', in B. Stocker (Ed.), *The Post-Analytic Tractatus*, Aldershot: Ashgate, pp. 151–166.

Eagleton, T. (1997) *Literary Theory: An Introduction*, second edition, Oxford: Oxford University Press.

Eldridge, R. (2009) 'Introduction', in R. Eldridge (Ed.), *The Oxford Handbook of Philosophy and Literature*, Oxford: Oxford University Press, pp. 3–15.

Fish, S. (1980) *Is There a Text in This Class? The Authority of Interpretive Communities*, Cambridge, MA: Harvard University Press.

Gibson, J. (2007) *Fiction and the Weave of Life*, Oxford: Oxford University Press.

Harrison, B. (2015) *What is Fiction For? Literary Humanism Restored*, Indianapolis: Indiana University Press.

Johansson, V. (2014) 'Perfectionist Philosophy as a (an Untaken) Way of Life', *Journal of Aesthetic Education*, Vol. 48, No. 3, pp. 58–72.

Kuusela, O. (2008) *The Struggle Against Dogmatism: Wittgenstein and the Concept of Philosophy*, Cambridge, MA: Harvard University Press.

Wittgenstein, L. (1922) *Tractatus Logico-Philosophicus*, Trans. C.K. Ogden, London: Routledge & Kegan Paul.

Wittgenstein, L. (1953) *Philosophical Investigations*, fourth edition, Trans. G.E.M. Anscombe, J. Schulte, and P.M.S. Hacker, Oxford: Wiley-Blackwell.

Wittgenstein, L. (1980) *Culture and Value*, Oxford: Basil Blackwell.

9

RE-IMAGINING EDUCATIONAL THEORY

Anne Pirrie

Introduction to the extract

The extract below offers a critique of the notion of capacity building in educational theory. Broadly speaking, the term refers to a perceived need to engender a greater understanding of the role of theory in educational research, including in the presentation of research findings (Biesta *et al.*, 2011). The extract reflects the author's enduring fascination with the practice of educational research, and the cognitive and imaginative possibilities of language. It is driven by a desire for lightness rather than *gravitas*, and a resistance to modes of academic exchange that value *expositions of knowledge* over *demonstrations of thoughtfulness*. Italo Calvino (1988: 8) suggests that it is only by engaging with the 'lightness of thoughtfulness' that we are able to perceive 'all that is minute, light and mobile'. The extract below is an attempt to bring this lightness of thoughtfulness to bear on the notion of capacity building in educational *theory*. As Biesta *et al.* (2011) point out, the methods and methodologies of research have received rather more attention in recent years than has the quality of theorising. This is a significant gap because 'good research depends on a combination of high quality techniques and high quality theorising' (*ibid.*: 226). Biesta *et al.* suggest that there is a key role for theory in 'deepening and broadening understandings of "everyday" interpretations' and in 'exposing how hidden power structures influence and distort such interpretations and experiences' (*ibid.*). What happens when we subject calls for capacity building in educational theory to the same treatment? In the ensuing extract this is achieved by drawing attention to how we use language, and by considering the obverse of capacity, namely, *incapacity*, construed as a form of attentive non-doing. Is there a role for the latter in educational research? It is worth recalling the etymology of theory, which is derived from the Greek θεωρία, meaning contemplation, speculation, or the act of looking.

EXTRACT: ICARUS FALLING: RE-IMAGINING EDUCATIONAL THEORY[1]

Are the intentions behind capacity building as a means to re-invigorating educational theory as benign and altruistic as they appear? My aim here is to offer a more radical and daring alternative for re-invigorating educational research, one that foregrounds the engagement of the researcher by exploring the expressive, cognitive and imaginative possibilities of language as a means of exploring *incapacity* as an alternative basis for a re-enlivened educational research. After all, we have been asked by one of the main proponents of capacity building in educational theory to refrain from regarding a learner as 'the one who is not yet complete, not yet knowledgeable, not yet skilful, not yet competent, not yet autonomous' (Bingham and Biesta, 2010: 134). Perhaps incapacity and lightness rather than capacity and *gravitas* are the prerequisites for responsive and ethical research.

'Whenever humanity seems condemned to heaviness', Calvino writes, 'I think I should fly like Perseus into a different space' (1988: 7). Reading conventional educational research provokes similar feelings. Calvino reassures us that flying away does not mean 'escaping into dreams or into the irrational'. Rather, it means looking 'at the world from a different logic and with fresh methods of cognition and verification' (1988: 7). This seems a legitimate philosophical enterprise, one that may or may not involve elaborate initiatives in 'capacity building'. This is a situation in which less is more. Masschelein (2010: 49) suggests that 'critical educational research requires...a poor pedagogy, a poor art: the art of waiting, mobilizing, presenting'. It is useful to consider the dichotomy between capacity and incapacity in relation to Richard Rorty's well-known distinction between systematic or analytical philosophy and edifying philosophy (Rorty, 1979). As Richard Smith (2014: 35) explains, systematic philosophy aims at identifying definitive solutions for philosophical problems, 'so that [philosophers] can move on to other such problems that need solving'. The aim in systematic or analytical philosophy is to devise a system to deal with relevant problems efficiently and effectively. This means identifying explanatory gaps, nailing a point down, looking for additional descriptive resources that are not quite there (yet). The implication is that they are out there somewhere, if only we employ the correct conceptual apparatus, demonstrate sufficient ingenuity, or develop 'capacity'. Biesta *et al.* (2011: 227) suggest that 'theory becomes identified with knowledge of what is permanent and unchangeable in contrast to knowledge about the empirical world of change, flux and appearances'. But is it not precisely the world of change, flux and appearances that holds our interest?

Edifying philosophy may hold the key, as it 'returns again and again to addressing issues that always seem to have the power to bewilder us' (Smith, 2014: 35). In Rorty's terms, edifying philosophy works 'by substituting the notion of *Bildung* (education, self-formation) for that of "knowledge" as the goal

(Continued)

(Continued)

of thinking' (1979: 359). The hallmark of the best writing in this tradition is that it provides a plausible or defensible supplement to some more standard kind of discourse. Edifying philosophy acknowledges that there is eternal return, that there are no last words, no definitive solutions to particular problems, no 'solid metaphysical foundations for goodness and truth' (Smith, 2014: 34). We have to keep trying, to give more than we have, to confront our incapacity in respect both of the object of our enquiry and our interpersonal relations. In short, we have to work things out as we go along. This approach suggests a commitment to *improvisation* (process) rather than *innovation* (outcome), to *habitation* (a transient state) rather than *occupation* (mastery of a particular domain) (Pirrie and Macleod, 2010). Edifying philosophy invokes dialogic rather than dialectic conversation. Engaging in dialogic conversation is more like participating in a rehearsal rather than in the verbal jousting that is typical of conventional academic exchanges. Sennett (2012: 18) explains that 'in verbal conversation, as in musical rehearsal, exchanging is built from the ground up'. The ability to go on playing together 'comes from paying attention to what another person implies but does not say...in picking up on concrete details, on specifics...those small phrases, facial gestures or silences which open up a discussion'. Musicians are attuned to the minute, the light and the mobile. Their communication 'consists of raised eyebrows, grunts, momentary glances and other non-verbal gestures' (Sennett, 2012: 18). In contrast, in academic exchanges, there is scant attention to embodied presence, to visual and aural cues, and a retreat behind the written text. There is often an appeal to a supposed higher authority – Dewey, Kolb, Vygotsky, Bourdieu, Foucault – in order to 'add plausibility to empirical findings' (Biesta *et al.*, 2011: 226).

Demonstrating *thoughtfulness* differs substantially from engaging in an exposition of *thought*. The latter may involve a type of ventriloquism, a form of outsourcing thoughtfulness, as it were, by re-describing situations through the lens of particular theorists. Perhaps the prospect of not having a clear '-ism' with which to identify is unsettling in a climate that favours clear disciplinary allegiances, robust 'frameworks' and clear outcomes. Smith (2014: 34) observes that 'the responsibility of thinking lies in having the courage to have thoughts without anchors or criteria' (with the implication of being 'all at sea') and in refusing 'to fall in with established rules'.

Knowingness

If Calvino considers the literary virtues of exactitude and lightness, then Smith (2014: 49) has turned his attention to what he calls 'knowingness', namely the ability to move 'surely and successfully along the path of enquiry'. He also observes that '*acquiring* knowledge is often less important than *learning to live with our knowledge'* (2014: 51, my emphasis). Knowingness comprises a twofold paradox. It is not necessarily more awareness or knowledge that is lacking (although this is implied by capacity-building initiatives). 'There is no cure by information', Smith tells us (2014: 50). The problem seems to be that *one cannot yield to what one knows.* Knowingness also implies a failure to recognise that the human intellect is ordered to a reality that it *cannot* know. It is perhaps this ineffability that Smith has in mind when he refers to 'the slow cure for knowledge', the kind of discourse or *logos* 'that is written together with knowledge in the soul of the learner (*Phaedrus*, 276a, 5–6)' (Smith, 2014: 51).

The remedy for knowingness (it is perhaps over-optimistic to talk of a cure) is to recognise that what is required is not necessarily a more exhaustive description or a more ornate theoretical framework. Rather, it is an explicit acceptance that the issues that confront continue to interrogate us. Metaphor can provide a useful register for speaking in this situation, as it involves accepting uncertainty and looking for a discourse that we can acknowledge between speakers. It represents the search for truth 'in terms more familiar to the audience, and/or more memorable...in a way that calls for the audience to participate' (Haack, 1998: 78). Let us briefly examine the terrain occupied by the capacity builders, for they too issue an invitation to participate, albeit one of a different order.

Capacity and incapacity

Biesta *et al.* (2011: 231–232) describe how theory in interpretative and critical-emancipatory research 'can...be characterised by the ambition to make the strange – that is what is not known or not understood – familiar, that is bringing the strange into the sphere of what is already known and understood'. The implication is that the invocation of a higher authority will 'add plausibility to empirical findings' (2011: 226). In addition to making the strange familiar, theory also serves to 'make what is familiar strange' (2011: 232). They distinguish between forms of theory that 'add plausibility' to empirical research by explaining (in the Weberian sense of *erklärendes Verstehen*), or 're-describing' situations that 'make the actions of individuals and groups plausible', and 'autonomous theorising', which involves 'the *re-description* of educational processes and practices' (p. 233, emphasis in the original).

Biesta *et al.* (2011: 228) suggest that 'educational research shows a predominance of...descriptive, analytical and reflective contributions to policy and practice' and suggest that some of this research uses 'taken for granted categories as foundational, for example, teacher, learner, school, subject'. Capacity building might be another case in point. The authors observe that more attention has hitherto been paid to 'capacity building with regard to the methods and methodologies of research' than it has to educational theory

(Continued)

(Continued)

(2011: 225). In their view, the problem with educational research is that routine descriptions of what is the case fail to exhaust what needs to be said. They are in possession of the antidote. Theory, they argue, plays a key role in interpretative research by 'deepening and broadening understandings of "everyday" interpretations and experiences'. It provides extra leavening, elevating the pedestrian to the 'robust'. In critical theory, the aim is to expose 'how hidden power structures influence and distort such interpretations and experiences' (Biesta *et al.*, 2011: 226), with a view to offering:

> *better* interpretations than those generated by the social actors themselves, on the assumption that such first person interpretations might be distorted as a result of the workings of power, or, in more traditional critical language, as a result of the social position of actors.
>
> *(Biesta et al., 2011: 231)*

The striking thing about this extract is that the authors appear to have flown like Perseus into another, more exalted, space (a laboratory, perhaps). It appears that they breathe a more rarefied air than the 'social actors' of whom they speak. They do not appear to consider the possibility that their own activities and practices may be distorted by the exercise of power. This might take the form of identifying a 'lack of capacity' in educational theory, and proposing the remedy: namely, 'systematic empirical and historical investigations into the kinds of theory and forms of theorising that are being used in educational research' (p. 234). The 'agenda for research and practice in capacity building' contains linguistic talismans ('systematic', 'empirical') that are likely to appeal to funding councils. The scope of this mission is slightly surprising, given the perceived lack of 'high quality theorising' in educational research. The authors state that what is required is not 'more theoretical or philosophical reflection on the uses of theory' and suggest that 'maybe most of the work currently available is confined to such reflection' (2011: 234). This raises the question of what they mean by 'systematic', if investigation of philosophical and reflective work is to be ruled out *prima facie*. The exclusion of 'theoretical' work on theorising is puzzling, to say the least. Perhaps the only course of action left is to dart out of the darkness and to tell a cautionary tale.

The Bucket Rider

Calvino concludes his essay on lightness by re-telling a mysterious tale by Kafka. This encapsulates the qualities of lightness he identified in the work of Dante's contemporary, Guido Cavalcanti. It is in the highest degree light; it is in motion (and it is also about motion); and it is a vector for information. It also represents some of my misgivings about the notion of capacity building.

Written in 1917, the point of departure of *Der Kübelreiter* is the lack of coal in the last winter of warfare. The protagonist goes with an empty bucket in search of coal to fire the stove. The empty bucket serves as a horse, and they fly up as far as the second floor of a house, only to discover that the coal-merchant's store is below ground. The coal merchant seems disposed to heed the bucket rider's desperate cries, although his wife refuses to help. The bucket is so light that it flies off with its rider and disappears behind the Ice Mountains.

This enigmatic story is open to a number of interpretations. First, there is the idea of an empty bucket raising you 'above the level where one finds both the help and egoism of others; the empty bucket, a symbol of privation and desire and seeking, raising you to the point at which a humble request can no longer be satisfied' (Calvino, 1988: 28–29). Moreover, the fuller the bucket, the less it will be able to fly. Perhaps we should let Calvino have the last words on the issue of 'capacity building', for his is a more ambitious version of utterance, namely the rebirth of what is given in another context of meaning or another medium of showing. Astride our bucket, we should not hope 'to find anything more in it than what we ourselves are able to bring to it. Lightness, for example, whose virtues I have tried to illustrate here' (1988: 29).

Note

1 This extract is taken from a longer article, published as Pirrie, A. (2015) 'Icarus Falling: Re-imagining Educational Theory', *Journal of Philosophy of Education*, Vol. 49, No. 4, pp. 525–538.

References

Biesta, G., Edwards, R., and Allan, J. (2011) 'The Theory Question in Research Capacity Building in Education: Towards an Agenda for Research and Practice', *British Journal of Educational Studies*, Vol. 59, No. 3, pp. 225–239.

Bingham, C. and Biesta, G. (2010) *Jacques Rancière: Education, Truth, Emancipation*, London: Continuum.

Calvino, I. (1988) *Six Memos for the Next Millennium*, Cambridge, MA: Harvard University Press.

Haack, S. (1998) *Manifesto of a Passionate Moderate: Unfashionable Essays*, Chicago: University of Chicago Press.

Kafka, F. (1917/1971) 'The Bucket Rider', Trans. Edwin and Willa Muir, in *Franz Kafka: The Complete Stories*, New York: Schocken Books, pp. 450–453.

Masschelein, J. (2010) 'E-ducating the Gaze: The Idea of a Poor Pedagogy', *Ethics and Education*, Vol. 5, No. 1, pp. 43–53.

(Continued)

(Continued)

Pirrie, A. (2015) 'Icarus Falling: Re-imagining Educational Theory', *Journal of Philosophy of Education*, Vol. 49, No. 4, pp. 525–538.

Pirrie, A. and Macleod, G. (2010) 'Tripping, Slipping and Losing the Way: Beyond Methodological Difficulties in Social Research', *British Educational Research Journal*, Vol. 36, No. 3, pp. 367–378.

Rorty, R. (1979) *Philosophy and the Mirror of Nature*, Princeton, NJ: Princeton University Press.

Sennett, R. (2012) *Together: The Rituals, Pleasures and Politics of Cooperation*, London: Allen Lane.

Smith, R.D. (2014) 'Re-reading Plato: The Slow Cure for Knowledge', in M. Papastephanou, T. Strand, and A. Pirrie (Eds), *Philosophy as Lived Experience: Navigating the Dichotomies Between Thought and Action*, Berlin: LIT Verlag, pp. 23–37.

Educational philosophy: reading and writing practices in this extract

The above extract offered a critique of the notion of capacity building in educational theory. The ultimate aim was to expose the false ontology of capacity and to explore and critique the taken-for-granted notion of capacity building through a close reading of a particular text (Biesta *et al.*, 2011). The line of argument was developed in relation to a consideration of *thoughtfulness*, as opposed to a demonstration of *knowledge* of theorists who are generally considered to provide a useful lens through which to consider matters that pertain to educational theory. A salient feature of the extract is that it drew on two types of sources. First, there are those that clearly belong within the realm of educational philosophy or theory, for example, Smith (2014) and Biesta *et al.* (2011). Second, there is a reliance on a text that *prima facie* has little to do with the philosophy of education (Calvino, 1988), and yet which can offer relevant conceptual resources. The rationale for its inclusion here is that it is 'written together with knowledge in the soul of the learner (*Phaedrus*, 276a, 5–6)'. The choice of sources is one feature of the reading practices at work in this extract. The style of writing is another, and this contribution concludes with a brief consideration of this dimension.

The extract is part of a longer essay that remains loyal to its etymological roots: a first attempt in learning or in practice, an endeavour. According to the psychoanalyst Adam Phillips (2013: 383), the essayist:

> is the writer who extricates theory from science, who can write about method without method, who can write truthfully without needing to know what the truth is…The essay [is] perhaps the form that keeps making links between curiosity and sociability.

Phillips also suggests that, for psychoanalysts, writing essays is a form of 'resistance, a protest, a refusal to meet certain criteria' and to remain 'fairly and squarely within the realm, and the cultural prestige of science' (*ibid.*). The extract also speaks to a curiosity that will not be satisfied within the framework of a single contribution, however singular. In *An Essay Concerning Human Understanding*, Locke (1690/1836) expressed a preference for 'dry truth and real knowledge' and exhorted us to 'speak of things as they are' (to call a spade a spade, as it were). He warned us that the purpose of figurative language is 'to insinuate wrong ideas and move the passions'. However, he was no stranger to the use of figurative language himself, observing that 'eloquence, like the fair sex, has too prevailing beauties in it to suffer itself ever to be spoken against' (1690/1836: 373).

I suggest that eloquence is under-represented in philosophy and theory in educational research (as indeed is the fair sex, but that is another matter entirely). I have also attempted to demonstrate, through recourse to Calvino's essay on lightness and Kafka's tale of the bucket rider, that figurative language enables us to give more than we have, to acknowledge our *incapacity*. Metaphor embodies – if that is not stretching things too far – the being-in-relation that is a hallmark of educational theory and practice. As Haack (1998: 77) points out, 'Metaphor is an interactive phenomenon, in the sense that it is an utterance which a speaker intends his hearer to amplify and adjust.' It is thus the perfect vehicle (there is no escape from metaphor) for making links between curiosity and sociability. In contrast, calls for capacity building appear to be about giving *less* than one has as an embodied subject; expecting *more* of what is not (yet) there in terms of descriptive or conceptual artillery. They also imply positioning oneself in a relationship of implied superiority rather than demonstrating thoughtfulness.

References

Biesta, G., Edwards, R., and Allan, J. (2011) 'The Theory Question in Research Capacity Building in Education: Towards an Agenda for Research and Practice', *British Journal of Educational Studies*, Vol. 59, No. 3, pp. 225–239.

Calvino, I. (1988) *Six Memos for the Next Millennium*, Cambridge, MA: Harvard University Press.

Haack, S. (1998) *Manifesto of a Passionate Moderate: Unfashionable Essays*, Chicago: University of Chicago Press.

Locke. J. (1690/1836) *An Essay Concerning Human Understanding*, London: T. Tegg & Son.

Phillips, A. (2013) *One Way and Another: New and Selected Essays*, London: Hamish Hamilton.

Smith, R.D. (2014) 'Re-reading Plato: The Slow Cure for Knowledge', in M. Papastephanou, T. Strand, and A. Pirrie (Eds), *Philosophy as Lived Experience: Navigating the Dichotomies Between Thought and Action*, Berlin: LIT Verlag, pp. 23–37.

10

MAKING VOICES VISUAL

Two images

Nancy Vansieleghem

Introduction to the extract

This contribution will be about visual research that makes us think about the issue of giving voice. The impetus for this is a project that I carried out in 2011. The project was commissioned by the Flemish Office of the Children's Rights Commission, which wanted to enquire into the increasing problematisation and medicalisation of young people and children who show disturbing behaviour. The Commission posed the question of how to deal with the increase in psychiatric diagnoses in developed countries and, more particularly, how children with behavioural problems themselves relate to this diagnosis. As a consequence, researchers were invited to conduct a project in which children diagnosed as children with Attention Deficit Hyperactivity Disorder (ADHD) were given a voice. In this extract I write about what it could mean to give children a voice by opposing two docufilms as forms of visual research: DISORDER and DIS-ORDER. The contrast between the approaches shown by the films is strong, precisely because we get to see something totally different, even though the research questions correspond, the same children participate in both research projects, and they took place in the same period of time. Hence, the focus of this extract is on a particular form of doing visual research, in which 'something' from the world we live in today (the discourse on children diagnosed with ADHD) is put on the scene to make it visible and an object of thought.

EXTRACT: DIS-ORDER: TWO IMAGES OF CONVERSATION[1]

The film DIS-ORDER wants to present a particular form of visual research. More specifically, a form that does not try to present an image of what we know or can know, but that makes us think about *how* we think and see. In order to do so I contrast this film with a similar one, DISORDER. Both films have the intention to give voice to children who are diagnosed as children with ADHD. In order to realise this, reflective and philosophical group conversations (DIS-ORDER) on the one hand, and individual life stories (DISORDER) on the other, are put on the screen. Although this might seem an obvious distinction, an important difference comes to light when we discuss the contrast between the two research approaches in relation to the question of giving voice to a group of people who are excluded from the common discourse and not heard. Therefore, this contribution is not in the first place a description of what children with ADHD think about their diagnosis, but an attempt to conceptualise a firm basis to think about the potentiality of visual research in regard to giving a voice to children. Or, to put it differently, this text is an attempt to draw attention to the potentiality of visual research in relation to emancipation. The questions that are dealt with are twofold: how do both research approaches differ in regard to their effect on children's emancipation? And what is the role of the researcher in realising emancipation and giving voice?

I start with a description of what DISORDER does. DISORDER is an account of four youngsters who tell their life stories. They talk about themselves and in particular about when their behavioural problems all began, when they experienced difficulties, how they cope with their diagnosis and what they like and don't like about their diagnosis. It is a research approach that informs us about the psychological and social problems which children diagnosed with behavioural disorders experience, and how they deal with it. Allowing individual young persons to tell their life stories, the spectator's attention is drawn to different needs, viewpoints, and passions of (labelled) children. The idea behind this is that when we focus on their label we don't see any longer the singularity of the child and its environment. To put it differently, what the film does is show that our society assigns too much significance to the label of ADHD. Consequently, the added value of the film is that it wants to make us think differently about the label ADHD, *viz.*, no longer interpreting it as an indication of a neurobiological disorder, but as a description of disturbing behaviour of children who sometimes and because of a specific social and psychological environment can be fussy and distracted. And so, in DISORDER we do not only see individual children telling their life stories and taking pills, but also images of youngsters who are playing, gaming, running, and dancing. These images have the intention to make us realise that children who are diagnosed as children with ADHD also have particular capacities, emotions, and passions, and that on top of that, they are often very creative and artistic. To show this, DIS-ORDER displays images of two intensive workshops on craft and drumming, which the researchers set up together. We see engaged artists and happy children playing music, dancing, and making craftwork. Soft background music and colourful fragments that harmoniously merge into one another are very

(Continued)

(Continued)

present in the film and have the intention to invalidate the idea that children and young people with ADHD are difficult to deal with. DISORDER has thus a specific goal, which is quite obvious for anyone watching this documentary, and uses images to realise it: the spectator has to be confronted with an image of the youngster with a behavioural disturbance and s/he has to realise how this differs from the view people commonly have. This different image, more positively spoken, comes down to the presentation of an affirmation that these children have particular capacities as well, but lack a positive environment and diagnostic potential in order to make these capacities visual. This way, rather than disrupting the dominant discourse on ADHD, DISORDER shows merely a research approach that substitutes one discourse with a similar one. This is because, although the makers of this documentary have chosen to film the children in their 'natural' environment, in the end this comes down to a specific way of giving shape to what is so called natural. The researchers have a clear goal in mind, as they want to make visible the youngster behind the label which seems to be a child with strengths, capacities, and ideas. From this point of view, relating ADHD with neurobiological problems would overshadow the development of individual capacities and talents. As such, more than exposing the dominant discourse on ADHD, DISORDER seems to present an image of how children with behavioural problems should be approached and talked to. DISORDER decides what the spectator has to think and directs him or her in a predefined way. The images themselves do not speak, since they are assembled or constructed in such a way that they do not show what emerges before the camera, but what the researcher has in mind.

In contradistinction to DISORDER, DIS-ORDER does not start from the desire to show the child behind the label, but starts from the assumption that there is no fable to be exposed in order to see the truth. The assumption to start from is that there is no real world as opposed to a false one, but that what we see is real. What often happens, however, is that we do not look at what we see, but at what we know, or can know. Therefore, what DIS-ORDER does is not to make visible what is invisible, but to re-see what is there to see, here and now. As such, the starting point is not the discovery of a hidden world – the latent capacities of 'the child with behavioural problems' – but the suspicion that what is presented as unknown and hidden, is not so strange as we believe and assimilates merely with the archive of what we already know (the dominant discourse). This means that DIS-ORDER is primarily exposing the assumptions of the current educational discourse on children with behavioural problems, and of making the discourse inoperative. A remarkable difference with DISORDER is that DIS-ORDER, by doing so, does not observe the children in their natural environment, but makes an intervention. DIS-ORDER creates an artificial environment – 'a classroom' or a time and space where children are taken out of their 'natural' context and their 'natural' way of speaking about ADHD – in order to put themselves – as a figure – on the scene and make it into an object of thought.

As such, the children in this documentary are invited to talk about the questions: Who is the mentally disturbed person? What does 's/he' think? What does 's/he' say and what does 's/he' do? Thus no questions are asked such as: Why are 'you' here? What is 'your' problem? What do people think of 'your' behaviour? How do they define it? How do 'you' deal with 'your' problem/diagnosis? What helps and what supports 'you'? Who or what does not support 'you'? What influence does medication have on 'your' life? How do 'you' look at 'yourself'? How would 'you' like others to look at 'you'? Can 'you' be 'yourself'? What is particular for these kind of questions is that the research object – children with behavioural disorder – is estranged from its usual image, and a new connection or a new way of speaking becomes possible. The children are used to speaking. Not only with the psychiatrist, the psychologist, and the therapist, but also in school; group-discussions are organised in order to expose personal problems and individual viewpoints. The conversations organised in DIS-ORDER, however, do not give space to articulate inner problems or perspectives. The starting point of the conversations is not individual problems, experiences, and perspectives, but rather the discourse that sets the stage of those who are included and those who are not. The conversations brought into play the discourse itself by introducing a way of speaking that does not meet the assumed practices and expectations. The conversations empty the subject-position – the position of the child as someone with ADHD or with a behavioural problem. They install, so to speak, the possibility to begin. There is no right or wrong answer. There is only the possibility to speak and say something about what is there.

Since the children are not used to speaking about the type of subject they 'do', *viz.* as actor, this opens the possibility to say and to think something different, something that is not immediately understandable or thinkable within the dominant discourse. In DIS-ORDER the researcher does not address the children as 'owners' of behavioural problems, but as actors that by doing what they do present the conditions for reality to exist: the hitherto constituted order that legitimises and captures particular ways of seeing, feeling, acting, speaking and being in the world with one another. It is about the visible that is made visible by the person who is diagnosed as a person with a behavioural disorder, who speaks with the words of an expert that he not only mimics and copies but also distorts and trivialises.

(Continued)

(Continued)

There is little evidence of the direction in which the researcher guides the children. Neither the researcher, nor the children know how to respond. Just like the camera, the researcher registers for the first time what the children say, without making a detour along a predefined idea. Instead, what appears is a heightening of specific expressive elements. Rather than a story that explains to the spectator how children with behavioural problems think and act and why they are acting and thinking the way they do, the organising principle in DIS-ORDER is offered by the spoken words and gestures of the children. It is gestures and movements, words and arguments that are in a sense indifferent to the dominant discourse that constitute the focus of the film. In short, where DISORDER wants to liberate the child from their label and artificial code by observing the children in their natural environment, DIS-ORDER starts from the assumption that the installation of an artificial environment makes it possible to bring the dominant discourse in another context through which it loses its significance. This makes, I believe, that what is said in the film also speaks. There is no predefined message to be heard. DIS-ORDER shows us voices and no scenario. In general it can be said that what the children utter reflects a kind of sorrow or pain. However, not the kind of suffering that is caused by 'their illness' (ADHD). It is not 'their' ADHD that makes them suffer, but the experience of being a 'part with no part' (cf. Rancière, 2007). As far as what the children say, think, and do has a meaning within dominant discourses, it is understood in terms of indications that (can) stimulate the children's capacity and motivation to learn (cf. DISORDER). In contradistinction, DIS-ORDER does not start from the assumption that there is a problem that needs to be solved, but that giving voice to those who are 'a part with no part' requires an artificial operation towards the dominant discourse in order to make it inoperative. By bringing the significant discourse in to another (artificial) space and time, it makes it possible to reveal what is seen and what can be seen and said.

In brief, DIS-ORDER gives voice. This is not to say that the film explains something or teaches a lesson. It puts the figure of the child with behavioural problems on the scene and as such turns that figure into a subject of thought. DIS-ORDER opens or creates a different dimension that entails a direct confrontation with what can be said and thought and with who has the ability to see and to speak. It produces an effect that chiefly testifies to the possibility of other or new ways of thinking, seeing, hearing, and speaking. Inviting youngsters to speak about those matters they normally do not speak about, DIS-ORDER stages an event that realises a confrontation with different questions than the ones that are evident within the dominant discourse and thus opens an experience of potentiality. The conversation links the autonomy of a person explicitly to the potentiality of becoming something else: of a different way of relating to oneself, others and the world. It is breaking with what is, in order to show what can be.

Note

1 The extract is taken from Vansieleghem, N. (2015) 'DIS_ORDER: Two Images of Conversation', in N. Vansieleghem, J. Vlieghe, and P. Verstraete (Eds), *Afterschool: Imagining Educational Research*, Leuven: Leuven University Press, pp. 35–50.

References

Rancière, J. (2007) *The Future of the Image*, London: Verso.

Educational philosophy: reading and writing practices in this extract

I want to call the kind of research I described above 'empirical philosophy', as research that is divided from classical philosophy and empirical research, but is an approach that is in need of empirical elements in which the researcher is actively involved (Mol, 2000). That I, by doing so, associated my contribution with a research tradition that already exists, a style of thinking and doing that is developed collectively, does not mean that I have tried to do justice to this research tradition in advance. What you can read above is my particular attempt to speak and write about something I have done. A story. I call it a story on purpose. A story refers to a possibility, not to an ideal. It is a word that suggests that there is also the possibility of singularity and imagination. Therefore, it is often related to literature or art, instead of science and research. Doing research, however, does not mean that singularity and imagination are not at stake. Imagination includes the promise that there are other possible ways of thinking and seeing. And it makes possible a better understanding of what research can do. I relate my reading and writing to empirical philosophy precisely for the reason that its practice cannot be integrated in a method or a programme with particular instructions that can be applied anywhere, and where any content can be inserted. The substantive question of empirical philosophy is not how to do research, but how to do difference. Furthermore, empirical philosophy not only tries to answer that question. It understands difference as a basic assumption and an experiment that has to be done time and again. Hence, philosophical research not only describes, convinces, interprets, or criticises. Empirical philosophy is first of all a doing. Where this activity comes from is not always clear. Activity is not a prerequisite for reading and writing practices. The starting point is that there is activity in reading and writing itself. The reading and writing do something. Reading and writing propose action. Each research (text or image) is an intervention in reality. So is my story.

I have written about two different kinds of visual research. I also highlighted them as interventions so that the reader can 'see' differences and can ask the questions: Where is there a place for emancipation? Where does the child speak for itself in both films? These questions can be situated in the sphere of the senses. I addressed the reader as a viewer, not an interpreter: someone who 'can see' things and who can talk and think about what he/she sees. Hence, in my writing I tried to bring the reader/viewer to the materiality of the objects, the words, the sentences, the arguments, and the ideas that are circulating, and I invited him/her to think about what kind of doing these sentences and arguments generate. This way, the arguments and ideas become detached from the context in which they are meaningful and become 'some-thing' that can get new meaning. Very concretely, this means that the visible is no longer subject to the speakable. The assumption I started from is that the speakable and the visible have a relationship of equality. By doing so, I broke with a representative order that determines what can be seen and thought (at least temporarily), and I opened a space of thought. In addition, I also invited the reader/viewer not only to pay attention to what is said, but also to pay attention to the gestures, facial expressions, and voices. In DIS-ORDER, movements, facial expressions and hesitations take the place of identities and categories, leading to a blurring of identities and categories. They transform characteristics and categories into substantial situations.

Therefore, contrary to what is the case within the empirical research tradition, this kind of research starts from the assumption that the eye does not know in advance what it sees, what to think of it, and what to do with it. It is a way of doing research where the viewer is exposed to the question: what now? Hence, the intention of this contribution is not so much to focus on the final results of both films. The question was not: did both films provide new and valid knowledge about children with ADHD? Rather, and more than this, I wanted to show how the research design, the kind of questions that are asked, the analysis of the output, the way the camera is used, and the way the movie is directed have an effect on what is presented as final results in both films. By contrasting two examples of visual research I have tried to make a difference. I opened the possibility to experience visual research not as an operation in which the pedagogical reality is represented, but as an operation in which something becomes real – research that makes something visible so that it can become a matter of concern or material fact. In other words, I have tried to make a difference between images (as form of visual research) that are obvious, but do not invite us to look at what there is to see, because we already know what we will see, and images or research that install a space where what we see invites us to look, and appeals to us in the sense that the viewer is touched by it. In other words, I tried to present research that makes something 'real' (as material) and that in that sense is 'empirical'.

In line with what I described above about what empirical philosophy is or does, I would like to add that this kind of research does not depend on the acquisition of the right expertise and competences. Within the tradition of empirical philosophy – as far as I can write about a tradition or discipline – there is no hierarchy of intellectual capacity. Much more than knowledge and skills, you need to ask the question, time and again, whether there is a space and time in which the researcher and the viewers are addressed as actors or beginners (perhaps we can say children). In line with what Rancière (2007) says about this, I think that it is only possible to make something visible when things are detached from their context and brought together again in a different way. As he writes: 'Whoever looks always finds. He does not necessarily find what he was looking for, and even less what he was supposed to find. But he finds something new to relate to the thing he already knows' (Rancière, 1991: 33). Hence, this does not imply competences in the first place, much more it is about being focused on what is there now.

References

Mol, A. (2000) 'Dit Is Geen Programma. Over Empirische Filosofie', *Krisis*, Vol. 1, No. 1, pp. 6–25.

Rancière, J. (1991) *The Ignorant Schoolmaster: Five Lessons in Intellectual Emancipation*, Palo Alto, CA: Stanford University Press.

Rancière, J. (2007) *The Future of the Image*, London: Verso.

11

LANGUAGE, TEACHING, AND FAILURE

Ian Munday

Introduction to the extract

This research derives from my experience of working as a teacher in an English Comprehensive school during the noughties. During that time I felt as though a particularly weird and sceptical approach to language had insinuated itself into the culture of schooling. This manifested itself in a number of troubling ways. At that time, Ofsted (the school inspectorate in England and Wales) gave four grades to both individual teachers and schools. We could be marked as 'unsatisfactory', 'satisfactory', 'good', or 'outstanding'. I recall a talk in which the Headteacher informed us that 'satisfactory' was no longer satisfactory, and that the majority of teachers should aim to be 'outstanding'. This sort of scepticism in the face of language (where one can no longer rely on words to mean what they ordinarily mean) had its corollary in approaches to language in the classroom. As teachers, we were told that we should not talk too much, and what we did say should be utterly transparent if learning objectives were to be met. In the meantime we were expected to ensure that certain contextual factors (such as seating plans) were in place so as to achieve maximum control of the learning environment. The aim of the research presented in the extract is to bring the work of Jacques Derrida on the performative dimension of language to bear on issues regarding the role played by contextual factors when establishing whether or not teaching fails or succeeds. Derrida was a French poststructuralist philosopher of language whose writings revolutionised the philosophy of language.

EXTRACT: THE PERFORMATIVE UTTERANCE[1]

The philosophical material that guides this discussion derives from Jacques Derrida's reading of J. L. Austin's theory of the performative utterance that appears in his famous essay 'Signature, Event, Context' (Derrida, 1988). Let us begin with Austin. In *How to Do Things With Words* (Austin, 1976) Austin attempts to distinguish constative utterances that 'state' things from performative utterances that 'do' things. Constative utterances are true or false. If I say 'the cat is on the mat' this either is or is not true. Such statements assume a distance between language and world, between words and actions. In contrast to constatives, performative utterances cannot be thought of purely in terms of truth and falsity. Such utterances include 'I christen this ship the...' and 'I now declare you man and wife'. With such utterances, whereby I 'do' something by saying it, the division between word and world, doing and saying breaks down. To speak is to act.

By focusing on the kinds of utterance that 'do' something Austin is obliged to consider the 'constraints or conditions that they operate under which ensure they communicate or do their work as perfectly as they do, as perfectly as the most unobjectionable true-or-false statements do theirs' (Cavell, 2005: 158). Austin argues that the success of performative utterances (though not divorced from questions of truth and falsity) is subject to conditions of infelicity or unhappiness. Infelicity/unhappiness occurs when the performative utterance fails to achieve its intended effect. Such failure results from some lack or inadequacy within the total speech situation. An example might be a wedding in which the person presiding over the ceremony does not have the legal authority to marry the participants. This contextual factor means that the speaker's words do not have their intended effect, and the performative utterance is therefore unhappy.

Having recognised that a distinction can be made between constative and performative utterances, Austin comes to see that it begins to break down. Although constative utterances represent truth claims, constatives are subject to conditions of infelicity; if the cat is under the mat, then the statement 'the cat is on the mat' (Austin, 1976: 9) is clearly unhappy. In the case of performatives, if I warn you that 'the bull is about to charge' and it isn't, then concerns with truth infect performative utterances (p. 6).

Ultimately Austin comes to argue that to think of truth claims operating within some purified zone of stating is a fundamentally flawed vision of language. After all, if I 'state' something then I am doing something. Claims of essential or abstract truth are positioned by contextual factors that take over the whole speech situation. Austin is not saying that we cannot speak of truth. However, he demonstrates that conditions applicable to the language of doing apply to the language of stating; that in a complex way, constative statements are necessarily performative and performatives are bound up with truth claims.

(Continued)

(Continued)

Austin, Derrida, and context

Derrida's interest in Austin's project derives in part from the latter's recognition that in identifying the ways in which words can do things the focus moves away from thinking of language in terms of signification where words stand as markers for ideas, for some truth external to language, to an emphasis on 'communicating a force through the impetus [impulsion] of a mark' (Derrida, 1988: 13). We should note here that, for Derrida, the notion of the mark acts as a replacement for the sign. The sign, with its binary distinction between signifier and signified, remains trapped within the metaphysics of presence. It assumes some origin of meaning and a fullness that precedes the signifier. Derrida's 'mark' is the written word stripped of signification (emptied out of meaning) that indicates a presence in the form of a trace. The mark indicates presence, yet in Derrida's terms it exists as the absent origin – the mark stripped of meaning. Meaning/concept is an effect produced through the force (the impetus) of the mark. To understand things in this way is to understand all meaning as textual – there is no outside text.[2] When Austin shows how issuing a performative utterance is not to report on language, but to indulge in it, he appears to recognise the impossibility of adopting a stance that is external to language. This is why Derrida notes that:

> As opposed to the classical assertion, to the constative utterance, the performative does not have its referent (but here the word is certainly no longer appropriate, and this precisely is the interest of the discovery) outside of itself or, in any event, before and in front of itself. It does not describe something that exists outside language and prior to it.
>
> *(Derrida, 1988: 13)*

Derrida argues that Austin has shattered the concept of communication as a purely semiotic, linguistic, or symbolic concept. Communication is no longer considered in terms of 'transference of semantic content' or fixed in its orientation towards truth. Derrida praises Austin's patience and openness, the fact that the work is in constant transformation, that it acknowledges its impasses.[3] Nevertheless, despite the fact that for Austin meaning no longer has a 'referent in the form of a thing or of a prior or exterior state of things', Derrida argues that Austin undoes all his good work by missing something important about the structure of locution which effects the ternary distinction between locutions, illocutions, and perlocutions.

What does this amount to? It seems to have everything to do with the importance to Austin's project of an exhaustively determined context. One of the essential elements to this 'remains, classically, consciousness, the conscious presence of the speaking subject in the totality of his speech act'. Performative communication is bound up with intentional meaning:

> The conscious presence of speakers or receivers participating in the accomplishment of a performative, their conscious and intentional presence in the totality of the operation implies teleologically that no *residue* [*reste*] escapes the present totalisation.
>
> *(Derrida, 1988: 14)*

I take this to mean that Austin, having shown how the outside to language invoked by the 'referent in the form of a thing or a prior exterior state of things' (*ibid.*) breaks down in the colonisation of the constative by performative concerns, then goes on to reinstate external presence in the figure of the speaking subject. The success of an utterance depends on whether or not my words do what I intend them to do: 'therefore we find an exhaustibly definable context, of a free consciousness present to the totality of the operation, and of absolutely meaningful speech master of itself: the teleological jurisdiction of an entire field whose organising center remains intention' (*ibid.*). If my intentions succeed, they must do so with due 'correctness' and 'completeness'. This can only be accomplished if other factors (felicity conditions external to the utterance) are in place. If the priest is not qualified to marry me, then I will not be married. Derrida notes that Austin's procedure is:

> rather remarkable and typical of that philosophical tradition with which he would like to have so few ties. It consists in recognizing that the possibility of the negative (in this case, of infelicities) is in fact a structural possibility, that failure is an essential risk of the operations under consideration; then in a move which is almost *immediately simultaneous*, in the name of a kind of ideal regulation, it excludes that risk as accidental, exterior, one which teaches us nothing about the linguistic phenomenon being considered...Thus, for example, concerning the conventionality without which there is no performative, Austin acknowledges that *all* conventional acts are exposed to failure: 'it seems clear in the first place that, although it has excited us (or failed to excite us) in connexion with certain acts which are or are in part acts of *uttering words*, infelicity is an ill to which *all* acts are heir which have the general character of ritual or ceremonial, all *conventional* acts: not indeed that *every* ritual is liable to every form of infelicity (but then nor is every performative utterance)' [Austin's emphasis].
>
> *(Derrida, 1988: 15)*

(Continued)

(Continued)

Derrida notes, and applauds, Austin's interest in the 'negative', in communicative failure. In this respect, Austin's project seems in line with non-analytical strands of philosophy. However, Austin then seems to take a step backwards by focusing solely on the contextual surroundings 'the conventionality constituting the *circumstance* of the utterance' (*ibid.*). Derrida's point is that Austin misses the conventionality intrinsic to what constitutes the speech act [locution itself]. He notes that: 'Ritual is not a possible occurrence, but rather, *as* iterability, a structural characteristic of every mark' (*ibid.*). What does this amount to? It seems that words, if they are to mean anything at all, must be repeatable and repeated as ritual. Derrida's point is that language is itself performative and exercises force in its own right. Austin's mistake is to move away from the 'wordness' (the 'graphematic' aspects) of language to concentrate on forces that enact themselves on language and are thought to be somehow exterior to it. For Derrida, words are subject to an internal force and movement. It is not the case (as Austin might have it) that the context determines the force of words. Rather, an unlimited number of possible contexts are internal to the words themselves. The word or concept is never at one with itself. Derrida insists that he is not referring to the polysemy[4] of language but its iterability. If we perceive the forces in language to be external, then the context determines meaning.

For Derrida, context is not something that sits behind words but operates through them. Moreover, the reiteration of words means that they find themselves in unexpected places, doing unexpected things that are not under anyone's direct control. Consider what has happened to the word 'queer'. For a long time queer was used to 'capture' a rather negative form of peculiarity. It then came to be used in another negative sense in relation to homosexuality. However, the gay community proudly (think about what has happened to the word 'pride') reappropriated what had been (and continues to be) an instance of hate speech. We cannot say that these different uses of the word are somehow discrete. Rather the older contexts/meanings of the words haunt the newer ones. For Derrida, in different ways, what has happened to 'queer' and indeed 'gay' or 'pride' is true of all words. Moreover, whatever I may intend to mean by using a word in a particular way cannot be unaffected by the various contexts/meanings that are internal to that word. I cannot choose whether or not something 'arrives' in language.

Lessons and events

When considering what Derrida's discussion surrounding iterability and context have to do with teaching and learning, we might begin by drawing an analogy between what is currently regarded (in Britain) as 'successful learning' and the notion of infelicity or unhappiness that plays such an important part in

Austin's theory of the performative utterance. A successful or happy lesson as it conventionally understood[5] nowadays must take on board numerous contextual factors (felicity conditions?). So, for example, a good teacher will do the following things (this is not an exhaustive list):

1. She must place the learning objectives/outcomes on the board and make it clear from the beginning of the lesson exactly what it is that is going to be learnt that day.
2. The teacher should ensure that the learning outcomes are differentiated at the outset so that different things are required of different learners with different abilities.
3. Tasks should be differentiated in accordance with both ability/attainment levels and different learning styles, kinaesthetic, auditory and visual.
4. The lesson should incorporate group tasks and individual tasks in which learners work independently.
5. Students should be provided with the tools to assess their work.
6. Behavioural issues should be accounted for through the use of various techniques for example a seating plan that locates students in accordance with their behavioural needs.
7. Activities should be timed in accordance with the anticipation that students may go off-task.
8. Whether or not learning has taken place should be assessed at the end of the lesson through adherence to the learning objectives/outcomes.

The above list represents examples drawn from the set of contextual factors that should be in place for successful (happy?) learning to take place. This notion of success is built into the idea that more old-fashioned pedagogies (if they even deserved the name) failed to account for all sorts of factors necessary to successful communication. Indeed, there are good reasons for thinking that adherence to these contextual factors represents progress in the realm of pedagogy. It seems likely that taking account of different abilities, attributes and behavioural characteristics will prevent the kind of confusion, boredom, or chaos that simply ignoring such factors might engender. Equally, there is surely much to recommend the inclusion of different kinds of task, which encourage group or independent learning. What should be noted (and we will return to this) is that most of the things listed above are things we do with words – which is to say things we *do* with words.

This chapter does not aim to debunk the predilections of contemporary pedagogy. However, through adherence to Derrida's reading of Austin, we might see that current approaches to teaching and learning miss something

(Continued)

(Continued)

important about context, and how what is missed out is not wholly dissimilar to what is left out of Austin's philosophy when he talks about the total speech act situation. For both Austin and adherents of the contemporary pedagogical norms, context is thought of solely in terms of factors (that are not thought of as linguistic) that need to be in place for successful communication to take place.[6] So for example, the didacticism attributed to traditional forms of teaching is criticised because it is felt that if teachers simply talk to the class or discuss issues with them, then only a certain kind of student (able, auditory, good at concentrating) will benefit. It appears that what is at issue here, is the teacher's role as a kind of master – the teacher knows what he is talking about and understands the truth of what he professes yet things go wrong (or become unhappy) because simply speaking to the class will not ensure that whatever is in the teacher's head will end up in the student's heads. It should, however, be noted that the contemporary teacher is also expected to be a master, but it is more important that this mastery involves control over contextual factors than knowledge (the teacher's knowledge is taken for granted). Consequently, we might note that constative/truth concerns are not at issue here, it is the successful transmission of the constative that is at stake. The assumption here is in keeping with a view of knowledge that sees it as something that floats above us waiting to be communicated in either a successful or unsuccessful way. It is this view of language that had been undermined by Austin in his discussion of the performative aspects of speech.

We might argue that taking the constative for granted in this way represents a deep suspicion of language. Teachers are often told not to speak too much and when they do speak they should be as clear as possible, otherwise meaning will go awry; their utterances will not be understood. This is surely to acquiesce in securities that are unwarranted. Is there 'always' a danger that students will misunderstand what has been said?

The issue that is at stake here concerns whether when teachers speak (particularly when they, heaven forfend, speak 'for a long time'), they are generally misunderstood. To recognise the iterability of language does not lead to scepticism (which would be based on a false metaphysics of the constative) but openness to the flexibility of language and meaning. To speak of flexibility is to take a positive stance on linguistic complexity. If we are constantly afraid that meaning will 'go awry' we will be bound by the kind of value judgement about failure implicit to Austin's argument. It repeats the suspicion of writing and literariness that runs through the tradition of Western philosophy. Yet, as Derrida shows, the very possibility of communication is dependent on the iterability of language, and this iterability requires a necessary division that means words are not at one with themselves. Consequently, trying to pin words down through excessive adherence to clarity is destined to failure, but this is only 'failure' because communication is thought of here as something that must be full and transparent. I am not suggesting that teachers should give up on clarity, but rather that they should be aware of its limitations. Moreover, clarity as such is not simply a contextual quality that can be brought in from outside, or ticked off on a list, it is a quality that pertains to the utterance itself – a facet of a certain way in which we indulge in language.

Conclusion

In this chapter I have tried to bring critical attention to the ways in which notions of 'success' and 'failure' are applied to teaching and learning in English schools. We have considered Derrida's reading of Austin's theory of the performative utterance. Derrida maintains that, having shown how truth claims are bound up with performative concerns, Austin takes a step backwards by fixating on external contextual factors that must be in place for the performative utterance to be happy. This ignores the iterability of language and the ways in which words are ultimately bound neither by the intentions of the speaker, nor by any other aspect of the environment in which the utterance takes place. The current thinking in regards to successful teaching and learning invites a comparison with Austin's treatment of context – for a lesson to be successful a set of contextual factors must be put in place. In this chapter I have argued that treating teaching and learning in these terms represents an overdetermined understanding of 'success' and 'failure' that sees language as something to be tamed by context.

Notes

1 This extract is taken from: Munday, I. (2011) 'Derrida, Teaching and the Context of Failure', *Oxford Review of Education*, Vol. 37, No. 3, pp. 403–419.
2 This is a literal translation of Derrida's famous formulation '*Il n'y a pas de hors-texte*'. As Attridge notes, 'This phrase does not mean "the things we normally consider to be outside the text do not exist" but "there is nothing that completely escapes the general properties of textuality, différance etc."—that is, as Derrida goes on to explain, no "natural presence"' that can be known "in itself". But it is also true that there is no inside the text, since this would again imply an inside/outside boundary' (Attridge in Derrida, 1992: 102). The more famous (though less exact) translation is 'there is nothing beyond the text'.
3 In his essay 'Truth', Austin writes: 'in philosophy the foot of the letter is the foot of the ladder' (Austin, 1964: 19). Here there is a clear affinity between Austin and Derrida.
4 Polysemy comes into play when a word that has two or more similar meanings. Consider the phrases 'the house stood at the foot of the hill' and 'he liked to stand on one foot'.

(Continued)

(Continued)

5 It should be noted that the 'happiness' referred to here relates to 'effectiveness' and is not meant to allude to positive psychology's treatment of the former.

6 It is important to recognise that several things distinguish Austin from the pedagogues. To begin with, the latter take the constative for granted whereas Austin does not. Also, the 'extra-linguistic' factors that Austin refers to are somewhat different to those that are a feature of modern pedagogy. As mentioned earlier, people do get married. When they fail to do so, this is due to a fairly exceptional set of circumstances. Moreover, the contextual factors Austin alludes to are not annexed to utterances in a forced manner. The manipulation of context that characterises fashionable teaching methods is of a rather different order to the treatment of context in Austin's work. We do not wilfully construct authenticity. That said, Austin's philosophy still presents an overly simplistic and overdetermined treatment of context.

References

Austin, J.L. (1964) 'Truth', in G. Pitcher (Ed.), *Truth*, London: Prentice-Hall, pp. 18–31.

Austin, J.L. (1976) *How to Do Things With Words*, Oxford: Oxford University Press.

Cavell, S. (2005) *Philosophy the Day After Tomorrow*, Cambridge, MA: Harvard University Press.

Derrida, J. (1988) *Limited Inc.*, Evanston: Northwestern University Press.

Derrida, J. (1992) *Acts of Literature*, New York: Routledge.

Educational philosophy: reading and writing practices in this extract

As I mentioned in the introduction, the chapter came about as a consequence of particular anxieties I had (and still have) about the language of schooling. I found a voice that addressed these anxieties in Derrida's paper 'Signature, Event, Context' (1988). Much of this chapter and the article on which it is based are concerned with a close reading of Derrida's paper, which is itself an original reading of sections from J. L. Austin's *How to Do Things With Words* (1976). I find it impossible to distinguish reading from writing when approaching the work of philosophers as difficult as Derrida. To get any purchase on what is going on I have to find my own ways of wording Derrida's argument and this 'writing' becomes a more fruitful form of reading. I believe much secondary poststructuralist literature (in philosophy of education and elsewhere) presents the work of Derrida, and others, in a rather undigested fashion that attempts (and usually fails) to emulate its sources as regards 'style'. I do not feel as though I have any grip, however loose, on Derrida's writing unless I can rephrase it, or perhaps, 'translate' and then be 'translated' by it. This is necessarily a slow and immersive process. I find that examples, drawn from educational situations, help in this regard. However, it is important, in my view, that the examples are not instruments for serving the philosophy. Rather, the philosophy and examples live through (or give life to) one another. Ultimately, the 'educational' significance of the argument is the primary concern. When I write, I have a dim, perhaps vain, sense that I would like teachers to engage with what is being said. The notion of audience is a much more significant and complex issue for educational philosophers than it is for 'straight' philosophers.

Though I hope the chapter is relatively accessible, the reader may feel that there is a certain dissonance between the various registers that are handled; the language of complex philosophy, the language of schooling with its strange mixture of technical terminology, and finally 'ordinary' language. This leads to a jarring of discursive registers that will probably seem strange and perhaps 'inappropriate'. I want, for the sake of scholarly seriousness, to thematise this 'inappropriateness' and see it as a critical dimension of the chapter – critical, that is, as critique. The dissonance in question points to the ways in which language can open up, house, or foreclose different ways of seeing the world. The philosophy introduced here is home to ways of seeing that educational discourse is necessarily blind to (I make this point despite the fact that terms like 'deconstruction' and 'performativity' are regularly employed and hollowed out in schools and education departments). This is not to say that the philosophy introduced here is meant simply to negate educational discourse or show up its narrow mechanistic character. Rather, I want dissonance to be 'affirmative'. Indeed, the kind of philosophy presented above is not (or at least not wholly) adversarial. Rather, it is affirmative and productive. Derrida's philosophy embraces the messiness of language and the hurly-burly of the form of life. Much educational discourse flourishes on cleaning up the mess, and enquiries are raised to the circuits of a frictionless medium of thought. To challenge that narrowness and shallowness, we should perhaps resort to messing up the clean at least, to making it better earthed.

References

Austin, J.L. (1976) *How to Do Things With Words*, London: Oxford University Press.
Derrida, J. (1988) *Limited, Inc.*, Evanston, IL: Northwest University Press.

12

ON PROVOCATION, FASCINATION, AND WRITING IN PHILOSOPHY OF EDUCATION

Morwenna Griffiths

Introduction to the extract

The article from which my extract is drawn explores a way of re-reading Jean-Jacques Rousseau and Mary Wollstonecraft's influential eighteenth-century books on education, with the aim of re-thinking how social justice is relevant in educational practices. It compares and contrasts how concepts of nature and of education are brought together in the work of these two writers. It then shows how their different conceptions have some implications for how teachers should relate to their students and to the curriculum, in ways that enhance the possibilities of social justice in the classroom and, ultimately, in the world. Thus the extract also contributes to the increasing body of work in educational philosophy that examines educational relationships.

The argument expressed in the article is the result of bringing together a number of ideas that had provoked and fascinated me. This process lasted three years or more, taking sometimes unexpected directions, depending on what I was reading and teaching, and in which conversations I took part. Most of these provocations/fascinations arose during teaching. A doctoral student of mine was focused on philosophy and outdoor education. Both he and the co-supervisor introduced me to a body of scholarship and educational practice around ecology, place, the outdoors, and so on, that both interested and challenged me. Other doctoral level teaching brought me into contact with some explicitly posthumanist theories. I also taught a Master's course centred on philosophical writing that has been influential on educational theory and practice – and how it might relate to the students' current practices. The course included Rousseau's *Émile* (1762/1979) and Wollstonecraft's response to it in her *A Vindication of the Rights of Women* (1792/1994). I had always been irritated by *Émile*, ever since

I first encountered it, but it was hard to avoid it because it is by a very famous philosopher, and it is a book that has had a lasting influence on educational thinking right up to the present time.

Rousseau and Wollstonecraft both lived in the eighteenth century. Rousseau was a central contributor to the revolutionary changes in the thinking and the imagination of the time, with his books on equality, the social contract, and, not least, education. He put forward the ideas that nature is good, society is corrupt, and that a boy taught in accordance with nature, and in close contact with it, would turn into an ideal man and thus be a perfect citizen for an ideal society. The education of girls was very different. Sophie is the female equivalent of Émile. She is to stay at home, learning to be docile. The adult Émile has the virtues of a man: an autonomous, rational citizen in control of his emotions. The adult Sophie has the virtues of a woman: a dependent, obedient, loving partner. Wollstonecraft, who was about 30 years younger than Rousseau, was herself very influenced by his work. However, as an early advocate of equal rights for women, she was appalled by his views on the education of girls. She had already written *A Vindication of the Rights of Men* and she followed it up with another, more famous book on the rights of women. She argues against Rousseau's educational proposals. She advocates equal education for both boys and girls, to the benefit, she argues, of both sexes. She was an early advocate of equality for men and women in schools and in workplaces, a position that was shocking to many people at the time. (Horace Walpole, a well-known Member of Parliament at the time, called her 'a hyena in petticoats'.)

Teaching *Émile*, especially in conjunction with the polemic of the *Vindication*, inspired me to reflect on why one infuriated, and the other delighted, me. In my article I focused on their different approaches to concepts of nature, something central to Rousseau and to his continuing influence on how we think and imagine our place in the world. At the time I was thinking about all this, I came across the essayist Kathleen Jamie. I read her simply for enjoyment at first, but while I was writing, I found that what she was expressing in her essays was relevant to my reflections on terms such as 'nature' and 'wilderness'.

EXTRACT: EDUCATIONAL RELATIONSHIPS: ROUSSEAU, WOLLSTONECRAFT AND SOCIAL JUSTICE[1]

I consider educational relationships as found in Rousseau's *Émile*, and the critique of his views in Wollstonecraft's *A Vindication of the Rights of Women*. I argue that we can benefit not only from her critique of Rousseau but also from her alternative approach. I argue that their educational approaches point to a significant difference in their understanding of social justice. I begin by placing

(Continued)

(Continued)

the two authors in their historical contexts and then go on to outline how their views of educational relationships differ. Finally, I consider relationships between human beings and the more-than-human. These relationships are seldom recognised as contributing to a more socially just education so I consider them at a little more length, drawing from observations by Kathleen Jamie and using an example from outdoor education to suggest possible implications for educational practices.

Between human beings and the more-than-human

Rousseau uses 'nature' or 'natural' in more than one way, for instance describing the more-than-human world, the physical and psychological development of human beings and in distinguishing artifice from what is authentic. However, as Wain points out:

> These are not, however, contradictory or inconsistent uses but complex ways of using the same term in different contexts of meaning. It is neither necessary nor usual for a word to carry one constant meaning whenever it is used, provided that the different uses are clearly signalled by the context.
>
> *(2011: 47)*

In short, Rousseau's view of nature is Romantic. He re-theorises nature as good, against views of his time that the rationality or spirituality of human beings is manifested in a transcendence of nature. Rousseau's view, radical at the time, was significant because, if nature is the source of our goodness, then a natural man can trust his conscience which will not have been corrupted by society. Nature has a double use. It is needed to allow a boy to develop into a man. Then, as a man, he can return to Nature as a source of sublime feelings and restoration. Taylor describes Rousseau's approach:

> We return to nature because it brings out strong and noble feelings in us...Nature is like a great keyboard on which our highest sentiments are played out. We turn to it, as we might turn to music, to evoke and strengthen the best in us.
>
> *(1989: 297)*

Rousseau sees nature as something that draws a response from the solitary individual of sublime appreciation. Nature requires him to be able to deal with its challenges with rugged strength, endurance and courage. All of this is evidently a nature that is always, and necessarily, other than human except for the natural boy or man who experiences it. This nature, at least as found in man, is perfected by civilization (as is made clear both in *Émile* and in the *Discourse on Inequality*, 1755/1983). Ironically, this understanding is reminiscent of a rational, scientific Enlightenment that Rousseau rejects. It could be argued that he advocates using nature, just as a rationalist like Bacon wanted to use it, for the benefit of men. In both cases the preservation of nature can be understood as enlightened self-interest. For followers of Rousseau this means advocating outdoor education in order to experience a response to nature (Jickling, 2009; Bonnett, 2007); for followers of Bacon it means advocating Sustainable Development because the ecosystem needs to be preserved if human beings are to survive at all (Kopnina, 2013).

Wollstonecraft offers a different approach from either of these. For her, nature nourishes the spirit in several ways, all of which are to be found through a proper education. In her pedagogical proposals she does not impose a sharp demarcation between what is inside walls and what is outside them, neither does she distinguish a wild nature from one influenced by human beings. The sublime is significant, as is also clear throughout her *Letters Written in Sweden, Norway and Denmark* (1796/2009) where she describes the Scandinavian landscape. However, she is also attentive to the (more social) pastoral landscape as well as the (non-human) sublime. For Wollstonecraft, nature is both good and bad, restorative and dulling. The outdoors provides the pleasures of being in shady lanes or sitting on stiles, and the nuisance of muddy lanes and wet weather – and the pleasure of returning home, out of it. She writes of her spirits being restored by lakes, fir groves and rocks, but she also writes of being 'bastilled by nature' (1796/2009: 69) in a place where rocks and sea shut people out from finer sentiments.

Sublime nature can be enhanced by human additions. She mentions with approval a carefully placed stone seat (1796/2009: 21). She remarks how the place 'bastilled by nature' becomes 'extremely fine' when viewed from the sea: 'In a recess of the rocks was a clump of pines, amongst which a steeple rose picturesquely beautiful' (1796/2009: 70). But the non-human is not there simply for our exploitation. Kindness to animals is a significant virtue for her, partly, though only partly, because it connects with the treatment of one human being by another:

> Humanity to animals should be particularly inculcated as a part of national education, for it is not at present one of our national virtues. Tenderness for their humble dumb domestics, amongst the lower class, is oftener to be found in a savage than a civilized state...where they are.
>
> *(1792/1994: 258)*

(Continued)

(Continued)

She wants book learning and the real things to be integrated with play in the outdoors, valued not only for itself, but also because:

> These relaxations might all be rendered part of elementary education, for many things improve and amuse the senses...to the principles of which, dryly laid down, children would turn a deaf ear.
>
> *(1792/1994: 253)*

These relaxations also allow natural animal spirits to improve body and mind:

> With what disgust have I heard sensible women, for girls are more restrained and cowed than boys, speak of the wearisome confinement, which they endured at school. The animal spirits, which make both mind and body shoot out, and unfold the tender blossoms of hope, are turned sour and vented in vain wishes or pert repinings, that contract the faculties and spoil the temper.
>
> *(1792/1994: 248–9)*

Wollstonecraft's educational proposals suggest the relevance of the more-than-human in the education of children in ways that are neither in the long shadow of Rousseau's Romantic conception, nor in its converse of rationalist instrumentalism.

Wilderness and the outdoors: Human beings in relationship with the more-than-human

In this section I draw attention to how the world can be described using the terms which do not fall easily on one side or another of Rousseau's dualist distinctions between Nature and what is natural, on the one hand, and what is social and civilised, on the other hand. There is an alternative to seeing ourselves as distinct from an innocent, good, wild, non-human nature; instead, like Wollstonecraft, we need to employ no sharp demarcations between what is indoors and outdoors, what is wild from what is social. Kathleen Jamie's two recent books of essays (2005; 2012) demonstrate a way of understanding our natural selves that is much closer to Wollstonecraft's perceptions than to Rousseau's. As Jamie puts it in her trenchant critique of Macfarlane's *The Wild Places* (2008), the dominant imaginary in the Romantic tradition of nature writing is, following Rousseau, a 'lone enraptured male' in search of the spiritual resources of remote places seen as 'wild' (Jamie, 2008). Her work asks us to notice that nature is more complex. It is all of: organic, inorganic, indoors, outdoors, and both; of our bodies, in our bodies and beyond them; made/

created/formed by people; growing, inanimate; beautiful, grim; huge, minute, and all sizes between; mysterious, wild, ordinary, unspoilt, worked over, innocent, and a force to be struggled with. Like Wollstonecraft, she thinks that what we term 'nature' is not there to be exploited, though it is to be engaged with; that it can seem benign or malign; and that it demands an ethical response from us.

Jamie's essays may seem to be just simple, careful, attentive descriptions of her observations. But each of them is an implicit criticism of the dominant Romantic approach to descriptions of nature. She challenges the usual distinctions made between indoors and outdoors; the wild and the common place; the wild and the domestic; attention to what is non-human and attention to human beings. For instance, in her essay, 'Peregrines, Ospreys, Cranes' she does all of this. She begins by noting the call of a peregrine both outside and inside the house: 'The sound enters my attic room through its window, and if I turn from my desk to glance out of that window I see the hill' (2005: 29). She writes: 'Between the laundry and the fetching kids from school, that's how birds enter my life. I listen' (2005: 39).

In 'Skylines', she demonstrates the artificiality of Rousseau's dualism. The outdoors is linked to buildings, people, passers-by, her own everyday working life, the weather, geology, history and, most of all, to looking with attention. She starts an article about looking at Edinburgh skylines through a telescope on Calton Hill, by saying: 'One afternoon last November I was crossing Charlotte Square and, happening to glance up, saw a comet...this beautiful brass comet, a shining ball towing a deeply forked tail' (2005: 147).

In her essay, 'Pathologies', Jamie blurs another set of distinctions; the wild and the outdoors, the wild and ourselves. When her mother dies, somebody uses a phrase about nature taking its course. Shortly after, she attends a conference where people are pontificating about humanity's relationship with other species, and how we have to 'reconnect with nature', as if, she notes, we are not bodily, mortal beings, using vaccinations and eating meat. She thinks more about this issue, and gets permission to attend some biopsies. She looks at bacteria grazing on a stomach lining: 'It was an image you might find in a Sunday-night wildlife documentary. Pastoral but wild, too...in the wilderness of our stomachs' (2012: 35).

The outdoors in educational practice

The influence of Rousseau on education in the outdoors is clear. Orthodox educational approaches see the outdoors as providing real experiences in order to meet the pre-defined objectives of the science, geography or history curriculum. Alternatively, it provides adventure and a chance to develop physical skills in

(Continued)

(Continued)

response to risk. Or it allows children to find the spiritual resources missing when they are suffering from 'nature deficit disorder' (Louv, 2008; Moss, 2012).

The critique presented by Wollstonecraft and Jamie suggests that a better approach would be to acknowledge the rich complexity of human life in and of the world. It would be to acknowledge that nature is not only 'out there' but also 'in here' and 'around here'. Within education an approach like this would mean asking students to pay attention and then reflect using various forms of symbolisation and expression. However, as Randolph Haluza-Delay (2001) argues, this needs to be done in familiar places and in the midst of ordinary social events, acknowledging them, not bracketing them. Attention and reflection can be done alone or in a group, but in either case it thrives on conversations whether in the moment or remembered, and then on collaborative reflections, learning with peers as well as with tutors, in order to come to independent, unforced ways of understanding ourselves, in and of the world.

Note

1 This extract is taken from a longer article, published as: Griffiths, M. (2014) 'Educational Relationships: Rousseau, Wollstonecraft and Social Justice', in *Re-imagining Relationships: Ethics, Politics, and Practices*, Special Issue of *Journal of Philosophy of Education*, Vol. 48, No. 2, pp. 339–354.

References

Bonnett, M. (2007) 'Environmental Education and the Issue of Nature', *Journal of Curriculum Studies,* Vol. 39, No. 6, pp. 707–721.

Griffiths, M. (2014) 'Educational Relationships: Rousseau, Wollstonecraft and Social Justice', in *Re-imagining Relationships: Ethics, Politics, and Practices,* Special Issue of *Journal of Philosophy of Education,* Vol. 48, No. 2, pp. 339–354.

Haluza-Delay, R. (2001) 'Nothing Here to Care About: Participant Constructions of Nature Following a 12-day Wilderness Program', *The Journal of Environmental Education,* Vol. 32, No. 44, pp. 43–48.

Jamie, K. (2005) *Findings,* London: Sort Of Books.

Jamie, K. (2012) *Sightlines,* London: Sort Of Books.

Jickling, B. (2009) 'Sitting on an Old Grey Stone: Meditations on Emotional Understanding', in M. McKenzie, H. Bai, P. Hart, and B. Jickling (Eds), *Fields of Green: Restorying Culture, Environment, and Education,* Cresskill, NJ: Hampton Press, pp. 163–173.

Kopnina, H. (2013) 'Forsaking Nature? Contesting "Biodiversity" Through Competing Discourses of Sustainability', *Journal of Education for Sustainable Development,* Vol. 7, No. 1, pp. 47–59.

Louv, R. (2008) *Last Child in the Woods: Saving Our Children from Nature-Deficit Disorder,* Chapel Hill, NC: Algonquin Books.

Macfarlane, R. (2008) *The Wild Places*, London: Granta.

Moss, S. (2012) *Natural Childhood*, Corsham, Wiltshire: National Trust.

Rousseau, J.-J. (1755/1983) *A Discourse on Inequality* (Ed., Trans., and Notes Maurice Cranston), Harmondsworth: Penguin Books.

Rousseau, J.-J. (1762/1979) *Émile or On Education* (Ed., Trans., and Intro. Allan Bloom), New York: Basic Books.

Taylor, C. (1989) *Sources of the Self*, Cambridge: Cambridge University Press.

Wain, K. (2011) *On Rousseau: An Introduction to His Radical Thinking on Education and Politics*, Rotterdam: Sense Publishers.

Wollstonecraft, M. (1792/1994) *A Vindication of the Rights of Woman* and *A Vindication of the Rights of Men* (Ed., and Intro. Janet Todd), Oxford: Oxford World Classics.

Wollstonecraft, M. (1796/2009) *Letters Written in Sweden, Norway, and Denmark* (Ed., Intro., and Notes Topne Brekke and Jon Mee), Oxford: Oxford University Press.

Educational philosophy: reading and writing practices in this extract

Reading and writing practices in educational philosophy are associated with particular approaches to philosophy. However, the extract above does not draw on any single philosophical tradition. Rather it works at the edges of several different ones, by assembling them and then teasing out the connections between them. It draws on my own trajectory through different traditions of educational philosophy: analytic, phenomenological, feminist, post-modern, and post-human. As I explain elsewhere (Griffiths, 2014), this trajectory has taken me very far from my initial starting point during my doctorate, in which I took a broadly Anglo-Saxon, analytic approach, though with some phenomenological elements. Since then I have worked within feminist and postmodernist philosophy, and now in this article, with posthumanist approaches. The trajectory is more of an orbit than a straight line. The influence of all of these traditions affected how I wrote the article.

At the start of the article I explained the argument in outline before I presented it in detail, using the words 'I consider', 'I argue', 'I begin by', 'and then go on to outline how', 'Finally, I consider', and 'so I consider'. I set out the stages of my argument and the connections between each stage. This outline was written again and again as I worked out my ideas. It was a way of checking that what I was writing made an argument and came to a conclusion. Each paragraph is also carefully structured. I try to include a 'topic sentence', which is usually the first sentence. It summarises what the paragraph is about, before making a more detailed explanation. I hope that a reader can successfully skim the article by reading just the first one or two sentences of a paragraph. In this extract I have nearly achieved this, but not quite!

The beginning of the argument is very standard. I set up the two different views I wanted to discuss: first, the one I will disagree with, and then the one I will prefer. I was careful to demonstrate the accuracy of my views. I did this by summarising my understanding of what they had said. For Rousseau, I also quoted commentaries by respected writers, largely because I was aware that he is still influential and my criticisms of him might upset my readers. For Wollstonecraft, I needed to use many quotations, partly because she is less well-known, but also because her educational ideas are scattered through the book as well as being found in her chapter on education. Towards the end of the extract I again needed to use a lot of quotations in order to demonstrate how I understood what Jamie was expressing. And then I ended with a conclusion about the relevance of these abstract ideas to educational practice.

The literature I use is not confined to philosophy, or even to educational philosophy. I am committed to the view that philosophers of education need to engage with other educational theorists and with particular issues of practice as well as to philosophy more generally. Indeed, I read widely and make connections across disciplinary boundaries. This for me is one of the pleasures of working within education. Education, practically and theoretically, is so complex that it necessarily engages with a range of other disciplines in the humanities and social sciences. What I write, and, I hope, what I do professionally, are also influenced by the importance I attach to issues of social justice within education.

The article shows the influence of my reading within philosophy, and beyond it, about feminism, social justice, and outdoor education, as well as reading simply for enjoyment. The references in the article show this range of influence. I have been strongly influenced by feminism. It is no accident that I am writing about Mary Wollstonecraft, an early advocate of women's rights. My references here include philosophers not concerned with education, such as Charles Taylor (1989), and philosophers of education, such as Kenneth Wain (2011). There are also a number of philosophical and non-philosophical writers on nature or the environment, including Michael Bonnett (2007) and Helen Kopnina (2013).

The writing is influenced by my approach to educational philosophy. Something I love about this field is the way it can bring abstract theory and specific practices and contexts into dialogue with each other. Each can be interrogated and informed by the other in a continuing iteration. Value is attached to personal descriptions of specific contexts as well as to grand theory. (For instance, see Griffiths, 2003.) The extract uses extensive quotations and specific examples from the two main protagonists and elsewhere, as in the Jamie quotations, as a deliberate strategy to include the specificity of perspectives and place them in the context of abstract theory about justice and nature.

References

Bonnett, M. (2007) 'Environmental Education and the Issue of Nature', *Journal of Curriculum Studies*, Vol. 39, No. 6, pp. 707–721.

Griffiths, M. (2014) 'My Life as a Vixen', in L. Waks (Ed.), *Leaders in Philosophy of Education*, Vol. 2, Rotterdam: Sense Publishers, pp. 85–98.

Kopnina, H. (2013) 'Forsaking Nature? Contesting "Biodiversity" Through Competing Discourses of Sustainability', *Journal of Education for Sustainable Development*, Vol. 7, No. 1, pp. 47–59.

Rousseau, J.-J. (1762/1979) *Émile or On Education* (Ed., Trans., and Intro. Allan Bloom), New York: Basic Books.

Taylor, C. (1989) *Sources of the Self*, Cambridge: Cambridge University Press.

Wain, K. (2011) *On Rousseau: An Introduction to His Radical Thinking on Education and Politics*, Rotterdam: Sense Publishers.

Wollstonecraft, M. (1792/1994) *A Vindication of the Rights of Woman* and *A Vindication of the Rights of Men* (Ed., and Intro. J. Todd), Oxford: Oxford World Classics.

13

IMAGINING IMAGINATION AND *BILDUNG* IN THE AGE OF THE DIGITIZED WORLD PICTURE

Anna Kouppanou

Introduction to the extract

With my PhD thesis I attempted to give a critical account of human existence as conditioned by digital technologies. The connection between human existence and technology was foregrounded by the twentieth-century German philosopher Martin Heidegger, whose seminal work *Being and Time* (1927/2008) addressed human existence as an ever-changing situatedness conditioned by the world, language, and technology. Indeed, with this work, Heidegger laid the foundation of thinking about technology in terms of mentality instead of instrumentality. For Heidegger, technology – modern technology especially – is above all a way of perceiving the world. My research attempted to respond to Heidegger's abstract assertions about the essence of technology, and also to look at the specificities of this critique. A closer reading of the philosopher's earlier thought allowed the refocusing of my research on image, which happens to be one of the most prevalent features of current digital technologies. Delving deeper into the literature allowed me to detect several etymological and theoretical connections having to do with image (*Bild*), imagination (*Einbildung*), and education (*Bildung*). This, in turn, helped me discuss the potential contribution of Heidegger's thought to several educational issues.

Indeed, for Heidegger, there are two notions of image that relate to truth in specific ways. The first notion refers to technologically re-produced images that represent the world in terms of correspondence and correctness. In other words, these images reproduce the world according to predetermined notions. The other notion of image is poetic and transformative. It does not represent the world, but rather opens up possibilities of relating to the world in new ways. This type of image derives its force from the realisation that death is inescapable. In turn, this realisation can lead us into a state of awareness concerning our freedom to live our lives authentically and not according to predetermined notions of what our lives should be. This second type of image relates to truth understood as *alētheia*, that is, the Greek word for unconcealed-ness that denotes the possibility of revealing things in their real dimensions. For Heidegger, education (*Bildung*) should aspire to the latter type of truth, that is, technologically unmediated connectedness to the world that allows for authentic living. In this particular piece of research I challenge the correctness/*alētheia*, technological representation/immediate presence, and authenticity/inauthenticity dichotomies through a critical discussion of Heidegger's thought in connection to other more recent theories. In the extract that follows I shed light on technology's tendency to condition our world, and also begin to discuss the possibility to be educated transformatively in a world dominated by digital technologies.

EXTRACT: IMAGINATION AND *BILDUNG* IN THE AGE OF THE WORLD PICTURE[1]

Introduction

In 1938 Martin Heidegger (1977a) described his time as *The Age of the World Picture*. This succinct description meant not only that the world was obsessed with pictures, but also that the world itself was 'conceived as picture'. In other words, the world had become a *Weltbild* (world picture) (p. 129). For Heidegger, conceiving the world as picture meant that the western philosophical tradition, and especially Plato's legacy that sustained a technological understanding of all beings, had marginalized any other possibility for understanding the world. This metaphysical frame, Heidegger (1977b) argued later, gave rise to modern technology's essence as Enframing, that is, the way of thinking that reveals the world as mere representation and object. This kind of relatedness to the world appears to bring it near but things still remain out of reach. We thus watch the world instead of inhabiting it. And as we watch the world, we are also watching ourselves watching it. We, like the world, become picture. Heidegger (1977a) toys with the expression '[t]o get into the picture' which is suggestive of the structure of which we gradually become a part (p. 129). We are becoming enframed by technology. In reality, 'to get the picture' is to get into the picture; to be real is to be picture. However, what is the structure we are referring to? Where is this thought taking us? What does it mean to get the picture, especially in today's world, which is saturated with images?

Even if we are not quite sure what the phrase means, we intuitively feel that we are part of the picture. Let us consider an example: a teenager, let us call him Dave, watches his favorite artist performing on stage while recording the performance on his mobile phone. His perceptual frame is now the lens of the phone camera. Its perceptual limits are his limits; its affordances are his way of seeing. At first glance, as it were, this does not seem so different from

(Continued)

(Continued)

previous forms of recording. Dave is recording the curiosities of this world, just as previous generations of spectators and explorers have done. As soon as a satisfactory piece of recording is collected and perhaps modified through the phone's applications, Dave decides to post it online on his homepage on a social network. It becomes a status update, Dave describes it, comments upon it, likes it, and pins himself on a specific location so that whoever wants to 'connect' with him either online or offline is aware of his presence in a particular time and place. If Dave does not provide constant news feed, he will lose much of his presence and much of his connectedness. In other words, Dave does what he does so that others will get the picture about him immediately and unequivocally, so that he and others will ultimately get into the same picture or the same network. It seems that the immediacy of new digital technologies offers a new form of potentiality for the self to move from image to image, from representation to representation. This movement, it can be argued, enables a concealment of the self or at least the 'true' self. However, it is also possible that it is in fact all these iterations that constitute the becoming of a self.

The discussion concerning the possibility of a true self can of course be sustained by an analysis of the existential type, or can even be challenged by a more deconstructive approach. In this chapter, I aim to work through the first but I will also be looking at the same time towards the second. Martin Heidegger's thought, which was the starting point of this discussion, can allow for multiple readings with regards to technology, the possibility of authentic time, self and thinking. This is a discussion that needs to address the role of the image (*Bild*) for the formation of thought. Image, or the process of getting the picture refers to a process of formation or education (*Bildung*). This is mediated by technology and eventually limits that which should be limitless, namely, imagination (*Einbildung*). The fact that all three words (*Bild, Bildung, Einbildung*) come into the picture is not a mere word play. Their etymological relationship suggests the need for a dialogue concerning the possibility of education in the age of the world picture, the possibility of thinking in the age of image-formation and the connection between imaging and imagining.

Bildung and technology

As Paul Standish (2002) points out, the German term *Bildung* can be rendered as 'liberal education', but 'such a translation would...lose connotations that are important to the idea – for example, the origins of the term in medieval mysticism (*Bild* as the image of God) and its transformation through the Enlightenment into a neo-humanism' (p. iii). By maintaining the original German term we become sensitive to the different connotations that the term's etymology and history bring about. Standish goes on to detect one such connotation, which has to do with the need for alienation in order to grow and gain autonomy. *Bildung* requires a certain feeling of 'alienation' in order to come into sight. Quoting Hans-Georg Gadamer, Standish says that *Bildung* demands '[t]o seek one's home in the alien, to become at home in it' (*ibid.*). Just as the term commands a degree of alienation, so can its constituent parts provide the means through which education can rethink itself. It refers to what education could be if it were transformed.

Let us then take advantage of the alienating factor of the term and return to one of its literal renderings. *Bildung* 'contains the word *Bild* (image) in the sense of "sign" and of "reproduction". As a process, *Bildung* refers to the 'reproduction of a pre-given form (*Gestalt*), externally as well as inwardly' (Schwenk, 1989, p. 209, cited in Bauer, 2003, p. 133). For this reason, it is commonly translated as formation. Formation, though, of what and how? According to Katherine Hayles (2007), modern technologies that offer the possibility of constant change of attention have produced a cognitive mode she calls 'hyper attention' that entails 'switching focus rapidly among different tasks, preferring multiple information streams, seeking a high level of stimulation, and having a low tolerance for boredom' (p. 187). On the other end, there is the more traditional cognitive mode, that is, 'deep attention' which is 'traditionally associated with the humanities' and 'is characterized by concentrating on a single object for long periods (say, a novel by Dickens), ignoring outside stimuli while so engaged, preferring a single information stream, and having a high tolerance for long focus times' (*ibid.*).

Hayles (2007) sees ADHD (Attention Deficit Hyperactivity Disorder) as the extreme, but now common, manifestation of hyper-attention. Drawing on research from brain imaging studies she also infers that the use of different media causes synaptogenesis to progress in different ways. To put this in other terms, different technologies – the book, the video game – wire the brain differently (p. 192). Taking this into the context of our discussion, it seems that technology is literally formation; it is the formation of our minds and ways of thinking. To quote Nietzsche: 'Our writing tools are also working on our thoughts' (cited in Kittler, 1999, p. 200).[2] But it is not merely writing tools that have this effect. Tools work with different affordances that extract different types of embodied reactions, rhythms of thinking and ultimately modes of perception that define the limits of that which can be anticipated and imagined. The philosopher Bernard Stiegler (1998) argues that perception always relies on accumulated secondary memories in order to form anticipation, which ultimately defines what is to be perceived. In the case of digital technologies, however, what counts is not simply the content of the chosen memories that underlines the specificity of a certain set of criteria, but also the modes of attention and thinking they allow to emerge. In this light, thinking is a response to the tools we use and at the same time the very factor that

(Continued)

(Continued)

conditions and constructs our site of existence or our being there. This account takes us, however, back to Heidegger's existential analysis in *Being and Time*.

In his magnum opus Heidegger (1927/2008) names the human being *Dasein*, that is, being-there or being the *there*. What *Dasein* constructs and is constructed by is its relation to the world. *Dasein's* 'there' is both *Dasein's* unique site as a self and one site among the many sites of the world that inter-connect and communicate. *Dasein* becomes its own there through a process of individuation that allows it to be part of the community and repeat creatively its past. *Dasein* inherits its past, is thrown in an 'already-there'[3] which according to Stiegler (1998) was not created by *Dasein* but inherited by it. This 'there' contains memories on which *Dasein* relies in order to form decisions. However, what kind of decisions can *Dasein* make if its own 'there' is programmed to be identical to the others' 'there'? What if *Dasein's* site is the site of public opinion, and its words the words emitted by the media? *Dasein* needs to experience anxiety, have an uncanny impression that the world is not there, and that it itself is not at-home in order to seek for itself. Heideggerian thought, and much of the literature on *Bildung*, underline that the feeling of alienation is necessary for transformation, but inhibited by technology. Technology causes numbness as it distracts *Dasein* from grasping the possibilities of time. Time for *Dasein* is a process towards death, that demands careful consideration and questioning. Death is the undetermined we aspire to forget (Stiegler, 1998). But thinking through death is what brings about authentic time or *alētheia* as that form of truth that uncovers what is forgotten. On the other hand, time lived as concern towards the completion of projects, that is, towards an artificial and provisional end, is time measured by the clock, recorded by writing and calculated by technologies; it is the inauthentic time of truth as correctness.

Just as Heidegger distinguishes between authentic time as *alētheia* and inauthentic time as time mediated by technology, discussions about *Bildung* make a distinction between authentic education and a kind of inauthentic technologically-mediated learning that has already formed the mind and its ways of knowing the world. René Arcilla (2002) for example relies on this distinction pointing to the fact that 'what stimulates such learning (*Bildung* as liberal learning) is radical questioning of our deepest assumptions, and such questioning is apt to be obstructed by the very technology of the mass media, including the World Wide Web' (p. 457). When these distinctions are not taken into consideration, and misleading understandings of technology supporting its neutral instrumental nature are taken for granted, *Bildung* can be veiled and not even perceived as possibility.

When technology is understood as an external supplement that aids formation after the central images-aims of *Bildung* have been sketched, then technology claims its definite role as the one that does the forming. This takes us back to the etymology once more. *Bildung* describes a kind of education or individuation that is guided by *Bild* (a vision, a paradigm, an image). Sven Erik Nordenbo (2002) for example explains that the term *Bildung* refers to 'an image – a model – of which somebody or something is to become an image or model' (p. 341). He nevertheless points out that:

> In the educational context...it is not clear whether the person possessing *Bildung* has generated this himself or herself, or whether it is a consequence of somebody or something else. However, according to the standard German understanding of the concept as an educational idea, a person has acquired *Bildung* only if he or she has assisted actively in its formation or development. In other words, in the educational context, the concept of *Bildung* contains a reference to an active core in the person who is *gebildet* (educated, cultured).
>
> *(p. 341) (parenthesis added)*

So in this respect, technology can be the cause of formation but if the individual has not contributed to this formation, then this process is not *Bildung*. The individual needs to be allowed to individuate themselves, and this means that they need to have a considerable knowledge of what is causing them to be formed in a certain way. In our current context, this makes a demand for technology and media literacy that goes beyond superficial understandings of media representations. It is a demand for the understanding of the technological *Bild* (image) that causes formation and probably obstructs *Bildung*.

Notes

1 This extract is taken from: Kouppanou, A. (2014) 'Imagining Imagination and *Bildung* in the Age of the Digitized World Picture', in M. Papastephanou, T. Strand, and A. Pirrie (Eds), *Philosophy as a Lived Experience: Navigating Through Dichotomies of Thought and Action*, Berlin: LIT Verlag, pp. 78–89.
2 For the original reference, see Colli and Montinari (1978).
3 The term belongs to Stiegler.

References

Arcilla, R.V. (2002) 'Modernising Media or Modernist Medium? The Struggle for Liberal Learning in Our Information Age', *Journal of Philosophy of Education*, Vol. 36, No. 3, pp. 457–465.
Bauer, W. (2003) 'Introduction', *Educational Philosophy and Theory*, Vol. 35, No. 2, pp. 133–137.

(Continued)

(Continued)

Colli, G. and Montinari, M. (1978) *Nietzsche Briefwechsel: Kritische Gesamtausgabe*, Berlin and New York: Walter de Gruyter.

Hayles, K. (2007) 'Hyper and Deep Attention: The Generational Divide in Cognitive Modes', *Profession*, Vol. 1, pp. 187–199.

Heidegger, M. (1977a) 'The Age of the World Picture', in *The Question Concerning Technology, and Other Essays*, Trans. W. Lovitt, New York: Harper and Row, pp. 115–154.

Heidegger, M. (1977b) *The Question Concerning Technology and Other Essays*, New York: Harper and Row.

Heidegger, M. (1927/2008) *Being and Time*, Trans. J. Macquarrie and E. Robinson, Oxford: Blackwell.

Kittler, A. F. (1999) *Gramophone, Film, Typewriter*, Trans. G. Winthrop-Young and M. Wutz, Stanford, CA: Stanford University Press.

Kouppanou, A. (2014) 'Imagining Imagination and *Bildung* in the Age of the Digitized World Picture', in M. Papastephanou, T. Strand, and A. Pirrie (Eds), *Philosophy as a Lived Experience: Navigating Through Dichotomies of Thought and Action*, Berlin: LIT Verlag, pp. 78–89.

Nordenbo, S.E. (2002) '*Bildung* and the Thinking of *Bildung*', *Journal of Philosophy of Education*, Vol. 36, No. 3, pp. 341–352.

Schwenk, B. (1989) 'Pädagogische Grundbegriffe: Volume 1', in D. Lenzen (Ed.), *Bildung*, Reinbek: Rowohlt, pp. 208–221.

Standish, P. (2002) 'Preface', *Journal of Philosophy of Education*, Vol. 36, No. 3, pp. iii–iv.

Stiegler, B. (1998) *Technics and Time, 1: The Fault of Epimetheus*, Trans. R. Beardsworth and G. Collins, Stanford, CA: Stanford University Press.

Educational philosophy: reading and writing practices in this extract

With this piece of research I addressed questions posed both by philosophy of technology and philosophy of education. Both fields discourage the understanding of technology as means to an end, and investigate its impact on the user, its thinking, and the world. I thus attempted to show that when technology is not understood instrumentally, namely, as the one serving education's internal purposes, but as a supplement that forms thinking, analysis becomes more demanding. In order to respond to this kind of challenge I read the Heideggerian text quite closely, either by directly addressing the question of technology, or by addressing the question of technology in connection to human existence. Finally, I related this reading to the phenomenological investigation of current digital technologies that promote a kind of immediacy that does not allow the user any critical distance from the construction of its self. I proceeded to this analysis through Heidegger's own phenomenological accounts. My own phenomenological accounts of current digital technologies attempted to make the Heideggerian theory clearer, and indeed prove that digital technologies construct the user in ways that do not encourage critical reflection.

Evidently, this research approach pays close attention to language. Heidegger, himself, understood language as revealing hidden aspects of phenomena, and in this extract I took into account the etymological hints that reveal the relation between image (*Bild*), education (*Bildung*), and imagination (*Einbildung*). This investigation showed that both Heidegger's existential analysis of technology and the *Bildung* literature are based on the premise that individuals need critical distance in order to be truly educated. It also showed that for Heidegger, and of course other philosophers, this critical distance is obstructed by technology. This kind of research invites the researcher to think about the theoretical traditions that bring the notions in question to the fore and to also discuss the contextual role of these traditions and the possible connections that exist between them. Heidegger, for example, discussed the way technology forms thought and criticised modern technology precisely for this reason, that is, for tearing the human being away from its authentic self. He therefore detected a necessity for an education (*Bildung*) that is transformative and cultivates authenticity beyond the restrictions of technology. When Heidegger's take on this specific subject is put into dialogue, however, with other aspects of his own work, the empirical evidence discussed here by Katherine Hayles, and the argumentation concerning the always-already technological nature of thinking provided by Bernard Stiegler, the possibility for a kind of thought that is not conditioned by technology comes crashing down. This is because these contemporary thinkers offer readings of the human/technology, representation/presence, idea/matter binaries in a deconstructive way. Deconstruction is among other things a type of close reading suggested by the twentieth-century French philosopher Jacques Derrida, who asserts that the structural opposites of a binary do not simply oppose each other but rather construct the possibility of their difference through the interaction that constitutes them. My own deconstructive reading of Heidegger, as pursued in the rest of this chapter, attempts to show that Heidegger's own correctness/*alētheia* binary cannot be understood as a system of completely separated conceptual realms, precisely because technology is always already involved in both, and thus education, even transformative education, cannot escape this relation.

Addressing the human/technology relation through this particular mode of reading transforms the understanding of the matter and the way it may be addressed in matters of educational importance. Currently, several perspectives inform educational initiatives that hold in my opinion a rather restrictive understanding of technology. These assert among other things that:

(a) Technology is a mere means to an end and that technologies used for any aim are interchangeable.
(b) Technology enhances learning, even though there have been many illustrious initiatives that attempted to do precisely that without procuring the desired results.
(c) Technology allows the student-user to engage better with others and contribute to its environment even though technology's own role for the constitution of the user's milieu is not taken into account.

(d) Technology replicates thinking as it happens with computers. This position does not take into account that the design of technologies is a selective process that incorporates normativity and thus contributes to the reproduction of certain mentalities.

Most of the time these positions are supported by an unfounded belief about the potential of new technology that is supposed to ameliorate learning. On the contrary, the kind of writing I employ here denotes that the human/technology binary is a rather complicated relationship that conceals at times certain possibilities of thinking, and at others makes the observation of thinking through its exteriorisation possible. When educational policy takes this kind of reading and writing into account, decisions concerning the use of technology become even more difficult. Indeed, these decisions cannot be driven simply by the desire to change things and without real knowledge about technology's impact on thinking.

Reference

Heidegger, M. (1927/2008) *Being and Time*, Trans. J. Macquarrie and E. Robinson, Oxford: Blackwell.

14

READING BETWEEN THE LINES

Richard Smith

Introduction to the extract

I have for some while been struck by a number of strange features that modern philosophy, especially analytic philosophy, displays. It is sober and well–ordered, showing few of the flights of fancy, the poetical language, the irony or even the personal voice that can often be found in philosophical writing from Plato to Descartes, and from time to time beyond. It seldom reflects on its own literary style, the idea of which would probably alarm most modern philosophers, committed as they seem to be to repudiating style in favour of what they think of as a straightforward relationship between the words they use, on the one hand, and, on the other, the arguments they use and the truths they seek (as if that was not itself a distinctive style). Otherwise, they might ask, how would there be a clear distinction between philosophy and other genres such as autobiography or the novel? Then too there is the mysterious way in which philosophy now commonly falls neatly into packages of around 6,000 words, just what the academic journals require; even books on philosophy tend to look very much like collections of these familiar packages. It can be taken for granted, of course (some will suspect irony here), that philosophy is to be written and read, rather than spoken or argued aloud, in a dialogue between or among embodied persons, among friends, in the university seminar or tutorial, in the café or the bar.

At any rate this chapter concerns how to write philosophy, despite its title, which I have given it not least because the reader might like to read in full the text (a 6,000-word article, naturally) on which it is based, 'Between the Lines: Philosophy, Text and Conversation' (2009). Learning to write and learning to read go hand-in-hand. The original piece emerged in response to an invitation from Claudia Ruitenberg, of Canada's University of British Columbia, who was editing a Special Issue of the *Journal of Philosophy of Education* (2009) entitled 'What

Do Philosophers of Education Do? (And How Do They Do It?)'. I readily agreed, partly in order to find out what I was doing and how I was doing it, and because such invited articles, being effectively accepted in advance (unless the author writes something particularly outrageous), are an opportunity to be more expansive and push harder at the boundaries of convention than is normally the case.

The text imagines, or reports, or looks forward to, a seminar for which a group of some 20 final year undergraduate students have read the first three chapters of Richard Rorty's (1989) *Contingency, Irony, and Solidarity*. The points of interest are Rorty's vision of philosophy, the idea of truth, postmodernism, and whatever else the students find interesting. The module began with Plato's dialogue *Phaedrus*, which George, the tutor, thinks is a very good way to get to grips with some 'postmodern' ideas. It also raises puzzling questions about dialogues and texts. George, if anyone wants to know, both is, and is not, myself: teaching often feels like that, and so does writing, as other people's words sometimes have a way of changing you as they flow through you and onto the page.

EXTRACT: BETWEEN THE LINES[1]

Ben: ...and your view of philosophy, George. Do you think of yourself as a postmodernist, are you a Rortyan, or what? I can see a bit why you always avoid this question, because you don't see yourself as having any kind of method, as if there was a 'here's how to do it' that you could teach us and we could take it away and use it like a handbook.

Jane: Because the idea of method is at the heart of modernity – Francis Bacon and his *Novum Organum*, precisely the manual for the new inductive method, or he wanted it to be. And Descartes.

Anna: Descartes? Why Descartes?

Aisha: His *Discourse* is the *Discourse on Method*, Anna. On *method*. Full title: *Discourse on the Method of Rightly Conducting the Reason, and Seeking Truth in the Sciences*. It's got method, reason, truth and science – the whole modernist package!

Ben: Alright, George, you don't have a method. Some of us had suspected that for some time. But some of this Rorty stuff sounded a bit like you. If only the irony.

George: OK. I'll try to give you some idea of what kind of philosophy I like, in as far as I have a clear idea myself, or could give any kind of satisfactory account of how it's different from other kinds of writing. But let's make a gentle start. Would anyone like to remind us why Richard Rorty came up with this title, *Contingency, Irony, and Solidarity*? What about the first word?

Ilse: Well, he starts with language. It's just a matter of chance – of contingency – what language you grow up learning to speak. So, the example we thought of last week, back home in Germany we say *Geisteswissenschaften*, which means, literally, understanding the human spirit, but here you say 'social science'. So you grow up with assumptions about there being a scientific method, about the necessity of measuring and quantifying things, that we don't have to the same extent.

Mike: Or if you lived in the time when they had the theory of the humours, and you took it for granted that people were either phlegmatic or choleric and so on, and they were made that way and couldn't change. Or the way they talk of *erôs* in the *Phaedrus*, it has associations of passion and madness that our word 'love' doesn't have.

George: Just staying with the contingency of language for the moment – because of course Rorty has chapters on the contingency of community and selfhood as well – what are the implications of all this for the idea of truth?

Louise: Yeah, that's what I don't really get. He doesn't believe in truth, does he?

Tom: If he's saying there's no such thing as truth then –

Jane: We know, we know: 'then it must be true that there's no such thing as truth. Which is self-contradictory.' Spare us the cheap analytic shot. That's a method if ever I saw one!

Sam: He doesn't say there's no such thing as truth, he says that truth is a kind of empty compliment we pay to statements, or sentences – I can't remember which – that help us get things done. Help us achieve our ends.

George: And that is because he's a – ?
           (Silence)

Rachel: Nutcase? Professor?

George: I detect that, not for the first time, I have phrased my question badly. I was trying to prompt the response that he is a pragmatist, and a notion of truth as what helps us get where we want to go is a pragmatist theory.

Louise: As opposed to – ?

George: As opposed to the idea that a true sentence is one that accurately reflects the world, holds up a mirror to nature, to echo the title of Rorty's earlier book.

Jane: So the point of the contingency of language is that there is never anywhere a perfect language that tells us how reality is. There is something in the world that we call love and the Greeks called *erôs*, but there is no way of knowing it outside of these words.

Amy: This really does my head in. Surely it's either true that Socrates fancied Phaedrus or it isn't?

(Continued)

(Continued)

Mike:	What, like as a historical fact, when they are characters in a story, a dialogue?
Sam:	Doesn't this example make the point perfectly? Even if the *Phaedrus* reported real events, it would make all the difference whether we said Socrates loved Phaedrus, or had *erôs* for him –
Ben:	Or the hots...
Mike:	Or Phaedrus turned him on.
George:	Which is to say, before things deteriorate even further, that it's very hard to find language that isn't shot through with metaphor. Different metaphors, different realities. 'Turned him on', for instance, suggests a very mechanistic view of human relationships. And if language is heavily metaphorical, ineliminably metaphorical, then it can't be conceived as a nice, clear and neutral set of signs that accurately reflect reality.
Emma:	Sometimes I almost think I've got it, and then I think: surely there was either a big bang at the start of the universe or there wasn't? So to say that there was is either true or not true.
Rachel:	What, literally big? The way you said 'that's a big ask' when I tried to touch you for a fiver the other evening? Or the way that's a big tree outside? *That* big?
Ilse:	And that's before we get onto 'bang', as opposed to whether it was more like a very loud 'pop', and how there can be a bang when there's no-one to hear it.
George:	On a pragmatist theory, to call that particular theory of the origin of the universe 'true' is to say it's part of a story which helps us do things: to understand the age of the earth and make sense of the fossil record, for instance. Though I have to confess I personally still have an urge to say that the creationist account just isn't *true* in the sense that what it describes didn't happen. Still more so when we come to controversial historical events. Some people think Napoleon was poisoned, for example, and one day we'll find whether that's true or not. Or in the Orwellian kind of example, either Jones was at the meeting with the other party high-ups, and they doctored the photos later when he fell out of favour to make it look as if he wasn't there, or he never was actually there in the first place.
Rachel:	What I have a lot of trouble with in Rorty is that it all seems to come down to agreement. Instead of looking for the truth and knowing when we've found it, we sit around having civilised conversations about our aims and purposes. So we agree that we want more human solidarity – another of the words from the title – and less cruelty, and

whether this or that counts as more solidarity or a world with less cruelty is just a matter of whether we think it does. Not of whether it really does or is. OK, let's accept that there are problems with the idea of truth in just the way that Rorty says. But it can't be nothing but whether or not we agree, can it? What if we all agree but only because we are dead smug and complacent and reach a cosy consensus? And who are 'we', anyway? Well-paid academics with white hair like the picture on the back of the book? No offence, George.

George: I wish, the first part of that description. Look, what Rachel has done is turn the discussion to where I thought we might find ourselves going today. It's one of our nine themes of postmodernism, neatly bullet-pointed in the module outline: the ideal of conversation comes to replace that of knowledge.

Ben: Which is why we started with the *Phaedrus* and have ended up with Rorty.

George: Yes. And now we have to take seriously Rachel's question. When is a conversation or dialogue, one of these events that we are replacing the pursuit of knowledge with, a good or successful conversation, one that takes us somewhere, however we want to put this, and when is it a bad one? Think of those conversations you have into the small hours in your disgusting shared student houses with mysterious damp patches, or of course think of a university seminar, including this one.

Ilse: This is the difference between Rorty's systematic, and edifying philosophy, isn't it? We're talking about philosophy as edification, aren't we?

Louise: Come again? I think I was away for that.

Ilse *(Takes file from bag, shuffles through it and reads aloud):* 'Systematic philosophy, of which Anglophone analytic philosophy is a prominent example, tries to solve problems in a way that produces a body of successful philosophical solutions. Edifying philosophy takes the gadfly path, from Socrates to Derrida. It aims at continuing a conversation rather than at discovering truth. It is educative, in the sense of *Bildung*, as a matter of forming the character of the individual. It is not concerned, or much less concerned, with the "discovery, elucidation and justification of a core of fundamental truth"'.[2]

Mike: Because of course Rorty has a problem with truth.

George: Which is...? Anyone?

Ilse: On the systematic view, philosophy is a kind of master-discipline that addresses the relationship between language and reality. It's very often tempted by the idea of truth as a matter of holding up a mirror

(Continued)

(Continued)

	to nature, in the title of Rorty's earlier book, that is to say representing it. By contrast with philosophy as edifying conversation.
Louise:	Oh, representation again. Everything on this module seems to come back to presence and representation. Rorty's against it, Lyotard seems to think it leads to totalitarianism,[3] and then there's Derrida and the metaphysics of presence. So if truth and meaning aren't about – aren't about – saying 'here's reality' –
Aisha:	Then they're about going on some endless conversational trip. Is that right, George?
George:	Endless, yes, in more than one sense…
Aisha:	Here it comes, the bloody Derridean deferral of meaning again!
George:	… but I'd have to say a few things about the idea of it being a 'trip'…
Tom:	I see. I get it now. We're having an edifying seminar, aren't we? The point isn't to get to the truth but to go round in circles.
Emma:	But in an edifying way!
Tom:	Seriously, George, is this your vision of what we're doing here, of philosophy, if this is philosophy? Is this what philosophy means to you? You've often hinted at your reservations about the kind of philosophy you were taught. Which was analytic, systematic in Rorty's view?
George:	Reservations, yes. There was a sense when I was studying philosophy at university that the object was to identify and get beyond certain wrong turns in philosophical thinking, such as the idea that ethics just comes down to expressions of feeling – emotivism – for instance, or to see just why some of Russell's paradoxes are seductive but flawed. At the same time the way I was actually taught was quite Socratic: one-to-one tutorials where any question you asked of your tutor was likely to be answered with another question. Which was often exasperating, but one eventually and slowly began to realise that philosophy wasn't a discipline where the whole point was to learn the answers and reproduce them to order.
Tom:	But there were exams, and you had to get the answers right?
George:	Of course. So sometimes you wondered if the edification – not that we used that word at the time – wasn't entirely serious, or if the Socratic approach was something you could really go in for properly only if you could afford not to worry about getting the good degree that would mean a job at the end. And then of course the dons, as they were known in those days, went off in the vacations to write their books, and you thought this must be the real philosophical business, in contrast to showing undergraduate students that there were no easy answers. Because those books and articles that they wrote held answers, didn't they, even if not easy ones?

Jane: That hasn't changed, has it. Our lecturers are always telling us they need to get on with their research and write their books. For promotion, or just so they don't lose their jobs.

George: Quite. Anyway, so much for the philosophical education of George, such as it was. To be honest, I find all this hard to think about clearly, partly, I suppose, because of the autobiographical element and partly, I think, because the difference between getting the conversation, the Socratic dialogue if you like, right and getting it wrong in various ways is very slight, a dividing line that it's easy to cross without noticing it. Often just at the point where you begin to think you're getting it just right, you realise you've fallen into one trap or another. In this it's a bit like more familiar forms of therapy, where it's notorious that the patient can unconsciously use his intelligence to avoid looking at things he doesn't want to look at, or the therapist's extensive experience and knowledge of the theory of therapy can get in the way of properly listening to, attending to, the patient in front of her.

Notes

1 This extract is taken from a longer article, published as: Smith, R. (2009) 'Between the Lines: Philosophy, Text and Conversation', *Journal of Philosophy of Education*, Vol. 43, No. 3, pp. 437–449.
2 Gutting (1999: 189).
3 See the last paragraph of Lyotard's *The Postmodern Condition* (1979/1984).

References

Gutting, G. (1999) *Practical Liberalism and the Critique of Modernity*, Cambridge: Cambridge University Press.

Lyotard, J.F. (1979/1984) *The Postmodern Condition: A Report on Knowledge*, Trans. G. Bennington and B. Massumi, Minneapolis, MN: University of Minnesota Press.

Rorty, R. (1979) *Philosophy and the Mirror of Nature*, Oxford: Blackwell.

Rorty, R. (1989) *Contingency, Irony, and Solidarity*, Cambridge: Cambridge University Press.

Smith, R. (2009) 'Between the Lines: Philosophy, Text and Conversation', in C. Ruitenberg (Ed.), 'What Do Philosophers of Education Do? (And How Do They Do It?)', Special Issue of *Journal of Philosophy of Education*, Vol. 43, No. 3, pp. 437–449.

Educational philosophy: reading and writing practices in this extract

It may be disconcerting, in a book whose major theme is practices of reading and writing in educational research, to find the idea of 'method' problematised as it was at the beginning of the extract.[1] The student interlocutors were receptive to the idea, however, partly because they understood that there are some things that can hardly be turned into a method – conversation or a good seminar being two of them – and partly because most of them had taken compulsory 'research methods' courses in one social science department of the university or another. Here they saw the limitations of learning such 'methods' as a substitute for a deep critical engagement with a particular topic or issue. It was revealing, as one student observed in a different seminar, that the lecturers, claiming research methods as their area of expertise, naturally lacked substantial understanding of any topic or issue that the students were interested in investigating, and were surprised to find that some students wanted to read more deeply than was necessary for a superficial 'literature review'. 'We were told that this would stop us getting on with the actual research', said another, in bemusement. It was also odd, said the same student, that these 'methods' were presented as democratically available for anyone to learn, take away and deploy: as if the way in which you talked with, say, school refusers about their lives might not be connected in complex and important ways with the kind of person you were; as if method was a substitute for sensitivity, insight, sympathy, judgement, tact, and delicacy. The students had come to see that methodolatry, the veneration of method, is a trope of modernity, closely related to imagining that all kinds of capacities are 'skills':[2] the 'employability skills', for instance, that are now supposed to be embedded in all their modules. 'Wouldn't it be better if university actually made you unemployable', Sam asked, 'that is, the kind of person whom a dodgy or corrupt employer wouldn't dream of taking on? Someone who might stand up against the way it was trashing the planet, or exploiting people on zero-hours contracts?'

None of this is to say that doing and writing philosophy cannot be learned: only that you cannot learn it in the way that apparently you can learn to do participant observation from a couple of lectures, or the way that you can acquire the skill of filleting a fish from watching *MasterChef* and then practising until you've got the knack of it. It is both slower and harder than that, and so it can be more profoundly fulfilling. To make another comparison, it is like learning to build an intimate relationship with someone, rather than picking up the techniques for seducing them. The contrast runs through Plato's *Phaedrus*; the young man from whom the text takes its title, and whose name means 'sparkling' or 'dazzling', still hasn't quite seen the point by the end of the dialogue, where he seems to think that sitting at the feet of Socrates for a day – willing to be dazzled by him and hoping Socrates is dazzled in return – makes him Socrates's friend and equal.

Jane (interrupts):   I don't think this is going to be very helpful to people starting out in philosophy of education. And your characteristic touches of irony will just confuse them. Anyway, didn't Socrates have a method, the maieutic approach, irony, the *elenchus*?

George:	*(or whoever it is that she's talking to):* Where did you come from? This isn't the dialogue part, this is the bit where I step out from the text and talk about the text. Come to think of it, though, you all learned to join our conversation without my teaching you a method, didn't you? Well, learning to do philosophy is a little like that. But you shouldn't be here at all now!
Jane:	Did you think you could be shot of us – push us out of the conversation – so easily?
George:	I was only trying to do what the editors told me to do. Oh, and the idea that Socrates has something like a method is shaky, the invention of later writers who couldn't think of Plato as a philosopher unless he had a system.
Jane:	No doubt Plato was being ironic. You were always quoting that comment of Rorty's, that we're still trying to work out which bits of Plato are the jokes.[1] Seriously, though, how do you expect this chapter to help people?
George:	Seriously? I suppose I was trying to say – I've never got this entirely clear in my own head – that doing philosophy is rather like having a conversation. There's no alternative but to listen for a while, read for a while, and then begin to join in when you feel ready. I hoped too that it would come across that there is something special in both, in conversation and in philosophy, in the listening and the talking, the reading and the writing. A special kind of joy, something to celebrate.
Jane:	Something to hold up against our mechanistic, utilitarian world, you used to say, with its obsession with skills and method!
George:	Well, let's pray that something of that will still be around when they've replaced me with an online learning package and you and the others have gone off to boost the University's graduate employability statistics. Something to put off the day when the books sit unread in the library and the conversation stops.
Jane:	I'll join you in that prayer!

Note

1 'The permanent fascination of the man who dreamed up the whole idea of Western philosophy – Plato – is that…after millenniums of commentary nobody knows which passages in the dialogues are jokes…' (Rorty, 1980: 369n.).

Reference

Rorty, R. (1980) *Philosophy and the Mirror of Nature*, Princeton, NJ: Princeton University Press.

Notes

1 For more on the strange idea of 'research methods', see Chapter 3, 'The Idea of Method', in Smeyers and Smith (2014).
2 See Hart (1978).

References

Hart, W.A. (1978) 'Against Skills', *Oxford Review of Education*, Vol. 4, No. 2, pp. 205–216.
Rorty, R. (1989) *Contingency, Irony, and Solidarity*, Cambridge: Cambridge University Press.
Smeyers, P. and Smith, R. (2014) *Understanding Education and Educational Research*, Cambridge: Cambridge University Press.
Smith, R. (2009) 'Between the Lines: Philosophy, Text and Conversation', in C. Ruitenberg (Ed.), 'What Do Philosophers of Education Do? (And How Do They Do It?)', Special Issue of *Journal of Philosophy of Education*, Vol. 43, No. 3, pp. 437–449.

PART III
How to proceed?

15

READING AND WRITING

Reading and writing for, and as, research

Amanda Fulford and Naomi Hodgson

When it comes to research, and to the textbooks, websites, and study skills resources that support it, much attention is given to writing. This is not surprising. For many novice researchers, and even experienced academics, the processes of writing, of publishing, and of putting one's ideas in the public domain for scrutiny, can be difficult ones. Reading, however, tends not to be seen in the same way. Of course, there are the perennial problems of tackling the seminal texts in one's field (especially those that might be considered difficult, or whose ideas are strongly contested). There is also the sheer amount of material that there is to read, to which online portals and databases now provide access, and which link to yet more material. But writing – especially academic writing – remains the more difficult skill for many. It is not surprising, then, that many of the research methods textbooks that we discussed in Chapter 2 devote more space to discussions of the process of *writing* (the different sections of one's research report or dissertation), than to what is entailed in the practices of *reading* for research. We will return to practices of writing later in this chapter, but our focus first is on reading. Initially, we will consider how some of the research methods texts perceive the place of reading in the research process (in terms of what it *is* and *when* it is undertaken, i.e. what it is *for*). We then turn attention to how reading tends to be understood in educational philosophy, exemplifying some of its practices with reference to our colleagues' contributions in Part II.

Reading-for-research

Even a cursory glance at the index of many supporting texts for research reveals that entries for 'reading' are notably absent. A closer consideration of these texts shows that reading is rarely addressed as a practice in itself, but rather as concomitant with writing. Reading is only mentioned in the chapters advising on how to write a literature review, which must, of course, entail reading of the sources that inform it. But despite this, the language in which reading is often discussed raises some interesting questions about what comprises 'reading'. First, reading seems to be equated with technical processes of information retrieval, and many texts include detailed sections on identifying educational gateways and databases (see, for example, Newby, 2010: 204ff.), and on how to evaluate different sources of information (see Thomas, 2013: 60ff). Second, the language in which reading is discussed tends to prefer terms such as 'searched' (Machi and McEvoy, 2009: 5), 'surveyed' (*ibid.*: 6), or 'reviewed'. Of course, these terms do not preclude the idea of literature being read, but present a certain idea of reading. Anthony Coles and Jim McGrath put it like this: 'Selective reading is the key. It's a good idea to consider what you want to get out of a source before you read it' (2010: 43). This is the kind of reading that is 'efficient' (Wilson, 2013: 50), in that it limits the amount of what is read, thus enabling the neat compilation of an overview of any particular field. Such an approach requires what David Silverman refers to as the deployment of 'the tricks of the trade' (2010: 323). 'Your aim', he goes on, 'is usually to "fillet" a publication in terms of your own agenda' (*ibid.*). To continue with the 'fishy' metaphors, Gary Thomas writes: 'Try to develop the skill of speed-reading, "gutting" an article or book for the material you need' (2013: 67).

These kinds of approach often advise the reader to focus attention on the structural elements of a given text (the abstract, or the sub-headings, for example), to enable the reader to skip those sections that might seem irrelevant. In some cases, a reader is advised to give attention only to the conclusions of an article (Silverman, 2010) in order to judge whether it is worth reading the rest. The rationale for using such techniques is that close attention to the text is unnecessary in many cases, especially since, as Thomas claims: 'Academics write in strange prose that is sometimes meaningful only to the limited group of people who work professionally in that area, and if you spend your time trying to decipher it all you will go mad' (2013: 67–68). Thomas' comment may be somewhat tongue-in-cheek, but it is important to understand what is at stake here. It is not that skimming texts in the ways suggested is necessarily a bad thing, or inappropriate to a certain kind of research. There are many approaches to reading, and these need to match the purposes for which one reads in any particular situation. If the object of writing a literature review is to situate a research project in the context of existing published findings in any given field – in Newby's words, to 'create a bond between our research results and what is already known' (2010: 193) – then scoping the field methodically seems entirely appropriate. Part of the work of writing a good literature review is to include sources that *have a direct bearing on* the project's research questions and findings, and to exclude extraneous material. In summary, reading in this way is a 'winnowing of the information to only the data that provide the strongest evidence to support the thesis' (Machi and McEvoy, 2009: 5).

This kind of broad survey approach to reading is suggested for preparing the litera-ture review, common in many types of research. In what we have already covered, the *purpose* of reading, and its general approaches (to 'fillet' and to 'gut'), are clear; but what does this say about the specific *practices* of reading? Here, the textbooks present readers with a methodical approach – a kind of 'roadmap...known procedures and skills that you can use to make the task easier' (Machi and McEvoy, 2009: 1). These tend to be laid out in broadly similar ways, often described in terms of stages: locating the literature; managing the sources; effective reading; critical reflection and evalu-ation of the texts, and the subsequent writing of the literature review. Machi and McEvoy's model has six stages (the subtitle of their book identifies these as the 'six steps to success'). Adherence to the model seems crucial to success. They write: 'Study carefully the literature review model...memorize it if possible. Use this figure to keep yourself on track' (*ibid.*: 10). Much of this is highly technicised, and outcome-driven. In a further iteration, Thomas advocates what he calls the SQ2R method of speed-reading and taking notes (the use of the almost algebraic acronym is suggestive of a proven formula). This is a model that Thomas adapts from an earlier SQ3R technique (Robinson, 1970). Thomas' model entails: surveying a text; remembering the 'key nuggets' (Thomas, 2013: 68); asking questions of what is read to ensure that what you are reading is directly relevant; reading the whole text again and annotating what is important; and recalling what has been read and making notes.

Of course, when starting out in research, these texts provide a useful overview of what is expected of work submitted as part of an accredited course, or indeed for publication. The approaches that we have outlined as highly technicised and outcome-driven do provide a structure and method that will undoubtedly be of use to many readers. But, before moving on, there are two further points to be considered in relation to these kind of approaches. First, there is a sense in many of the research methods textbooks that reading as part of research is an activity that is started – and completed – at the outset of the research. Getting the reading sorted out as early as possible ensures that the researcher has a clear conceptual framework to help focus the research. Indeed, the texts advise that: 'You need to *begin* with the knowledge that other people have acquired' (Furseth and Everett, 2013: 47, ital-ics ours). Andrew Brown and Paul Dowling make a similar point when they state: 'The first phase of development...involves making explicit a nebula of debates and theories and, indeed, empirical findings about the area of your concern' (Brown and Dowling, 1998: 20).[1] This idea of 'reading first' leads on to a second issue: that read-ing tends to be seen solely as a support, or a scaffolding, for the 'real' research of data collection and analysis. This suggests an unhelpful distinction between the practices of reading, and the practices of research, as if the two were not inextricably linked.

We turn now to consider how the practices of reading as set out in the research methods literature relate to forms of research that we referred to in Chapter 1 as 'educational philosophy'. In doing this, we will draw attention to our colleagues' reflections on the way that they read sources, and how these inform their research in educational philosophy.

Reading-as-research

Each of our colleagues' contributions in Part II of this book comprises three parts: an introduction to a short extract of their writing in educational philosophy; the extract itself; and finally, an analysis of the reading and writing practices used in preparation of the extract, and that constitute their research. In this final element, each contributor reflects on his/her particular approaches to reading-*as*-research. We can distinguish this from what we have termed reading-*for*-research. The notion of reading-as-research, especially in the field of educational philosophy, highlights that method (in this case, reading), and the substantive questions about, or approach to, the subject matter, are one. Within educational research, which tends to be concerned with the direct applicability of findings to policy and practice, and with empirical methods, the value of such an approach is not well understood. Richard Smith's contribution in Part II (Chapter 14) (which takes the creative form of a seminar conversation between a tutor and his students) points to this fact, and gives an account of how university lecturers were surprised that students wanted to read more deeply than was necessary for a literature review. In his account, the students report that "'We were told that this would stop us from getting on with the actual research'" (p. 136). Other reflections on reading-as-research in Part II suggest that there are particular practices of reading in educational philosophy that merit attention. These relate, first, to what counts as a source to be read, and second, to how such sources might be read. It is to these issues that we now turn.

What counts as a source to be read in educational philosophy?

In Chapter 7, her contribution to Part II, Andrea English seeks to address the place of the teacher in matters of moral education, and to her role as listener. She does this by reading Johann F. Herbart's theory of moral guidance. She acknowledges that Herbart was not developing any explicit theory of listening, but she chose to use his work as a source because she finds in his writing 'implicit notions of what it means to be a teacher, including how a teacher should listen' (p. 72). English's approach is to read a text to assess the extent to which it can contribute to the exploration of questions she is trying to answer. She goes on to say: 'I am also using my own questions to frame what I pay attention to in the text' (*ibid.*). We might ask at this point if this approach is any different from those that Silverman and Thomas suggest, to skim, to gut, and to fillet, to read only what is of significance. Perhaps not, if English's purpose was to find the salient points of Herbart's theory, and apply it directly to teaching as it is. But in important ways, it is different. English's approach is more open. It is about a detailed attention to the reading of a *whole* text. It is only by focussing on how Herbart understands and articulates what is pertinent to moral guidance that she is able to see what is relevant to her project and to the questions raised by today's classroom. Indeed, she admits that she would not have seen the relevance of what she was reading in Herbart to listening were she not concentrating on other aspects of his work.

Writing in Chapter 12, on social justice in educational practices, Morwenna Griffiths compares notions of nature and education in the work of two eighteenth-century writers, Jean-Jacques Rousseau and Mary Wollstonecraft. But what merits attention here is how she turns to read other literature in order to illustrate and develop her argument. Griffiths claims that she deliberately chooses to make use of sources that are not confined to education, or even to educational philosophy, preferring to make connections with literature from across disciplinary boundaries. Here she turns to the work of philosophers such as Charles Taylor, who isn't known principally for his concern with educational matters. She writes:

> I am committed to the view that philosophers of education need to engage with other educational theorists and with particular issues of practice as well as to philosophy more generally…Indeed I read widely…This for me is one of the pleasures of working within education. Education, practically and theoretically, is so complex that it necessarily engages with a range of disciplines in the humanities and social sciences.
>
> *(p. 118)*

Anne Pirrie makes a similar point in her work on capacity-building in educational theory (Chapter 9). While she seeks to draw on sources that clearly belong to educational philosophy and theory (such as Richard Smith and Gert Biesta), she also chooses to read texts from the writings of the Italian journalist and novelist, Italo Calvino. She describes this aspect of her work as 'a reliance on a text that *prima facie* has little to do with the philosophy of education' (p. 90). Her rationale for including this work is that it 'can offer relevant conceptual resources' (*ibid.*). Amanda Fulford's contribution (Chapter 4) is yet another example of the use of literature from sources not directly concerned with education (if we think of it only in terms of schooling and formal learning). Her work, critiquing the way that discourses of student satisfaction in higher education affect the talk between a university tutor and her student, draws not on educational or linguistic sources but on the work of the nineteenth-century American essayists, Ralph Waldo Emerson and Henry David Thoreau. She provides the following rationale for adopting this approach:

> It is important to point out that Emerson and Thoreau were not writing about the practices or outcomes of formal education, even less the idea of the tutorial conversation or of 'student satisfaction'. Their work, though, illustrates a particular mode of thinking about our lives. Put very simply, they are advocating a way of living in a state of dissatisfaction that drives us to a continual striving for a better self.
>
> *(p. 46)*

Her detailed reading of these works is evidenced not by the inclusion of a single citation to the respective authors, but by a more in-depth engagement with some of their key concepts – such as 'settling' and 'leaving' – that in turn requires a different approach to writing. We will consider this later in this chapter.

But sources that inform educational philosophy need not only be works of literature. Nancy Vansieleghem, in Chapter 10, writes about visual research and the issue of giving voice, and her writing more generally is often related to readings of works of art such as film (see e.g. Vansieleghem *et al.*, 2015). This use of different media is not uncommon. For example, in his attempt to take a different approach to addressing the environmental crisis as a topic in education, Paul Standish (2010b) provides a reading of the paintings of the contemporary German artist, Anselm Kiefer, in particular, his work *Nuremburg*. His reading also draws on Kiefer's use, in a number of his paintings, of ideas from the poetry of Paul Celan, a Romanian Jew, and in particular, his poem *Todesfuge* (*ibid.*).

What becomes clear from these examples is that it is not uncommon for work in educational philosophy to be informed by the reading of sources other than what Vansieleghem calls the more traditional sources of 'science and research' (p. 97). This is also the case for Viktor Johansson, whose Chapter 8 refers not only to a work of children's literature, but specifically a picture book, which he reads in terms of a particular type of storytelling and form of thinking. Here again we see research in educational philosophy informed by texts that, in themselves, are not overtly philosophical or, in this particular case, written as a work of academic scholarship. However, the value of non-philosophical texts in informing educational philosophy is clear here, as it was in Morwenna Griffiths' and also Anne Pirrie's extracts. Johannson emphasises this usefulness when he writes:

> The reading [of the picture book] is philosophical since…[it] is set in the context of a philosophical discussion…The literary experience thus changes the impression of the philosophical issue…The literary experience shows further ways of seeing a phenomenon and gives it new significance.
>
> *(p. 81)*

What is read to inform work in educational philosophy is, then, very broad-ranging. What we can also see from the contributions to Part II of this book is that the authors tend to read a limited number of sources, but do so in some depth; each text is highly significant. This illustrates something of a difference from the kind of reading undertaken for other kinds of research, where the tendency is to provide comprehensive literature reviews, through the use of multiple citations, in order to situate the project in the light of what is already known. What drives this difference is, to a certain extent, explained by the different scope of projects and the questions that drive them. Where a project is making use of the collection of primary data, the research question tends to be very specific, and to address a narrow, focussed concern. This is an eminently sensible way to proceed, of course, given that the research has to be manageable within the practical constraints of time, access to participants, the demands of data analysis, and so on. But in educational philosophy, the nature of the question, and so the potential literature to inform it, entail a greater depth of reading. Paul Standish puts it like this:

Because of its central concern with the nature of ideas [educational philosophy] is likely to draw significantly on a limited number of sources – perhaps on a particular philosopher…because very often the topic at issue is one that touches on such broad (and sometimes big) issues that one could never come to the end of.

(2010a: 11)

Research in educational philosophy is not concerned with providing an exhaustive literature review, but with a kind of reading that is not finite. This is not to say that reading never ends, but that while one might need to be selective, and narrow down the approach in the initial stages, that this is the very point at which questions open up that signal the need for a deeper reading of a select number of sources.

How are sources read in educational philosophy?

In attempting to provide some answers to this question, we turn again to the reflections of our colleagues who have contributed their work to Part II of this book. As we have seen, often a limited number of (wide-ranging) sources are used in research in educational philosophy. This is reflected in the significance given to them in the work and, therefore, on how they themselves are read. In Chapter 9, Anne Pirrie summarises this approach succinctly when she writes that her work 'explores and critiques a taken-for-granted notion…through a close reading of a particular text' (p. 90). In his contribution, Chapter 6, Joris Vlieghe writes about school practices and practising. He uses examples such as mastering the recitation of a poem by heart, of learning one's multiplication tables, or of performing bodily movements correctly in a physical education class. His work illustrates the kind of research that is characterised by a detailed engagement with texts (in this case, two texts: the work of the Italian philosopher, Giorgio Agamben, and that of the German philosopher and teacher, Otto Friedrich Bollnow). His experience of reading in this way, though, did not result in a gutting of the source and a mere reporting of the main relevant facts. Rather, Vlieghe says:

I engaged in a conversation with two other authors, but in a sense this is not accurate…It is perhaps more appropriate to say that this kind of work eventually consists in *a conversation with oneself*: looking at words and conceptual clarifications others have developed, one tests whether they make sense for oneself.

(p. 63)

Vlieghe refers to a consideration of words as a characteristic of the ways in which he reads a text in his educational philosophy. This attention to language is also part of the reading practices of other contributors to Part II. Anna Kouppanou, for example, in Chapter 13, writes of using this approach in her work on image, imagination, and education. In the introduction to her extract, she makes the point that her work is a 'close reading' of the work of the German philosopher, Martin Heidegger (p. 120). The close reading that she undertook (necessary given the generally accepted difficulty of Heidegger's philosophy), revealed 'important etymological and theoretical connections related to image (*Bild*), imagination (*Einbildung*), and education (*Bildung*)' (p. 120). This attention to the etymology of individual words allowed her to draw out the import of Heideggerian thought for education today. When Heidegger makes the claim that 'language speaks as the peal of stillness' (1971: 207), he is calling attention to the idea of language as evocation, calling forth, as address. Kouppanou's work recognises this, and her reading of Heidegger reveals aspects of the relatedness of notions of image, imagination, and education that, without such close attention to language, might not have been revealed.

In trying to make sense of the language of philosophy, and of what he reads, Ian Munday raises a different point in Chapter 11. His contribution questions the dichotomy of reading and writing. He writes:

> I find it impossible to distinguish reading from writing when approaching the work of philosophers as difficult as [Jacques] Derrida. To get any purchase on what is going on I have to find my own ways of wording Derrida's argument and this 'writing' becomes a more fruitful form of reading.
>
> *(p. 108)*

The contributions demonstrate that the sources that are read *as* research in educational philosophy, are not solely academic texts or works of philosophy and theory, but also novels and poems, or works of art. How they are read – in detail, with a focus on etymology and the particular use of language – is characteristic of work in this field. But such practices of reading require learning and development over time. Surely this process is not dissimilar from the acquisition of skills needed for reading in other forms of research? What is distinctive, though, about the reading practices in educational philosophy is that they are not a prior activity to the actual research, but rather *constitute* the research. As Vansieleghem puts it: 'The starting point is that there is activity in reading and writing itself. The reading and writing does something' (p. 97).

Writing-as-report, and writing-as-research

Having considered the different ways that reading is conceptualised as part of the research process in the research methods literature, we now turn to see how writing is discussed. Here again, there is a large variety of supporting texts. Some deal with the writing up of the research as part of broader discussions of the research process as a whole (Thomas, 2013; Wilson, 2013), while others take one element of a research report and consider this in much more detail. An example of this latter kind of work is Diana Ridley's (2016) text, *The Literature Search*. Other books address the issue of how to approach writing in a specific genre, such as Robert Kail's *Scientific Writing for Psychology: Lessons in Clarity and Style* (2014), while still others focus on writing successfully at a particular level, e.g. for completing an undergraduate dissertation (Greetham, 2014) or a PhD thesis (McMillan and Weyers, 2013).

Writing-as-report

Glancing through the contents pages of many of the research methods textbooks reveals something interesting about where their authors see the place of writing in the research process. In those books where the writing-up of the research is considered, the relevant chapters are located towards the end. Thomas sheds light on why this might be the case when he writes: 'You are now coming toward the end of your project…It is also the time when you will be doing most of your writing and tidying up' (2013: 285). There are many examples where writing is located within discussions of how to finish off one's research project, and issues related to writing are addressed at the end of the research methods textbooks. In Punch and Oancea (2014), the chapter entitled 'Research Writing' is the final one. In David Hopkins' *A Teacher's Guide to Classroom Research* (2008), it is not until Chapter 10 that a section is included on 'Reporting classroom research'. Similarly, Thomas (2013) does not discuss issues related to the writing up of the research until the final chapter, 'Concluding and writing up'. Writing is only addressed in a section entitled 'Finishing the research project' in Juliet Corbin and Anselm Strauss' (2015) book on qualitative research.

These examples suggest that conducting research, and then reporting on it through writing, can be thought of as a staged, linear process. Moreover, these examples show that a distinction is drawn between the practices involved in carrying out the research, and the subsequent reporting of it through writing for submission on a course, for publication, or for other forms of dissemination. Punch and Oancea hint at this when they write: 'A written proposal is required for the [research] project to commence, and a written report is required *after* the project' (2014: 354, italics ours). Thomas puts this more explicitly: 'When you have finished collecting data, analysing and discussing them, it is time to hammer them into shape in the chapters of your thesis' (2013: 288). This is clearly a dominant model for understanding the place of reading in the research process:

> In the traditional model of research writing, the write-up does not get done until the research is completed, and everything is figured out. 'I've done all the research, now I am writing it up'. Implicit in this is the idea that I don't start the writing until I've 'got it all worked out'. This is *writing to report*.
> *(Punch and Oancea, 2014: 369)*

It seems not to matter whether the research being reported is qualitative or quantitative, this distinction between research, and reporting of research through writing, seems to be maintained. The writing itself acts in some senses as a bridge; it is the route by which research that has been conducted is subsequently communicated to the research community, practitioners, policy-makers, and the wider public. Where writing is an adjunct to the research itself, and is given attention only because of its capacity to communicate existing findings, we see more clearly why many of the research textbooks focus so strongly on particular issues. These tend to be around matters such as clarity and awareness of audience when reporting on research. 'We have to know our audience', writes Newby, 'and pitch the tone of our writing to meet its expectations' (2010: 215).

Prescribing writing: the macro and the micro

The effective communication of findings seems to be both the driving force for, and the goal of, discussions of writing in many of the research methods textbooks. Support for the practices of writing that need to be developed to achieve efficient and effective communication seem to stem from a perceived need to 'reduce the complexity of the task' (Wilson, 2013: 211). Some texts, however, adopt a cautionary tone. Punch and Oancea (2014: 355) acknowledge that while there tends to be a 'conventional format' adopted in the writing up of quantitative studies, approaches to writing qualitative research tend to be more diverse, and utilise a broader range of strategies and models. They warn against using a 'tick box' approach to the elements and style used in writing up one's research, and point to the range of genres that are deemed appropriate across the disciplines. Similarly, while Strauss and Corbin acknowledge that some sections of a research report tend to use a standard pattern (they use the example of writing a methodology section), they prefer to offer only 'loose suggestions' for structure and style, preferring to avoid 'the rigidity of the process by dictating what to include, and how' (2015: 320).

The more common approach in many of the research methods texts, though, is to provide very detailed guidance on 'how to structure a research report and the content of each section' (Coles and McGrath, 2010: 17). The advice given tends to be at two levels: the macro and the micro. At the macro level, the texts address a range of issues, usually starting from the general expectations within a discipline, or research paradigm. Most provide some guidance on the overall structure or order of presentation of different elements of the research project. Indeed, getting the structure and order 'right' seem to be what writing up consists in: 'Since the advent of word processing…[and] the invention of the magical machines…writing has really become a process of getting things in order' (Thomas, 2013: 287). This is not only about the general structure of a thesis, dissertation, or journal article (that the introduction tends to precede both the statement of the problem, and the literature review, and that the methodology section comes before the presentation and discussion of findings), but also is concerned with how to ensure a logical structure *within* elements of the written research report. Thomas, for example (*ibid.*: 236), specifies six stages of writing the conclusions of a research project: (i) refer back to the introduction; (ii) chart the progress of any change; (iii) summarise briefly the main findings; (iv) acknowledge your project's limitations and weaknesses; (v) outline any recommendations; and (vi) outline points for further research. This kind, and level, of detail in the advice, are common. Wilson (2013: 215) takes a similar approach in detailing how one should structure the writing of an introduction, specifying that the writer should provide the following elements: (i) a justification of the significance of the substantive topic; (ii) a statement of the broad issues; (iii) a description of the context of the enquiry; and (iv) an outline of the rest of the study.

At the micro level, the research methods textbooks tend to focus on the technical aspects of writing related to style, register, and audience. Coles and McGrath (*op. cit.*), for example, give advice on the use of the first or third person, and on how many themes it is best practice to include in any given paragraph. Thomas (*op. cit.*) attends to issues of language, and of individual words, assessing the merits of the use of terms such as 'disabled' and 'impaired', and whether researchers should be referring to 'headmistress' or 'head teacher' in writing up educational research. Language is seen to be important for two reasons. First, researchers should ensure that they adopt the appropriate register. To this end, Thomas provides a detailed table (*op. cit.*: 39) that offers practical suggestions as to phrases and sentences that can be used to introduce different elements in a literature review, and to link ideas together coherently. Second, the use of correct, Standard English is vital if findings are to be communicated effectively; hence there is a strong focus on drafting and editing, but particularly on proof-reading. Thomas writes: 'Draft, proof-read and edit; re-draft, re-proof-read, and re-edit, then re-re-draft, re-re-proof-read and re-re-edit…and so on. Get it right' (*ibid.*: 291).

Providing a framework for writing in this way can be extremely helpful in supporting novice researchers and writers, and in inducting them into the conventional ways of writing within a discipline. However, the use of such approaches raises questions not only about whether they appropriately capture the educational reality they study, but also whether they support the development of independent thinking. The standardisation of research practices and students' induction into the language of research risks silencing other modes of inquiry and the student's own academic voice in the process as orthodoxies are further upheld (Fulford, 2009; Hodgson and Standish, 2007).

Writing-as-research

There is, however, a different way of thinking about writing than simply writing-as-report. This way of writing disrupts the separation between the conduct of the research and the phase of writing it up. Here, writing *is* the research, not just something tagged onto the end of the real work of research, of data collection and data analysis. Punch and Oancea hint at this when they write that we can conceive of writing 'as a way of learning, a way of knowing, a form of analysis and inquiry. This is the idea of "writing in order to work it out"' (*op. cit.*: 369). Writing-as-research is the kind of mode of enquiry typical of forms of educational philosophy that are our central concern here. Even when the research entails some empirical component, the process of writing in educational philosophy is integral to the enquiry, rather than merely a final reporting of its findings. Often, there are no specifically-gathered data as such to write up. It is rather that the writer is often engaging in detail with the sources that she has read, be these academic literature, works of art, or illustrative examples from policy and practice. This often necessitates more extensive – sometimes lengthy – quotations from the original sources.

Writing in educational philosophy tends to have, as its starting point, an educational concern that is pursued and analysed through the very act of reading and writing philosophically about it. This is by no means to say, however, that these concerns are abstract or purely speculative, but derive from educational policy and practice, as well as from our daily lives in which matters of educational significance abound, for example, in the relations between parents and children. Our colleagues' contributions to Part II of this book illustrated a variety of different ways in which writing in educational philosophy can be pursued. We turn again to these to further consider writing as research.

In reflecting on her contribution, Nancy Vansieleghem writes that 'philosophical research not only describes, convinces, interprets, or criticises…[it] is first of all a doing' (p. 97). The 'doing' is not necessarily in the selection and implementation of a certain methodology, in fieldwork and the collection of data, nor in the scrutiny and analysis of that data. It is rather that the activity of the research *is* in the writing of it. Vansieleghem puts it like this: 'Activity is not a prerequisite for reading and writing practices. The starting point is that there is activity in reading and writing itself. The reading and writing do something. Reading and writing propose action' (*ibid.*). Joris Vlieghe considers the nature of this action, of research-as-writing, when he considers the nature of his enquiry into the notion of 'practising'. He admits that one way of pursuing his study might have been to undertake a qualitative enquiry, mapping students' real experiences of practising some task or other. But he turns instead to 'a particular *philosophical* approach to educational issues, *viz.* phenomenology' (p. 62). His approach is phenomenological in that he wants to come to an accurate understanding of a particular phenomenon, namely, practising. The action he takes in doing this is to give a rich account, not by engaging with data in the form of students' experiences, but taking a common practice and thinking it anew through the work of other theorists; his approach is that of writing-as-research.

In some aspects, forms of writing in educational philosophy are no different (at both the macro and micro levels) from other forms of research reporting. Paul Standish (2010a) argues that some educational philosophy is highly structured, using logic to provide a systematic refutation of an established point of view. Morwenna Griffiths, in her contribution, draws attention to the specific structure she adopts in her extract. She notes how, at the outset, she explains her whole argument in outline, following this with a more detailed development of her ideas. She also points out that her approach is to use a topic sentence at the beginning of each paragraph. However, not all educational philosophy is like this. One of the characteristic features of some educational philosophy is that it is often 'more loose and less systematic in style, where the force of ideas (and the language used to express them) is allowed to evolve. Sometimes you don't know what you think until you have written it' (Standish, 2010a: 11). This draws our attention to a further dimension of educational philosophy; it is itself educational not only for the reader, but also for the researcher. This idea of the text as educative is highlighted by Ian Munday. He draws attention to the dissonances in his text that open up ways of seeing the world; such dissonances are themselves affirmative and educative. He writes:

Though I hope the chapter is relatively accessible, the reader may feel that there is a certain dissonance between the various registers that are handled; the language of complex philosophy, the language of schooling with its strange mixture of technical terminology, and finally 'ordinary' language. This leads to a jarring of discursive registers that will probably seem strange and perhaps 'inappropriate'.

(*p. 109*)

Language, then, is central to the writing of educational philosophy. This may sound obvious, and the point redundant. Indeed, language is central to *all* research whether it is written for publication, presented at a conference, or talked about in the public sphere. But this central focus on language in educational philosophy has a more sophisticated rationale than simply the need to ensure correct register and adherence to Standard English for effective communication of findings. As we noted above, there is a risk that when the language of research is prescribed through predetermined phrases, thought itself is stifled. Joris Vlieghe writes in his contribution to Part II: 'Language is not *just* a means of communication reporting on research results, but *itself* plays a part in the arguments philosophers make' (p. 63).

Anna Kouppanou's contribution to Part II, Chapter 13, illustrates how attention to language, through etymology, reveals a relatedness that was not previously apparent, between the words 'image' (*Bild*), 'education' (*Bildung*), and 'imagination' (*Einbildung*). This helps her to better understand technology's tendency to condition our world, and possibilities for being educated in a world dominated by digital technologies. In Chapter 4, Amanda Fulford similarly uses etymology to draw out an important distinction that she finds between 'conversation' and 'discussion' in her extract considering the nature of the university tutorial. She writes:

In the university tutorial, the conversation is characterised by such satisfying talk, the kind that is a form of settlement: of closing down and securing. Perhaps the etymology of the word 'conversation' is useful in illustrating the point here. The Latin roots indicate that in 'con-versation', we 'turn' (*vertere*) 'with' (*cum*) others. There is a sense of accord here that is entirely absent from conversation's common synonym, 'discussion' with its roots in the Latin *discutere* meaning 'to strike asunder' and from *dis* (apart) and *quartere* (to shake). Student satisfaction, in the tutorial context, derives from a conversation (rather than a discussion) which is based on the contentment derived from knowing exactly what is required to gain a pass mark in an assignment, or to achieve a certain degree classification.

(*p. 44*)

A further approach that similarly gives attention to language is a consideration of how subtle differences in the meanings of words in other languages can aid understanding of concepts in English. This is illustrated in Joris Vlieghe's contribution to Part II, where he considers the difference between 'learning' and 'practising' by turning to the work of Otto-Friedrich Bollnow (1978), and his claim that the object of learning is knowledge (to know something, *wissen*), whereas practising has to do with acquiring a skill (being capable of doing something, *können*).

In her research methods textbook for school-based research, Elaine Wilson (2013) advises that when writing up the conclusions of a research project (writing-as-report), you should use examples from your own findings to illustrate your interpretations and to link your findings to other studies (p. 219). Illustrating your analysis with examples from your collected data seems an entirely sensible approach. In educational philosophy, examples are used too. These are not, of course, extracts from data, as traditionally understood, but illustrations that, as Andrea English says in Chapter 7, 'help give us a picture of how an abstract idea connects to practice' (p. 73). This same approach is taken in a number of our colleagues' extracts. In Chapter 5, Stefan Ramaekers and Judith Suissa, for example, claim that the starting point for their writing is often the first-person accounts of parenting that they find in novels, magazines, or as a result of simply talking to parents. But such examples do not simply *illustrate* the analysis of a datum, they *are central to* the argument that they are used to develop. In Morwenna Griffith's extract, illustrations are vital as they are 'the way it can bring abstract theory and specific practices and contexts into dialogue with each other' (p. 118).

There are, then, a variety of ways to approach writing in educational philosophy, and the examples here are by no means exhaustive. If there is any commonality, however, it is perhaps that they do not follow what Standish calls the 'standard pattern' for writing-as-report (2010a: 11). But how does one learn to write 'philosophically'? We do not intend this text to serve as a 'how to' guide for writing educational philosophy, but is there still a need for the philosophical equivalent of the research methods textbook? Richard Smith, in Chapter 14, offers this advice:

> None of this is to say that doing and writing philosophy cannot be learned: only that you cannot learn it in the way that apparently you learn to do participant observation from a couple of lectures, or the way that you acquire the skill of filleting a fish from watching *MasterChef*, and then practising until you've got the knack of it. It is both slower and harder than that, and so can be more profoundly fulfilling.
>
> *(p. 136)*

To further explore the practices of reading and writing in educational philosophy, we consider below how these practices are conceived in the field, and in philosophy, more broadly. We start with reading, before turning again to writing. This draws our attention to the personal work, the labour, of reading and writing, in contrast to the procedural, technical accounts found in the research methods literature.

'What do you do?' The practices of reading in educational philosophy

Reading educational philosophy is often a challenging task. Ian Munday reminds us of this in reflecting on his reading of 'the work of philosophers as difficult as Derrida' for his own extract in Part II (p. 108). This might be for a number of reasons, which John Gingell has set out (2010). First, the kind of reading that is required is not simply a matter of acquiring factual knowledge on a subject; it is demanding in that it asks us both to engage with the content, and at the same time to re-examine our own position in relation to it. In reading educational philosophy, the fact that we ourselves might undergo education – a transformation, however subtle – means that our previously fixed ideas and our preconceptions are likely to be challenged in profound and sustained ways. Reading in this way is a 'difficult business' (*ibid.*: 147), Gingell writes, but perhaps all reading, not just in educational philosophy, should be like this.

A further challenge is posed by the way in which the subject might be written about; certain approaches confound us from the outset, unsettling our common understandings of the subject, and of its usual treatment. Gingell continues: 'Our natural expectations of what the subject may offer can be comprehensively frustrated by some philosophers' approach to the subject' (*ibid.*: 148). Anna Kouppanou's treatment of reading and metaphor is perhaps an example of this. But while her text demands our close attention, and might frustrate us, perseverance with it is a richly educative process. This tells us something about the demands of reading educational philosophy. Gingell puts it like this: 'Reading all philosophy is difficult. Partly this is because we are simply not used to paying close attention to a text that philosophy demands. Our "relaxed" reading style won't do' (*ibid.*: 147).

The work of some philosophers exemplifies particularly well the attention needed to read their philosophy attentively. Stanley Cavell, whose works span over half a century on Wittgenstein, J.L. Austin, scepticism, Shakespearian tragedy, opera, and Hollywood film, is a particular example. Paul Standish, whose educational philosophy draws on Cavell's work, writes of the: 'distinctiveness of [Cavell's] philosophical engagement and of the demands this makes on the reader' (2013: 51). He expands on this as follows:

> For there is no doubt that Cavell's approach is such as to prompt the reader to think for herself. This is evident, first, at the level of style. His writings are difficult in ways that are difficult to name. It is not that he writes in a specialised jargon, or in the received vocabulary of any particular scholarly tradition, and it is not that his writing is philosophically technical: if it had been complex in these ways, then perhaps this would have encouraged a certain kind of following, with adepts eager to show their proficiency in the master's words, and a reputation would have been more easily won. It is rather that his texts challenge the reader to read: this cannot be a process of simply assimilating the substance of what is said, as if the main points could

be noted and incorporated into an existing framework of judgements, for the force of the writing is to cause the reader to reappraise her relation to the words in use.

(2013: 51)

As for Cavell himself, he finds the same demands on the reader in some of the texts on which he draws. Cavell returns to the work of the nineteenth-century American philosopher and essayist, Henry David Thoreau, throughout his philosophical writings. In 1981, Cavell wrote a text that provides a reading of Thoreau's book, *Walden* (1854/1999), entitled *The Senses of Walden*. Thoreau devotes one chapter of *Walden* to the subject of reading. He writes this:

> The works of the great poets have never yet been read by mankind, for only great poets can read them. They have only been read as the multitude read the stars, at most astrologically, not astronomically. Most men have learned to read to serve a paltry convenience, as they have learned to cipher in order to keep accounts and not be cheated in trade; but of reading as a noble intellectual exercise they know little or nothing; yet this only is reading, in a high sense, not that which lulls us as a luxury and suffers the nobler faculties to sleep the while, but what we have to stand on tip-toe to read and devote our most alert and wakeful hours to.
>
> *(Thoreau, 1854/1999: 95)*

Thoreau is not presenting us with an elitist account here; it is not a privileging of a particular canon of literature. It is rather a claim that to read well – to 'read in a high sense' – is to recognise that reading is characterised by a particular relationship to the written word: one that awakens us to the further possibilities of language. For Cavell, to read *Walden* in a high sense is to be conscious also of its 'puns and paradoxes, its fracturing of idiom and twisting of quotation, its drones of facts and flights of interpretation' (1981: 16). This is the kind of reading that upsets our settled notions of the way things are, that awakens us to a different way of seeing things. To illustrate this, Cavell makes much of the image of the cockerel in *Walden*, and of how its crow facilitates more than a physical awakening. We need to be awake to this kind of reading, as it makes significant demands of the reader; it is of the kind required to read works such as *Walden* well. It is also required for the reading of (educational) philosophy.

'What do you do?' The practices of writing in educational philosophy

When we first had the idea for writing this book, and for including contributions from a range of international scholars in educational philosophy, we were keen to use examples that illustrated a breadth of styles and approaches. The examples we have used, however, would generally be more associated with what is termed the Continental tradition, or seen as straddling the Continental and analytic, or Anglophone, traditions (a distinction we discussed in Part I). As we worked with our colleagues, it became clear that they found little difficulty in selecting a suitable extract of their research that served to illustrate their particular philosophical interests and approach. However, there were more concerns, questions, and requests for clarification over what to include in the final section of each contribution. Here, we had asked our colleagues to reflect on their chosen extract of research and, in particular, to make explicit their practices of reading-as-research and writing-as-research. This, we thought, would be helpful to new researchers in the field, given that many of the existing research textbooks do not address these issues in relation to educational philosophy.

The difficulties our colleagues may have experienced here are not unique. What philosophers do, and more specifically, how they do it, have been the subject of recent interest and writing (Ruitenberg, 2010; Smeyers and Smith, 2015). Judith Suissa also outlines such difficulties in her reflections on being a philosopher, and having to teach a module on an educational research methods course for postgraduate and doctoral students. The following is a lengthy quotation, but serves to illustrate the challenges she faced in planning and delivering the module:

> I had the summer to plan the module, which was initially called 'Philosophical Approaches to Educational Research'. My confused struggle to articulate what I wanted to do, and to find some framework in the relevant literature that would help me to plan my approach, soon crystallised into a worry about the question of whether I should be thinking about the philosophy *of* educational research or philosophy *as* educational research; this, in turn, led to some further questions about the nature of philosophy and its relationship with educational theory and research. These questions did not go away but rather accompanied me throughout my teaching, often being reframed by the experience of teaching, often intertwining with each other, and often themselves becoming the focus of discussion in class.
>
> *(2007: 285)*

Given the difficulty of articulating, even in the most *general* terms, what research in educational philosophy is 'about', and indeed, how to 'do' it, it is not surprising that our contributors had similar difficulties with making explicit the *particular* reading and writing practices they used and why. If we take the example of writing, it is simply not the case that there is a formula, or even a single accepted approach, to writing educational philosophy. However, there are a number of characteristics that tend to be found in writing that reports more empirical forms of research in education and the social sciences. Our more detailed discussions earlier in this chapter attempted to lay some of these out. But to reiterate this point here, we might take the following as pertinent examples of *the* accepted approach that the research methods textbooks urge their readers to replicate: the genre of the literature review, the structure and content of an abstract, or the self-reflective articulation of one's positionality in the 'write-up' of one's research. This might seem too strong a claim to make – indeed, a broad generalisation. While we acknowledge that writing practices tend to be discipline-specific in some cases, there are some general approaches that are clearly distinct. Bas Levering (2003), in his analysis of research in the natural and in the human sciences, points to some of the broad distinctions that he finds between research published in these fields. He argues that the approach to research in these two fields is not different simply in terms of ontology and methodology (where the aim of the natural sciences is to explain, *erklären*, and of the human sciences is to understand, *verstehen*). He draws attention to the fact that the *writing practices* in these fields are also very different. Levering finds that writing in the natural sciences is characterised by 'a closed form of reasoning…in its search for undivided truth' (*ibid.*: 100). It is just these kinds of differences that the research methods textbooks do a good job in outlining for those new to the field.

But the range of approaches to writing in educational philosophy is arguably much broader, both at the macro level of structure, formulation of the argument, and use of sources, as well as at the micro level of language. In some cases, the approach might be familiar to the reader from works of ancient or medieval philosophy, and in others, the approach is highly individual. David Bridges points to this when he writes: 'Some philosophical writing describes or represents a particular methodology – Socratic questioning, Cartesian doubting, or linguistic analysis, for example – but a great deal more leaves it implicit or even invisible' (2003: 23). A number of scholars have attempted to draw attention to the differences, without suggesting that the approaches taken amount to any kind of formula that educational philosophers should follow. Levering, for example, draws a distinction between a mode of writing that he calls a 'study', which he finds generally adopted in the natural sciences, and 'whose argumentation runs according to the rules of formal logic' (2003: 100), and writing in social science, including education and philosophy.

This might suggest that writing outside of the field of the natural sciences (in educational philosophy, perhaps) is *not* characterised by logic and argument. This is not the case. Analytic forms of philosophy, which rose to dominance in the early twentieth century, especially in Great Britain and the United States, emphasise the formal language of logic. It is difficult, though, to characterise precisely the philosophical commitments of this phase of philosophy, as if it was a unified field, entirely separate from what is termed 'Continental' philosophy. R.F. Dearden, for example, describes it as 'slowly forming and finding sporadic expression' in the 1950s at least (1982: 57). Israel Scheffler, writing in 1973, argues forcefully that the type of analysis that proceeds from the logic of language has particular benefits:

> First, its greater sophistication as regards language, and the interpenetration of language and inquiry, second, its attempt to follow the modern example of the sciences in empirical spirit, in rigor, in attention to detail, in respect for alternatives, and in objectivity of method, and third, its use of techniques of symbolic logic brought to full development only in the last fifty

years…It is…this union of scientific spirit and logical method applied toward
the clarification of basic ideas that characterizes current analytic philosophy.

(1973/1989: 9–10)

A development of this idea of symbolic logic, brought to bear on educational
issues, is found in philosophy of education from the 1960s and 1970s. Richard
Smith (2010) draws attention to a pertinent example of the use of symbolic logic,
using this quote from Paul Hirst's *Knowledge and the Curriculum* (1974):

> A notion of learning which is not the learning of some particular X, is as
> vague as the notion of going somewhere, but nowhere in particular. Equally
> some particular person B is necessarily learning this X. Following the logical
> chain, it is therefore only in a context where both what is to be learnt and
> who is learning it are clear, that we can begin to be clear about teaching B, X.
>
> *(2010: 109)*

The work of Richard Peters and Paul Hirst from this era remains highly influential
in Anglophone, particularly British, philosophy of education. This approach to
philosophy of education still prevails in more recent work, though is not a focus
of this book (see, for instance, the recent Special Issue of the *Journal of Philosophy of
Education*, Cuypers and Martin, 2009).

In other forms of educational philosophy, as illustrated in this book, such formal
techniques of symbolic logic are not evident, and the writing proceeds more often
in the form of the essay. For Levering, this is a highly suitable approach. The essay
is the place where 'we literally try out an idea or thought' (2003: 100). Levering's
attention to the form of the essay for writing educational philosophy is rooted in
the etymology of the word. To 'essay' (from the French, *essayer*, to try or to test)
is to put something to the test; to test its worth, or to make an attempt. Here, the
end point is not the arrival at what he calls 'undivided truth' (*ibid.*: 101), but is a
pitching of an idea, or an argument, for public consideration in terms of its 'cred-
ibility or cogency' (*ibid.*: 101).

In our colleagues' contributions to Part II, there are other examples of the way
in which their extract, a part of a larger piece of writing, can similarly be seen to be
testing out an idea. Anne Pirrie writes this about her contribution:

> My aim here is to offer a more radical and daring alternative for re-invigorating
> educational research, one that foregrounds the engagement of the researcher
> by exploring the expressive, cognitive, and imaginative possibilities of lan-
> guage as a means of exploring *incapacity* as an alternative basis for a re-enlivened
> educational research.
>
> *(p. 85)*

Pirrie tests an alternative conception of capacity building. Another way of putting
to the test consists in testing the dominant language against the lived experience of

and ethical commitments entailed in human relationships. This is seen in this quotation from Stefan Ramaekers and Judith Suissa, who do this to offer an 'alternative picture' of the parent–child relationship than the one that has become dominant in the discourse of 'parenting':

> One of the main problems with the scientific discourse that dominates discussions of parenting is that it implies that there is a clearly-defined, objectively valid end-point of the parenting process and that the core of 'parenting' consists of forms of interaction that are causally related to achieving this. Implied in the language of this account is the idea that there is a right and a wrong way of parenting, and thus, in principle, a possibility of 'closure' or 'achievability' whereby one can be deemed to have succeeded as a parent. The alternative picture which we sketch out involves a focus, instead, on the particular quality of individual parent–child relationships, on the open-endedness of the process of being a parent, and on the sense in which the aims and goals that parents have cannot be unproblematically captured in a neutral, descriptive language, as they are infused with values and inseparable from the experience of individual parents within the shifting and dynamic context of their lives.
>
> *(p. 49)*

In the examples above and the chapters in Part II, our colleagues try out particular ideas, and illustrate the difference between this 'essaying' and the reporting of the results of research. In both cases, however, there is a conformity to the format required for peer and public scrutiny through publication. There is an assumption that the 'best' research in educational philosophy (indeed, in any field) is that which assumes the form we most easily recognise: the peer-reviewed journal article. The pressure to publish is strong in academia. That this is seen as the 'gold standard' is perhaps increasingly true in a culture, particularly in higher education, where publication of these kinds of articles assures tenure in some cases, and income generation through mechanisms such as the Research Excellence Framework.[2] The seductive appeal of the peer-reviewed journal article is clear. As Richard Smith puts it:

> It falls neatly into journal articles of around six thousand words or appears in books whose chapters are of roughly the same length. There is usually a respectable number of references to other publications, either foot- or end-noted, or set out in References at the end. The language is of a particular register: sober, decorous, grammatically orthodox, not much given to poetic flights of fancy (though the writer may, rather daringly, take examples from novels – or even more daringly – from film) – in short, the style is what we think of as *academic*.
>
> *(2010: 159)*

Richard Smith reminds us that systematic Western philosophy, at its start with Plato, was not shoe-horned into the 6,000-word written article, but was pursued instead through a form of dialogue. Through a mode of conversation, ideas were passed backward and forward; they were critiqued, refined, expanded, refuted, or dismissed. We only need to look to ancient Greek philosophy to find examples of this form of dialogue, particularly in Plato. Many of his works are in the form of dialogues, where the central protagonists discuss a topic through asking questions of each other. In the early dialogues, Socrates is the central character, in dialogue with others. *Euthyphro* is an example here, where Socrates is in dialogue with Euthyphro over the question of piety or virtue. In the later dialogues, such as *Meno*, this same dialogic form is used. Here, Socrates and Meno are the main two speakers, and the latter opens the dialogue with a question: 'Can you tell me, Socrates, whether virtue is acquired by teaching or by practice; or if neither by teaching nor practice, then whether it comes to man by nature, or in what other way?' What is clear about these dialogues is that they are not only in some cases *about* (moral) education, but are themselves educative texts. Richard Smith points to this aspect of the ancient dialogues when he writes about three notable examples, *Euthyphro*, *Gorgias*, and *Theaetetus*:

> If these three interlocutors…give themselves over fully to the process of the dialectic, the to-and-fro of question and answer, none of them will be quite the same by the end of the dialogue. Each will have been *educated* a little, or perhaps a lot, by the philosophy they have engaged in with Socrates. For this reason it seems fair to call these dialogues exercises in philosophy of education.
>
> *(ibid.: 160)*

Richard Smith's contribution to Part II of this book presents an extract written in the form of a dialogue. Just as in the example of Plato's *Meno*, Smith's dialogue, from an undergraduate seminar, also begins with a question from one of the students, Ben to another, George, the tutor:

Ben: Do you think of yourself as a postmodernist, are you a Rortyan, or what? I can see a bit why you always avoid this question, because you don't see yourself as having any kind of method, as if there was a 'here's how to do it' that you could teach us and we could take it away and use it like a handbook.

After a few interjections from other students attending the seminar, George continues:

George: OK. I'll try to give you some idea of what kind of philosophy I like, insofar as I have a clear idea myself, or could give any kind of satisfactory account of how it's different from other kinds of writing.

Then, in analysing the practices of reading and writing in this text-as-dialogue, Smith hears a 'student' – perhaps just a voice in his head – interrupt his thoughts with the comment:

Jane: I don't think this is going to be very helpful to people starting out in philosophy of education.

Smith's response to this thought is that he was just trying to do what the editors asked him to. By bringing in this voice, Smith questions the very legitimacy of what he is doing. Using (written) speech, to question what he is writing. His argument is made not by logical reasoning, but by showing, in practice, the nature of the questioning he seeks to invite through his writing and teaching. As with many of the extracts in Part II, he exemplifies in his writing the notion of education that he speaks for.

As editors, we had specifically asked contributing authors to analyse their own practices of reading and writing educational philosophy – their own 'methods' – and to make these explicit for the benefit of readers and researchers new to the field of philosophy and education. But perhaps we were in danger of trying to tie down, categorise, and neatly package what it is to do educational philosophy, in a way that is unhelpful for those new to the field. Perhaps the difficulty inherent in the task of capturing what it *is* to read and write educational philosophy is not something that should be overcome, as if it is a problem that needs to be solved in order to continue.

To focus on Smith's use of dialogue as a critique of the condensed form of the journal article, is not to suggest, however, that writing in this form diminishes educational philosophy. Far from it. As we have discussed, the process of writing *does* something. It is part of the process of thinking and, with reading, it constitutes the research itself. There are two important points to draw from the discussion of the essay versus the report, and from writing versus dialogue. The first refers to the possibilities that are opened up by acknowledging that when we write, we do something more than simply report objective knowledge or conclusions. The academic article, conceived as an essay, is not only a contribution to knowledge but to a public conversation, to be taken up by an interlocutor to refute, to develop, to rethink. Smith's contrast of the condensed journal article with the Socratic dialogue draws attention to the pedagogical dimension of educational philosophy: it can be put into practice in the classroom or lecture theatre. Smith intimates that to lecture students on what is the case, removes them from the conversation, presents matters as closed, and presents philosophy as a set of truths to simply apply. As we have shown, however, the educational value in writing in (educational) philosophy lies in its opening up for question matters that appear closed or taken for granted. Jan Masschelein writes specifically of the essay, as discussed above, as experimental, as a form of *in*discipline. Drawing on Hannah Arendt's notion of her work as exercises in thought, he writes:

> [W]e can understand such philosophy to be educational in three senses. First it is a kind of investigation that implies a bringing into play of the researcher herself (her thoughts): a self-education as 'work on the self' (Wittgenstein). But philosophy as an essay is, as well, a public gesture and is, therefore, also

educational in the sense that it can have a meaning for others who are invited to share the experience (to put themselves to the test, not to receive teaching). And lastly, such philosophy can be educational in the sense that the present at stake is the educational present.

(Masschelein, 2011: 358)

As a reader, you may well have reached this point in the book, and, with a sense of frustration, be asking, 'Well, what *is* different, then, about writing educational philosophy?' If many of the claims made for what constitutes a good piece of educational research are broadly similar for what makes for good educational philosophy, is the very problem that prompted the writing of this book dissolved? It is not good enough just to answer 'In some ways.' What we have attempted to demonstrate is that there is no definitive answer to the question 'What do you do?' when thinking about the practices of reading and writing in educational philosophy. Our colleagues' contributions in Part II illustrate this point clearly. Some are more sensitive to the essay form and trying out an idea. Others exhibit characteristics suggestive of a more dialogic form. This range of approaches leads Richard Smith to conclude that 'the separation between philosophy and writing cannot be established so easily, or perhaps cannot be established at all' (2010: 164). Some contributions begin with a question, others an assertion. The sources upon which they draw are not wholly philosophical; some are not strictly philosophical at all. Many favour metaphor, figurative language, and poetic devices over symbolic logic. All of this, claims Smith, 'may help us to imagine human life, and the learning and education that go on in it, more fully and more richly. There is no more important task for philosophy of any kind, as Plato knew, than that' (*ibid.*: 166). If the question of the difference between 'empirical' and 'philosophical' forms of research lies not so much in what is *done*, in terms of the practices of reading and writing, then it may be more clearly articulated by looking at ways to proceed in educational philosophy. It is to these that we now turn.

Notes

1 While many authors suggest that reading for (and the writing of) the literature review should come in the early phases of the research, David Silverman (2010) is a notable exception. Arguing that early reading can lead to much wasted effort (since a researcher will not know what she has found until after data analysis has happened), he advises researchers to leave a review of the literature until it is clearly known which literature is relevant to the substantive concern of the research, i.e. until the process of data collection and analysis is well underway.

2 The Research Excellence Framework is the system by which research is assessed in Higher Education Institutions in the United Kingdom. It was introduced in 2014 and replaces the Research Assessment Exercise which was last conducted in 2008.

References

Bollnow, O.-F. (1978) *Vom Geist des Übens. Eine Rückbesinnung auf elementäre didaktische Erfahrungen*, Freiburg: Herder.

Bridges, D. (2003) *Fiction Written Under Oath? Essays in Philosophy and Educational Research*, Dordrecht: Kluwer.

Brown, A. and Dowling, P. (1998) *Doing Research / Reading Research: A Mode of Interrogation for Education*, London: The Falmer Press.

Cavell, S. (1981) *The Senses of Walden*, San Francisco: North Point Press.

Coles, A. and McGrath, J. (2010) *Your Education Research Project Handbook*, Harlow: Pearson Education Ltd.

Corbin, J. and Strauss, A. (2015) *Basics of Qualitative Research: Techniques and Procedures for Developing Grounded Theory*, London: Sage.

Cuypers, S. and Martin, C. (Eds) (2009) 'Special Issue: Reading R. S. Peters Today: Analysis, Ethics, and the Aims of Education', *Journal of Philosophy of Education*, Vol. 43, Issue Supplement s1.

Dearden, R.F. (1982) 'Philosophy of Education, 1952–1982', *British Journal of Educational Studies*, Vol. 30, pp. 57–71.

Fulford, A. (2009) 'Ventriloquising the Voice: Writing in the University', *Journal of Philosophy of Education*, Vol. 43, No. 2, pp. 223–237.

Furseth, I. and Everett, E.L. (2013) *Doing Your Master's Dissertation: From Start to Finish*, London: Sage.

Gingell, J. (2010) 'Reading the Philosophy of Education', in R. Bailey (Ed.), *The Philosophy of Education: An Introduction*, London: Continuum, pp. 147–157.

Greetham, B. (2014) *How to Write Your Undergraduate Dissertation*, second edition, Basingstoke: Palgrave Macmillan.

Heidegger, M. (1971) *Poetry, Language, Thought*, Trans. A. Hofstadter, New York: Harper and Row.

Hirst, P. (1974) *Knowledge and the Curriculum*, London: Routledge & Kegan Paul.

Hodgson, N. and Standish, P. (2007) 'Induction into Educational Research Networks: The Striated and the Smooth', in D. Bridges and R. Smith (Eds), *Philosophy, Methodology, and Educational Research*, Oxford: Wiley-Blackwell, pp. 299–310.

Hopkins, D. (2008) *A Teacher's Guide to Classroom Research*, fourth edition, Maidenhead: Open University Press.

Kail, R.V. (2014) *Scientific Writing for Psychology: Lessons in Clarity and Style*, London: Sage.

Levering, B. (2003) 'From Schools of Thinking to Genres of Writing: New Roles for Philosophy of Education', in P. Smeyers and M. Depaepe (Eds), *Beyond Empiricism: On Criteria for Educational Research*, Leuven: Leuven University Press, pp. 93–103.

Machi, L.A. and McEvoy, B.T. (2009) *The Literature Review*, Thousand Oaks, CA: Corwin Press.

Masschelein, J. (2011) 'Philosophy of Education as an Exercise in Thought: To Not Forget Oneself When "Things Take Their Course"', *European Educational Research Journal*, Vol. 10, No. 3, pp. 356–366.

McMillan, K. and Weyers, J.D.B. (2013) *How to Research and Write a Successful PhD*, Harlow: Pearson.

Newby, P. (2010) *Research Methods for Education*, Harlow: Longman.

Punch, K.F. and Oancea, A. (2014) *Introduction to Research Methods in Education*, second edition, London: Sage.

Ridley, D. (2016) *The Literature Search: Strategies and Tools for Student Researchers*, London: Sage.

Robinson, F.P. (1970) *Effective Study*, fourth edition, New York: Harper and Row.

Ruitenberg, C. (Ed.) (2010) *What Do Philosophers of Education Do? (And How Do They Do It?)*, Oxford: Wiley-Blackwell.

Scheffler, I. (1973/1989) *Reason and Teaching*, Indianapolis: Hackett.

Silverman, D. (2010) *Doing Qualitative Research*, third edition, London: Sage.

Smeyers, P., and Smith, R. (2015) *Understanding Education and Educational Research*, Cambridge: Cambridge University Press.

Smith, R. (2010) 'Writing the Philosophy of Education', in R. Bailey (Ed.), *The Philosophy of Education: An Introduction*, London: Continuum, pp. 158–166.

Standish, P. (2010a) 'What Is the Philosophy of Education?' in R. Bailey (Ed.), *The Philosophy of Education: An Introduction*, London: Continuum, pp. 4–20.

Standish, P. (2010b) 'An Economy of Living: A New Economy of Education', *The Korean Journal of Philosophy of Education*, Vol. 49, pp. 99–113.

Standish, P. (2013) 'Rethinking Democracy and Education with Stanley Cavell', *Foro de Educación*, Vol. 11, No. 15, pp. 49–64.

Suissa, J. (2007) 'Shovelling Smoke? The Experience of Being a Philosopher on an Educational Research Training Programme', in D. Bridges and R. Smith (Eds), *Philosophy, Methodology and Educational Research*, Oxford: Blackwell Publishing, pp. 283–297.

Thomas, G. (2013) *How to Do Your Research Project: A Guide for Students in Education and Applied Social Sciences*, second edition, London: Sage.

Thoreau, H.D. (1854/1999) *Walden*, Oxford: Oxford University Press.

Vansieleghem, N., Vlieghe, J., and Verstraete P. (Eds) (2015) *Afterschool. Imagining Educational Research*, Leuven: Leuven University Press.

Wilson, E. (Ed.) (2013) *School-Based Research: A Guide for Education Students*, London: Sage.

16

HOW TO PROCEED?

Amanda Fulford and Naomi Hodgson

To conclude this book, we will try to offer some indications of how to proceed. We will try to answer an important question for those researchers in education who ask: 'Why would you do research in the field of educational philosophy in the first place?'. We will turn not to the research methods textbooks that have been the focus of much of this book, but to some of the literature that specifically addresses aspects of educational philosophy in order to address the tricky question of how, and why, to start work in this field.

'Why would you do research in the field of educational philosophy in the first place?'

In the Greek dialogue, *Theaetetus*, Socrates says: 'The sense of wonder is the mark of the philosopher. Philosophy indeed has no other origin.' This may be true, but perhaps another claim is also true; one that would help us to better understand the starting point for educational philosophy: philosophy begins with a sense of puzzlement. For those working, and researching, in education, the puzzlement may arise from the everyday aspects of working with children and young people. Richard Pring puts it like this:

> Philosophy begins when one feels puzzled about the meaning of what one is doing – its aims and purposes, the implicit values, the assumptions made about what is right or wrong, true or false, worthwhile or not. It is a struggle to make sense when others do not see the contradictions or unsound basis for action. And in that 'struggle to make sense', one tries to clarify what one means, finding that what previously was thought simple is really very complex.
>
> *(2015: 206)*

This kind of puzzlement is not the sort where one asks, perhaps as a teacher, administrator, or policy-maker, what will work best in any given situation. Concerns with what works lead the researcher down a different route in terms of her research. To illustrate this point, let us imagine the options for a secondary school teacher who is puzzled why so many of one particular year group in mathematics seem to struggle with the topic of algebra. Pupils in this group seem disengaged, do not see the relevance of studying algebra, are beginning to be disruptive in class, miss deadlines for handing in homework, and are not achieving at the levels they have been predicted. One of the most disruptive pupils has been excluded from the school. The teacher, currently studying part-time on a postgraduate course while working full-time, wants to investigate this issue for her dissertation. There are a number of options available to her for pursuing this research. She might plan to undertake a small-scale piece of action research by planning, implementing, and evaluating an intervention to re-engage the pupils, to try out different approaches to the teaching of algebra, and to improve levels of achievement. Equally, she might choose to conduct her research with a small number of the (most troublesome) pupils in the group, with the aim of better understanding their attitudes to mathematics, and the problems they face. This would surely help her to plan and deliver her lessons in a way that the pupils would find engaging, and would most likely lead to higher levels of achievement. Or she might adopt a different approach altogether, and decide to interview teachers of mathematics from a range of different schools in order to re-assess her own pedagogical approaches, and gain insight into methods of teaching and learning that she had not previously considered. All of these require her to collect her own primary data, to analyse it, thus enabling her to take action based on it. These, as the research methods textbooks tell us, would be highly appropriate empirical approaches to investigating this issue.

But the kind of puzzlement that Pring has in mind tends to concern matters of value, of ethics, of knowledge, and of educational aims. The difference is not to be seen in terms of the practical here, as if Pring's concerns have no immediate bearing on, or application to, the classroom. Indeed, the starting point for thinking about educational matters might be the same: the 'problem' mathematics year group. But the difference lies in the way that the concerns are expressed, and subsequently pursued. In the struggle to make sense of what is happening in the mathematics classroom, our teacher might ask instead: 'Should learning always be immediately relevant to students?', or 'What do we mean by "engagement" in learning?' The puzzlement might not lead to a question at all, but rather to the expression of something more open, such as 'The ethical dilemma of school exclusions'. There is something different about these kind of questions or issues, and Pring summarises them succinctly as 'problems which can only be described as philosophical' (2015: 206). To claim this may suggest to us that these kinds of 'problems' bear no relevance to practice. Some forms of philosophy do indeed proceed in more abstract terms. But philosophy since the ancient Greeks has also been concerned with a mode of enquiry that is about how to live the good life, that is, with the very practical nature of our daily lives. Meno's question to Socrates at the opening of the dialogue, *Meno*, cited above, illustrates this.

In a chapter entitled 'What is the Philosophy of Education?' (2010), Paul Standish similarly tries to lay out how research in educational philosophy might be distinct from other types of research that rely on the collection and analysis of empirical data. He also argues that the issue of where one starts, of the question(s) that drive the research, are simply not the same. He argues that the kind of concerns that tend to drive philosophical research are ones that are simply not empirically researchable. In laying out how these interests are different, and how they lead to the articulation of particular questions, he summarises the common interests of philosophical work: '[It is] centrally concerned with questions of meaning and value, with conceptual matters and with the coherence of ideas (whether they make sense, whether they are justified); quite often with some kind of struggle with ideas' (*ibid*.: 11). While these concerns might lead to a specific research question (to use the example above: 'What do we mean by "engagement" in learning?'), Standish points out that often the interests of philosophical research are 'concerned with an area in which one searches with less clear a destination' (*ibid*.: 11). The consequence of this is that it is difficult to provide a complete categorisation of possible topics for philosophical enquiry.

In what follows, we will draw on some of the areas in which Standish suggests that philosophical research might be pursued, and illustrate these with examples of topics and questions typical of these broad areas. These are not intended to be prescriptive of topics that research in educational philosophy *should* pursue. Indeed, some of the contributions in Part II of this book do not fit easily into any one of these broad categories, and many overlap a number of different ones. This illustrates the rich variety of work in this field that resists an unhelpful kind of 'pigeon-holing', or marginalising, of such work.

Issues relating to concepts

Paul Standish suggests that one broad area of philosophical enquiry in education is related to questions of conceptual clarification. He uses the example of quality in education, and how it can be assessed. But simply to *clarify* concepts is perhaps too narrow a categorisation. Research in educational philosophy is certainly concerned with concepts, but in a broader sense. In some research in this field, the concern is not so much with *clarifying* a concept, but rather in drawing attention to it in the first place. Standish suggests that educational philosophy 'allows us to see what is implied by terms in their current usage' (*ibid*.: 12). But it can also be more than this; it helps us to think about the concept in a different way, unsettling and opening up our ideas about the concept, rather than the settling down that comes from simply evaluating their current use. Anne Pirrie's contribution to Part II is an example of this. She starts out with considering the notion of 'capacity building' in educational research. Her aim, though, is not just to assess how this concept is currently used, but rather to disrupt those notions by 'drawing attention to how we use language, and by considering the obverse of capacity, namely, *incapacity*, construed as a form of attentive non–doing' (p. 84). Similarly, Stefan Ramaekers' and Judith Suissa's discussion of the notion of 'parenting' is related to the issue of concepts. Their research stems from a dissatisfaction with dominant accounts of 'good parenting', and of how such discourses 'were raising significant conceptual and ethical questions about which, as philosophers, we should have something to say' (p. 48).

A further critical dimension of philosophy lies in its production of new concepts to describe ontology and our experience of the world. The work of the poststructuralist philosopher Gilles Deleuze is an example of this (Deleuze, 2004). This relates to our discussion of the essay as test, as it entails putting our existing concepts to the test of the reality that we observe and experience. Amanda Fulford's extract aims to do this, with her testing of the concept of student satisfaction in the context of the contemporary university.

Issues relating to the work of philosophers and writers

We have already argued that research in educational philosophy gives particular attention to the sources that inform it. This tends to be through a detailed engagement with the source(s) rather than just through cursory forms of attention, or passing citation. Some forms of educational philosophy are structured in the form of a discussion of how the work of a particular philosopher or writer is significant for thinking about education. In some cases, the philosophers/writers chosen may have written extensively about education, such as John Dewey, for example; in other cases, authors may select philosophers/writers whose work is not explicitly (or even implicitly) about educational concerns, but in whose work they find significant educational import, such as Heidegger. Or, as we have seen, sources may be drawn from outside philosophy. Morwenna Griffiths' contribution to Part II is also an example of educational philosophy in this broad area. In Chapter 12, she takes the work of two eighteenth-century philosophers and writers, Jean-Jacques Rousseau, and Mary Wollstonecraft, to consider the concepts of nature and of education, and how these are brought together in the work of these authors to 'show how their two different conceptions have some implications for how teachers should relate to their students and to the curriculum, in ways that enhance the possibilities of social justice in the classroom and, ultimately, in the world' (p. 110). Anne Pirrie's work, on the other hand, engages with the work of the twentieth-century Italian journalist and novelist, Italo Calvino. She takes his idea of 'lightness of thoughtfulness', and in her extract, brings this to bear on the notion of capacity building in educational theory. We can see here, also, that the focus on a particular author is one approach to the analysis or generation of concepts, referred to in the previous section.

Issues relating to society and social justice

Questions relating to education's role in a creating a just society, and broader questions of social justice, are at the heart of enquiries in educational philosophy. Paul Standish provides the following examples of the types of topic that are envisaged here: children's rights; the nature of compulsory schooling; access to, and the funding of, higher education; inclusion; and the implications of multiculturalism (2010: 13). But here again we see an overlap with educational philosophy's concern with concepts that we addressed above. Of course, we are right to think of issues of inclusion and of multiculturalism as issues pertaining to discussions of social justice. But these concepts, especially in the way in which they tend to be discussed in education, are accepted as something of a given that ignores their complexity and context. To research these issues well means asking questions that open up these terms to consider questions of the values enshrined in them, their current, everyday use, and their political usage, but also their potentialities. Morwenna Griffiths' Chapter 12 addresses issues of social justice directly.

In her contribution, Nancy Vansieleghem discusses visual research and how this makes us think about the issue of giving voice. The notion of 'voice' in education is often used in relation to research on social justice and democracy, concerned with who does and who does not have a voice, whose voices are heard, and how and whether particular groups are represented (Fielding, 2004; Griffiths, 2003). Vansieleghem's Chapter 10, about giving voice to pupils with Attention Deficit Hyperactivity Disorder (ADHD), focuses on 'a particular form of doing visual research, in which "something" from the world we live in today (the discourse on children diagnosed with ADHD) is put on the scene to make it visible and an object of thought' (p. 92). By putting life stories on the screen, the spectator's attention is drawn to the pupils' voices in two different ways. In DISORDER, the first film discussed, social justice is understood not as giving voice to the children as 'children with ADHD' but as allowing *their* individual voices to be heard, as against a discourse that makes these children visual *in terms of* their ADHD. In DIS-ORDER, the second film, the first is shown to still conform to the standard discourse of ADHD; the children are accustomed to speaking about themselves, e.g. with therapists, and about their individual feelings. The second, therefore, asks questions that invite a new conversation on the subject and so gives voice not about something we already know, but that begins something new. This contribution, therefore, both addresses the way that society labels pupils with ADHD, and problematises the current understandings of the relationship between voice and social justice.

Issues of value and justification

Issues of value are commonly discussed in philosophy, whether in value theory in branches of moral philosophy, or in broader discussions of what is good and of value, in questions of how to live our daily lives. It is no surprise, then, to see that questions of value in education are ones that educational philosophy tends to address.

Questions relating to value and justification might relate to the curriculum that pupils follow, discussions that lead on to the broader question of the aims of education. We might ask, for example, if there is any justification for the inclusion of financial literacy education in the school curriculum, or citizenship education in an age of multiculturalism. Similarly, a study might discuss whether there is justification for sex and relationships education to be part of the school curriculum, or whether this is better left to families and carers to address. Such discussions open up onto very practical questions concerning the nature and aims of our education: Is there a case for a grammar schools? Should teachers be trained in universities, or in schools? Should university students pay fees? What should be the nature of an education in the early years? Should there be a national curriculum? Are there limits on freedom of speech in the university?

Let us take a further example from contemporary education. There is much talk in teacher education of 'resilience' as a quality seen to be desirable in educators (Gu and Day, 2013). Pupils too must be seen to be resilient when faced with difficult subjects or complex situations that take time and dedication to see through. But we might ask: What is the value of resilience in education? Or, we might say what is the justification for pursuing it? But we should also ask what it means as a concept. Is it the same as determination, or perseverance? Is resilience shown only in difficult situations, or does resilience have a more positive connotation – is it a synonym for endurance and staying power? And what does it mean today, in this particular usage? To pursue a study on resilience, then, in educational philosophy, requires not only attention to issues of value and justification, but also of language and the meaning of concepts.

A further dimension of the specific treatment of notions of value in educational philosophy is to consider the *educational* value of a practice. This entails understanding 'educational' not in terms of future employability, measures of well-being, better overall exam results in the future, but rather in terms of its potential for transformation. It is a subtle distinction, perhaps, but one that marks a distinctive critical dimension of the field. An example of this is given in Joris Vlieghe's Chapter 6, discussed further below.

Issues of pedagogy and classroom practice

In forms of educational research focused on the collection and subsequent analysis of data, there has been a focus in recent years on 'what works', driven largely by the improvement and accountability agendas of various governments and a focus on producing 'evidence-based' policy. Such research attracts funding and gains influence because of its perceived impact on the outcomes on schools and pupils' learning. This is unsurprising. Governments and policy-makers embrace studies that purport to provide evidence of interventions and teaching approaches that improve practice and will lead to enhanced achievements for pupils. Such studies often rely on hard, quantitative data, or longitudinal studies. Practitioners, of course, similarly embrace what they see as evidence-based practice to improve pupil outcomes and ensure that positions in league tables are maintained. This is not to present a cynical view of such research, but to point out its limitations. Various critiques have been written in the field of educational philosophy analysing why this incessant drive to secure evidence-based practice simply will not work (see e.g. Biesta, 2007; 2010; Smeyers and Depaepe, 2006).

As we have seen, we are not claiming that educational philosophy, which largely does not rely on the collection and analysis of empirical data, cannot contribute to debates on pedagogy and classroom practice. One example of how issues of pedagogy can be addressed in educational philosophy is found in Andrea English's contribution to Part II of this book. In Chapter 7, she writes: 'I seek to illuminate an essential role of the teacher in moral education that is not commonly addressed, namely, the role of the teacher as *listener*' (p. 65). This is a development of her research on the teacher-learner relationship that is deeply rooted in her experiences in the classroom. Her work provides a strong basis for other practitioners interested in the role of listening in the classroom. As such, her philosophical research has very practical import. She writes:

> The three guiding principles of listening can be described as follows: (1) listening to know where the learner is, (2) listening to know when to cultivate discontinuity in the learner's experience and, in turn, to support the learner's expansion of her circle of thought, and (3) listening to know when to end the task of moral guidance.
>
> *(p. 66)*

Whereas the force of English's work is concerned with exploring what she calls the 'guiding principles of listening', Joris Vlieghe, in his contribution to Part II, takes a rather different approach. He is interested in the notion of practising, and in what makes this a typically educational activity. He writes:

> In this text I deal with the *educational* value of activities that typically take place in school contexts. More precisely, I focus on practices such as getting to know the text of a poem by heart while reciting it, mastering the tables of multiplication by repeating the appropriate mathematical formulae ('four times nine is thirty-six'), as well as reiterating sets of the most elementary bodily movements during gym class. These concern the repeated and collective training and exercising of (basic) skills, under the supervision of a teacher who imposes a fixed rhythm.
>
> *(pp. 57–58)*

His work therefore starts with an established pedagogical approach – practising – and, through a reading of the works of Otto-Friedrich Bollnow and Giorgio Agamben, concludes with this central claim:

> If we stay true to what we *actually* experience, the most essential characteristic of this activity [practising] is *not* that it concerns the perpetual attempt of perfecting a skill (although this might hold true in many cases of practising), *but* that it consists in taking a certain (disempowering) relation towards skill or knowledge one (partially) possesses.
>
> *(p. 62)*

But here again we see that these categories, or general areas in which educational philosophy might be pursued, are not distinct. Vlieghe's account gives attention to a distinction in Bollnow's work between knowing something (*wissen*) and acquiring a skill (*können*). This is again a trying out, and a clarification, of concepts. Vlieghe writes that this kind of approach – that is a testing out of the uses of language by others to see if it makes sense for oneself – is a form of 'conversation with oneself'. This kind of work too has implications for practice that Vlieghe outlines:

> I do not think that philosophers of education should attempt to prescribe precise advice to teachers and policy-makers, or to critically assess pedagogies on the basis of some so-called 'deeper' insights that people without philosophical training lack. Nonetheless, philosophical work can be a valuable background when people in the field have to make decisions or have to give shape to their own role as a teacher.
>
> *(p. 64)*

Consideration of concepts or practices, then, is not, or not always, a matter of deriving general or universal principles or definitions to apply to education, but rather of identifying matters of common experience or concern and opening them up for new consideration. As a matter of common concern, this is also a rethinking one's own practice, as a form of work on the self, as Vlieghe shows.

Policy issues

Research in educational philosophy, as we have seen, contributes to debates that keep re-occurring – the aims of education is a good example here. But it is also able to bring to bear a critical viewpoint on matters of current institutional, national, or even international policy. Again, this is not a discrete area of research. If we take the question 'Should university students pay fees for higher education?', then this is clearly a matter of central government policy. It is also an issue of social justice, however, especially in terms of access to education, and the effects of debt on students after graduation. But, of course, this also raises issues of the justification for a market economy in higher education, and so leads us into discussions of value. Stefan Ramaekers and Judith Suissa note, in their contribution to Part II, that their work begins from a dissatisfaction with the discourses of parenting that abound not only in the self-help literature, but also that are also strongly evident in the policy literature.

There are, of course, numerous examples of the dominance of particular practices in education that can be traced directly to policy or good practice advice from a range of policy-making bodies and organisations with responsibility for monitoring quality in education. A pertinent example is the way that systematic, synthetic phonics are used for the teaching of children's reading in English schools. In this case, an excellent example of a response from the field of educational philosophy is Andrew Davis' research in the Philosophy of Education Society of Great Britain's IMPACT series (Davis, 2013). This series aims specifically to provide philosophical perspectives on issues of contemporary education policy.

These categories, as we emphasised earlier, do not comprise an exhaustive list. Paul Standish (2010) includes other areas that we have not explicitly covered here, such as questions concerning the nature of knowledge (he gives the examples: 'What is a literary education?' and 'The idea of transferable skills and their place in higher education'). What we have tried to show, however, is that these areas of interest for educational philosophy have very fluid boundaries, and individual studies may incorporate elements that can be identified with a number of areas. The benefit of laying out these areas in this way is to provide an idea of the possible starting points for research in educational philosophy, and how questions raised by contemporary policy and practice might be articulated and pursued in this field.

Concluding remarks

Reading, writing, and researching: educational philosophy in the margins

In conclusion, it is helpful to return to one of the themes for this book, which we first introduced in Part I, and that forms part of the sub-title for this text: the idea of the margin. As a brief re-cap, let us recall the points that we made in Chapter 1. When we think of something as 'being at the margins', we tend to think – in negative terms – of something at the extremes, or at the limits of acceptability (think of a person's conduct). To be at the margin of something is also to be away from the mainstream, at the edges, side-lined, and so not fully visible. In this sense, ideas can be marginal (in the sense that they do not conform to mainstream views), and people, practices, and institutions can similarly be marginalised (in the sense that they, or their contributions, are not considered to be of central importance). Both these uses of the 'margin' are imbued with a negative sense. But to think of the margin as the space around a text that is the place for comment, clarification, questioning – a space for debate – provides an altogether different, and more positive, picture. How then are we to think of educational philosophy in relation to the image of the margin?

Is this form of research at the margins of what is acceptable to the field of education? Are the kinds of research that are illustrated by our colleagues' contributions to Part II so far from the mainstream (either of educational research, or of philosophy) that they are considered unimportant? Or do these kinds of research illustrate the ways in which educational philosophy can provide a critical lens through which to view contemporary educational policy and practice? And is this of value? We argue that it is, because 'sometimes the approach to questions…requires a changing of the prevailing discourse in ways that fly in the face of common and professional understanding, precisely because it has become steeped in that discourse' (Blake *et al.*, 2003: 16).

As we have said, the dominant agenda in research in general, and in educational research in particular, is a concern with impact, and specifically with 'what works'. Research has value only if it is able to prescribe solutions to educational problems that will lead to effective interventions. Such research must lead to improvements in pedagogy (thought of simply in terms of teaching strategies); improve learning outcomes (in ways that are easily measurable); decrease disruptive behaviour in schools; lead to more valid assessments; and create 'better', more employable citizens. The kind of research that is needed, therefore, emphasises what works in order to provide a panacea for education's many problems, or the social problems that education is tasked with solving.

A similar agenda underlies the revised mechanisms for assessing the quality of research in higher education, illustrated, for example, in the UK Research Excellence Framework's (REF) requirement to demonstrate the impact of research, where impact is defined as 'an effect on, change or benefit to the economy, society, culture, public policy or services, health, the environment or quality of life, beyond academia' (HEFCE, 2015). Gert Biesta, in considering the drive to evidence-based practice, summarises the situation well in this extended extract:

> There is a real need to widen the scope of our thinking about the relation between research, policy, and practice, so as to make sure that the discussion is no longer restricted to finding the most effective ways to achieve certain ends but also addresses questions about the desirability of the ends themselves. With [John] Dewey I wish to emphasize that we always need to ask the question of whether our ends are desirable given the way in which we might be able to achieve them. In education the further question that always needs to be asked is about the educational quality of our means, that is, about what students will learn from our use of particular means or strategies. From this perspective it is disappointing, to say the least, that the whole discussion about evidence-based practice is focused on technical questions – questions about 'what works' – while forgetting the need for critical inquiry into normative and political questions about what is educationally desirable. If we really want to improve the relation between research, policy, and practice in education, we need an approach in which technical questions about education can be addressed in close connection with normative, educational, and political questions about what is educationally desirable. The extent to

which a government not only allows the research field to raise this set of questions, but actively supports and encourages researchers to go beyond simplistic questions about 'what works', may well be an indication of the degree to which a society can be called democratic. From the point of view of democracy, an exclusive emphasis on 'what works' will simply not work.

(2007: 21–22)

Where the emphasis is on immediate application of research evidence to improve practice, the place of educational philosophy may well be described as marginal. While such work should remain accessible to a wide audience, the ability to simply apply its 'results' is not how the value of such research should be judged. Blake *et al.* write:

> It is a mistake to suppose that research [in educational philosophy] must always be styled in this way. Sometimes complex philosophical enquiry is needed to expose and unravel the conceptual knots in which the discourse of educational theory and practice has become caught up.

(2003: 16)

Biesta shows us that there is a huge task ahead in re-envisioning educational research beyond the drive to investigate and publish simply 'what works'. Research on, and in, education must have a purpose beyond meeting the accountability measures of school effectiveness and school improvement. In this task, educational philosophy, with its concern for what is educationally desirable, has a central, rather than a marginal role. Indeed, Blake *et al.* argue that: 'A more coherent approach to the study of education involves a return to the disciplines of psychology, sociology, history, and philosophy of education' (*ibid.*: 14).

Such a return might bring educational philosophy out of the margins (in the sense of being marginalised or at the limits of acceptability). But in doing so it might also focus attention on the margins themselves, the borderline spaces that are usually out of our direct focus, but where the creative comment, the challenging question, or the critical debate can take place. This is not to conceive of educational philosophy as a corrective to other forms of enquiry (such as when a teacher writes a corrective comment to her student in the margin, to clarify her thought for her, or to identify a specific error). As Blake *et al.* state, the role of educational philosophy is not to 'stand itself on a different level of analysis, prescribing and proscribing *de haut en bas*' (*ibid.*: 15). Rather, it is to recognise that:

> More ambitiously, philosophy of education can engage in exploration of what education might be or might become…This is the kind of thing that Plato, Rousseau, and Dewey are engaged in on a grand scale. It can revisit but also problematize its canonical questions about such matters as the aims of education, the nature of knowledge, and the point of curriculum subjects, about human nature and human practices.

(ibid.: 15)

If this is the task of educational philosophy, then this is central to educational research more broadly. It has been our aim to show in this book that educational philosophy is vital to both the iterative debates on the aims of education – the 'canonical questions' (*ibid.*: 15) – *and* the raising of contemporary questions and concerns. As such, it cannot be thought of as either marginal notes – as *scholia* – or as a merely abstract form of thinking applying its teacherly judgement to practical matters. This would be to misunderstand how philosophy, from its earliest days in ancient Greece, has been inextricably connected with the practical daily issues of how we should live.

We have tried to show that the philosophical is always there in the questions that we have about the contemporary practices of education. A lecturer may have a question about how to get her undergraduate students to read seminal works in her discipline, rather than the summaries available on the internet. But this question opens onto other ones that relate to the nature of a higher education and the value of certain practices. And these are philosophical concerns. We have also shown how philosophy is woven throughout all the practices of our research in education; it is not something that we 'sort out' at the start of our research, before the 'real' work of research begins. In these senses too, philosophy is not marginal. Philosophy and theory are there at the centre of research in education, not aspects to be brought out of the margins, and then banished back there again once they have served our (research) purposes. Philosophy is not just another route to be chosen for conducting educational research, as if it is one among many possible methods. It cuts across all kinds of research in education. Having shown why, and how, educational philosophy is not a marginal concern, and made its practices a central focus of this book, we leave the reader to open and pursue her own educational inquiry in response to the educational conditions in which she finds herself, as researcher and perhaps as practitioner. In doing so, we hope this gives rise not to writing in the margin, but writing at the intersection.

References

Biesta, G. (2007) 'Why "What Works" Won't Work: Evidence-Based Practice and the Democratic Deficit in Educational Research', *Educational Theory*, Vol. 57, No. 1, pp. 1–22.

Biesta, G. (2010) 'Why "What Works" Still Won't Work: From Evidence-Based Education to Values-Based Education', *Studies in Philosophy and Education*, Vol. 29, pp. 491–503.

Blake, N., Smeyers, P., Smith R., and Standish, P. (2003) *The Blackwell Guide to the Philosophy of Education*, Oxford: Blackwell.

Davis, A. (2013) 'To Read or Not To Read: Decoding Synthetic Phonics', *Impact*, No. 20, pp. 1–38.

Deleuze, G. (2004) *Difference and Repetition*, London: Continuum.

Fielding, M. (2004) 'Transformative Approaches to Student Voice: Theoretical Underpinnings, Recalcitrant Realities', *British Educational Research Journal*, Vol. 30, No. 2, pp. 295–311.

Griffiths, M. (2003) *Action for Social Justice in Education: Fairly Different*, Maidenhead: Open University Press.

Gu, Q. and Day, C. (2013) 'Challenges to Teacher Resilience: Conditions Count', *British Educational Research Journal*, Vol. 39, No. 1, pp. 22–44.

HEFCE (Higher Education Funding Council for England) (2015) 'REF Impact', [Online], available at: www.hefce.ac.uk/rsrch/REFimpact/ (accessed 9 November 2015).

Pring, R. (2015) *Philosophy of Educational Research,* third edition, London: Bloomsbury.

Smeyers, P. and Depaepe, M. (Eds) (2006) *Educational Research: Why 'What Works' Doesn't Work*, Dordrecht: Springer.

Standish, P. (2010) 'What Is the Philosophy of Education?', in R. Bailey (Ed.), *The Philosophy of Education: An Introduction*, London: Continuum, pp. 4–20.

INDEX